Arnold Sweeney
August 29, 2005
Malta

NAVAL ACTIVITIES
OF THE
KNIGHTS OF ST JOHN
1530-1798

MALTESE SOCIAL STUDIES

1. Anthony Luttrell ed. — Hal Millieri: A Maltese Casale, its Churches and Paintings
2. Paul Cassar — Early Relations between Malta and the U.S.A.
3. S. Busuttil — Economic History of Malta 1939-62
4. John Attard Montalto — The Nobles of Malta 1530-1800
5. Henry Frendo — Party Politics in a Fortress Colony: The Maltese Experience
6. Godfrey Wettinger — The Jews of Malta in the Late Middle Ages
7. Carmel Testa — The Life and Times of Grand Master Pinto
8. Joseph Aquilina — 100 Maltese Profiles
9. Charles Savona-Ventura — Outlines of Maltese Medical History
10. Carmel Testa — The French in Malta 1798-1800
11. Joseph Muscat/Andrew Cuschieri — Naval Activities of the Order of St. John 1530-1798
12. Carmel Testa — Romegas

Naval Activities
of the
Knights of St John
1530-1798

Joseph Muscat

Andrew Cuschieri

Midsea Books Ltd
2002

Published by Midsea Books Ltd.
Carmelites Street, Sta Venera HMR 11, Malta
Tel: 2149 7046 Fax: 2149 6904
www.midseabooks.com

Copyright © Literary, Joseph Muscat/Andrew Cuschieri 2002
Copyright © Editorial, Midsea Books Ltd 2002

No part of this publication may be reproduced,
stored in a retrieval system or transmitted
in any form by any means, electronic, mechanical,
photocopying, recording or otherwise,
without the previous written permission
of the authors.

First published in 2002

This book has been published
with the support of the

MALTA MARITIME AUTHORITY

Produced by Mizzi Design and Graphic Services Ltd.
Printed at Gutenberg Press Ltd, Malta

ISBN: 99932-39-14-3

CONTENTS

Foreword	vii
Introduction	ix
The primary intention of the book	xi
Abbreviations	xiii
Chapter 1: The Maltese and their land	1
Chapter 2: Ships and their terminology	13
Chapter 3: Merchant Ships	89
Chapter 4: The search for Muslim ships	113
Chapter 5: The Fighting Tools	165
Chapter 6: Building and fitting-out of the Maltese galley	189
Glossary	209
Bibliography	221
Index	229

FOREWORD

The islands of Malta and Gozo cover an area of 316 square kilometres in the central Mediterranean. The sequence of events that shaped their past, that led up to their present and that will produce their future is, however, far vaster. Malta may be small in size but great in its history.

In every far corner of the islands, the past and the present are woven together like fine delicate lacework. On this small island one finds the remains of the great powers that ruled over the Mediterranean. Malta was fortunate enough to find herself in the very centre of the cradle of European civilization. At times she was called to play her part in the rise and fall of great powers who have chiselled a living testament in Malta's solid rock.

A little-known people, now lost in the dark recesses of prehistory, has left evidence of its beliefs on the hills and in the open spaces. The temples of Ħaġar Qim, Imnajdra, Ġgantija, and Tarxien[1] together with the underground temple-cemetery of the Hypogeum at Ħal Saflieni are solid and genuine reminders of the vision and skill of this stock. From the altars of these temples, there rose the smoke from the sacrifices of animals, immolated in thanksgiving to the gods in return for a safe return from the seas or in the expectation of life-giving rain and bountiful harvests. Those times have gone by but still the fragrant incense of thyme, pennyroyal, and narcissus still ascends to the living God, our merciful father.

The Phoenicians too left behind their burial places with remains of their art and their beliefs, while the Romans left a heritage in villas and baths, mosaic, countless items of pottery, and marble statues. Wherever one digs one finds the remains of the past – silent remains protected in the womb of mother earth.

The Order of St John left whole cities and impressive networks of fortifications, unique in Europe and the world. The different langues of the Order competed with one another to build bigger and more beautiful palaces. They are still there today, and they will remain there as a constant reminder of the greatness of our past.

The charm of Malta lies in the admixture of her buildings; close to the palace of the knight, one finds the rich man's villa or the farmer's age-old and patched-over farmhouse. It contains the small room where love was born and where it multiplied, and the open-air staircase leading to the small room where the children spent their care-free days playing until they grew old enough to help their father with the ploughing.

I remember one summer evening on Dingli cliffs. Far away the sun, a ball of fire, was setting, soon to be covered with a cool blue sheet. Sitting on a rock lost in thought, I imagined the galleys of the Order returning victorious – soldiers and sailors, most of them Maltese, tired and thirsty but glad because they were approaching their loved ones. Gone are the galleys, the galleots, and the tartanes... one after the other, they all disappeared. Only the caique of the Maltese fisherman with its weak, twinkling light has remained to bob on the waves in the endless struggle for survival.

Andrew Cuschieri

INTRODUCTION

The story of man resembles the waves of the sea. The wave rears up frighteningly, tears steel apart and swallows it up, only to disappear again in the sea. The same can be said of the history of the European nations. Over the years they rolled on each other like waves – and disappeared. Malta witnessed and played a part in this sequence of events.

Every power that wanted to control the Mediterranean had to seek control of the strategic island of Malta and its magnificent harbours. It was ruled successively by the Phoenicians, the Carthaginians, the Romans, the Byzantines, the Arabs, the Normans, the Angevins, the Aragonese, the knights of St John, the French, and the British.

Under foreign rule, the Maltese experienced the bitter realities of life and toiled to win their daily bread. The morrow was dark and hidden and therefore frightening; the expected was arduous. The Maltese, poor in number and wealth, always valued their wisdom highly. Though conscious of their relative insignificance, the Maltese never failed to show their bravery and ability in the face of the foreigner. The Maltese grew up in suffering and want but they never cowered cravenly under the foreigner's heel. Many a time they were prepared to shed their blood to uphold their reputation. When the sword was not available, they took up their scythes to fight the foreigner, or even their bare hands.

The Maltese of old proved their mettle to the Romans during the Punic wars. It is said that when the Maltese got to know of the uprising the Arabs were planning, they took up arms against them with the war-cry of 'Let's get the dogs.' Don Gonsalvo Monroy got the same treatment when he oppressed and ill-treated them. The Maltese also suffered, to some extent, under the knights of St John. Whenever the foreign ruler thought of laying a heavy hand on the Maltese, they rose up and presently curtailed the power and the haughtiness of whoever vainly thought he could suppress their legitimate aspirations. The story of Don Gaetano Mannarino is not the only proof of all this. Grand Master Francisco Ximenes clashed with one and all and attracted upon himself the odium of all quarters, particularly that of the local clergy.

Not even in the face of the violence and cruelty of Napoleon did the Maltese cringe; they rose and attacked their new rulers like lions. General Vaubois was shaken and dumbfounded and locked himself up in the shelter of the city-walls. The garrison Napoleon left behind were defeated and humbled by the local countrymen and, with the aid of the British and the Portuguese, they expelled the French for good. For 121 years, the British ruled with an iron hand and never allowed the Maltese to govern themselves until 1921, Malta was administered by a governor and a clique of yes-men. The British had come as friends full of vain and specious promises, but they brought a form of slavery worse than that experienced under the knights. The events of the uprising of 7 June 1919 will remain famous in Maltese history. There are, however, other instances when the Maltese stood up to the British, as in the case of the protests on canonical form of marriage of 18 July 1895. The British colonizer always sought to have servile bishops so that he could govern unhindered. He thought he could similarly deal with Bishop Caruana on the question of oath-taking. At least this particular bishop stood his ground and did not allow himself to be ordered about. Because of this incident, the British demanded a say in the selection of the Maltese bishops.[2]

NOTES

1   For the first evidence of ships in Malta, see J. Muscat, 'Maltese Ship Graffiti' in C. Villain-Gandossi, *Medieval Ships and the Birth of Technological Societies* (Malta, 1991), ii, 323-78 and J. Muscat, 'Ship Graffiti – A Comparative Study', *Journal of Mediterranean Studies*, ix, No.1 (1999), 74-105.
2   A. Cuschieri, *Chiesa e Stato in Malta* (Salamanca, 1971), 415, 416.

THE PRIMARY INTENTION OF THE BOOK

Many books have been published that deal with different aspects of Maltese history. Little has, however, been written about the Maltese and their connections with the sea. Life, for the Maltese, has been inextricably linked with the sea; herein lies the greater part of Malta's history. This book will attempt an account of the Maltese and the sea under the rule of the Order of St John.

These years, perhaps more than others, marked the period when Malta demonstrated her skills on the sea to the rest of Europe and beyond. During most of that time Malta was in a continuous state of war with the Ottoman empire and the Maltese had to prove themselves not only as sailors but also as soldiers. The Order and Malta became rich on the spoils of war. Gradually both the Order's and Malta's well-being came to rely almost exclusively on their warlike activities against the Muslims. When there was nothing else to be won the Order, and with it the economy of Malta itself, collapsed.

This book will deal with:
a) the types of craft the Maltese sailed,
b) their corsairing activities,
c) their life on the sea,
d) their fighting weapons,
e) a survey of the Grand Harbour.

Various books have been written that include references to the various types of local sea-craft, sometimes quite mistakenly or out of the proper context, perhaps because of the dearth of specialized knowledge. This book does not intend to supply the names of all the types of sea-craft in the Mediterranean during the Order's stay on the island as this would require a far bulkier volume and too many potentially-tedious details. It will, however, present a graphic representation of the most important craft that sailed round Malta.

If this book will become a work of ready reference, wherein one may look up information and pictorial representation on the various types of vessels in use during that period, then its purpose would have been attained. It will, perhaps, also help to discourage the mentality that anything goes in matters of reference to the terminology of ships and shipping. All this justifies the delving into the minutiae of the past.

ABBREVIATIONS

AFH		*Archivium Franciscanum Historicum, Florence*
AOM		Archives of the Order in Malta
Compendio Art.		'Compendio d'Artiglieria', MS at the Maritime Museum, Malta.
Lib.		Library MS at the National Library of Malta, Valletta.
MMM MS		Maritime Museum Malta manuscript
NLM		National Library, Malta
NAM		National Archives, Malta
LIB		Libretti
Bosio		G. Bosio, *Historia della Sacra Religione et Illustratissima Militia di S. Giovanni Giersolmitano* (Venice, 1695)
Dal Pozzo,	i.	B. Dal Pozzo, *Historia della Sacra Religione di Malta, Parte Prima* (Verona, 1703)
	ii.	*Historia della S. Religione Militare di S. Giovanni Gerosolmitano detta di Malta*, Parte Seconda (Verona, 1715)
ACM		Archives of the Cathedral Museum, Mdina

Chapter I

THE MALTESE AND THEIR LAND

The heritage of the Maltese is one of blood and sweat. A close look at the islands' history reveals a cruel endless struggle for survival. From an early age the Maltese became accustomed to tightening their belt and to hard work. With toil and endless patience, they cultivated their rocky fields to feed their dependants. Even when the sea decided to show its terrifying powers, they good-heartedly faced the storms and braved the elements to collect their fishing traps or to deliver their cargoes to foreign lands. Beautiful and alluring as the sea is when it is calm and serenely blue, it is awesome and terrifying when it shatters and erodes solid rock. Though the north-easterly winds brought St Paul and the light of the Faith to the island, it also claimed countless lives.

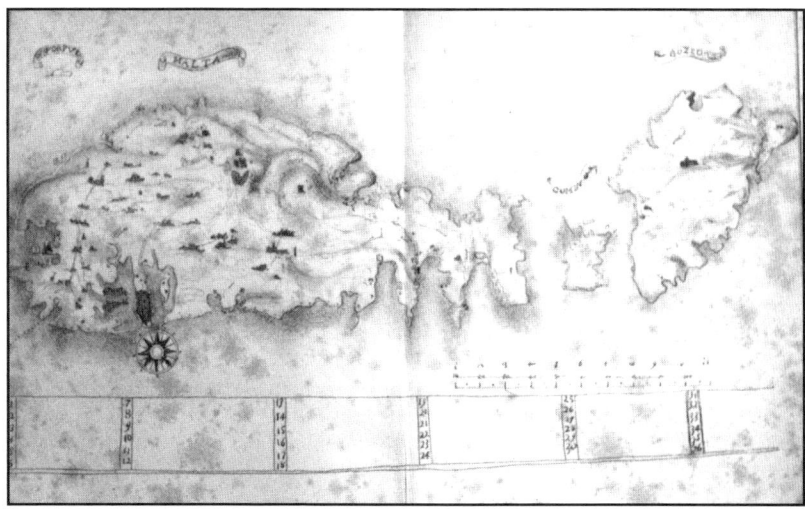

The Maltese Islands by Opizio Guidotti, Malta Maritime Museum

The sea plays about with the forsaken young man, swallows him up, only to return him out lifeless to his mother. Still the Maltese kept braving the sea: they really had no other choice.

The Maltese owe their livelihood to the sea. Their youth is passed light-heartedly playing on the sea-shore. On growing up, they have to learn to row and to climb the mainmast to fix the rigging. The sea fed the Maltese like a mother – it represented their daily bread, their field, their very home. This was the lot of the Maltese from the days of old. Though the knights after their arrival in 1530 brought the carrack, the galleon, and the galley with them, the Maltese harbours had welcomed cargo ships of all types and sizes from ancient days.

Long before the coming of the knights, the Maltese had learnt to unfurl their sails and earn notoriety as corsairs, plundering and looting on the seas round the island. Malta always had a high strategic value because of its central position and the Maltese had to show his skills with boats. The absence of fertile fields made the Maltese seek a hard living on the seas.

Many a time Malta faced starvation when the rains failed to come. Perhaps, the Maltese often toyed with the idea of abandoning this poor island for a kinder land. This, however, never happened and, in spite of the sufferings and sacrifices it entailed, the Maltese came to love their island.[1]

In addition to its proximity to Europe, nature also endowed Malta with safe and sheltered harbours. Because of its position and the protection it offered, Malta earned a reputation for the repair and maintenance of sea-craft. Under the knights, the industry of galley-building prospered. Great sea-faring powers such as Spain, Rome, and Naples built some of their ships in Maltese yards. Until the introduction of coal for the propulsion of ships, Malta had earned a good reputation in the making of sails.[2]

Malta in European history

In 1522 Suleiman II attacked Rhodes, defeated the Order of St John, and expelled it from the island. The Turks, however, acknowledged the heroism of the Hospitallers by according them full military honours. The Christian galleys sailed away from Rhodes on 1 January 1523 and

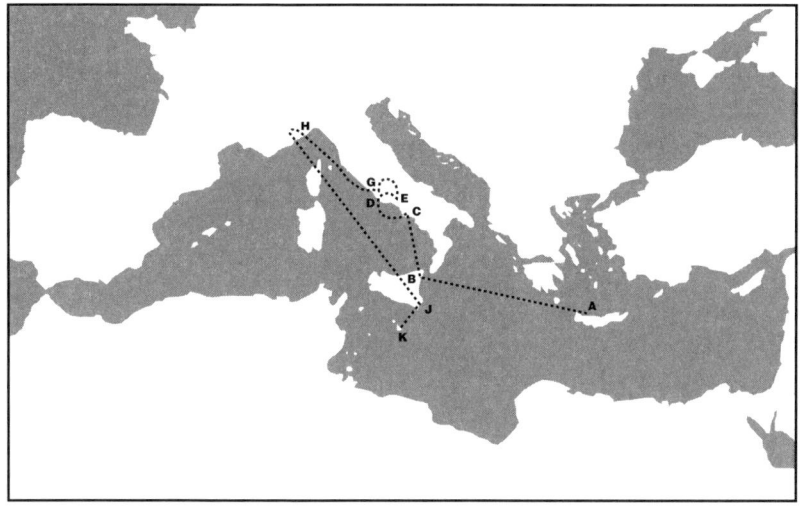

The itinerary of the Order round the Mediterranean before they settled in Malta

spent two months at Candia (Crete) where the knights repaired and patched their vessels as best they could. From Candia they went to Messina.[3] Very much against its will, the Order eventually accepted Malta as a fief from Charles V of Spain.[4]

The Order's itinerary, with the date of arrival of the knights, included:

Candia	5 January 1523
Messina	30 April 1523
Baia	22 June 1523
Civitavecchia	7 July 1523
Rome	14 September 1523
Viterbo	25 January 1524
Corneto	15 June 1527
Villafranca	3 October 1527
Nice	14 November 1527
Saragosa	7 October 1529

and then, '*con universale allegrezza di tutti giunsero a salvamento in Malta, mercoledi mattino a venti sei del mese di ottobre, dell'anno sopradetto mille cinquecento, e trenta a due hore di Sole*'.[5]

When the Frenchman Philippe Villiers de L'Isle Adam, the first grand master to reign in Malta, came ashore at Birgu he had one primary intention, that of remaining here for only as long a time as it took him to refit and re-equip his forces and recapture his beloved Rhodes. A few

Marble tablet showing the place where Grand Master L'Isle Adam died at the Ta' Ġieżu Friary, Rabat

months after his arrival in Malta, L'Isle Adam sent a squadron of six galleys and two Maltese brigantines with 1,200 sailors under Admiral Salviati to attack Modon in Greece from where they planned to strike at and capture Rhodes. Although Modon, Coron, and Patras were invested, it seems that Salviati was not successful in any of his attempts. On hearing of the knights' expeditions, Pope Hadrian VI sent word to L'Isle Adam to desist from harassing the Turks and to accept Malta as a permanent home.[6] Still the knights never gave up hoping to conquer the Holy Land once again and Rhodes was for them an ideal staging-post.[7]

After the Great Siege of 1565 many knights were of the opinion that Malta should be abandoned because the situation had become precarious and unstable while the future loomed uncertainly and inauspiciously. The knights expected quicker and greater assistance from France and Spain than they had received during the siege. They were prepared to go to Sicily or some other place only to preserve the Order.[8] Circumstances were, however, to dictate a long stay in Malta where, in a 268-year span, the island was to contribute signally to the fame and honour of the Hospitallers. Indeed the Order was to obtain its greatest moments of glory and honour in Malta.

With the assistance of the Maltese, the knights defied the mighty Turkish armada and humbled the forces of the Ottoman empire. Although the knights always got the laurels of victory after the Siege, an unbiased examination of the records reveals that it was the heroism of the Maltese that amazed Suleiman the Magnificent and made the Turkish forces sneaked away in shame and ignominy. The nineteenth-century historian Whitworth Porter is of the opinion that 'The Order was most ably seconded and supported by the bravery and resolution of the Maltese inhabitants. It must be borne in mind that the bulk of the soldiery was composed of the native element. The Maltese, whenever they have been tested, have shown themselves steady and resolute soldiers, and on this memorable occasion were not found wanting.'[9] Of the 10,000 casualties suffered by the besieged, 7,000 were Maltese men, women, and children.[10] Historians also agree that the battle of Lepanto would have had a far different outcome if the Turks had not been defeated at Malta.[11] This was not to be the last contribution of Malta to European history; for 268 years the Maltese heroically protected European interests from the challenge of the Muslim crescent.[12] The Order left Malta in 1798 when it was summarily expelled by Napoleon Bonaparte.[13]

When, barely three months later, the Maltese rose against the French, their leaders asked for the protection of the British. These, for their part, were half-hearted and doubted whether Malta would ever be of any strategic use to the British empire. General Acton wrote to Sir William Hamilton on 17 September 1798 giving a great deal of information on the situation in Malta and concluded that, 'These are the news I have been able to collect by my secret agents in that Island. I will not, however, answer for the absolute truth of them, considering the Maltese as a corrupted and suspicious people.'[14] Malta was, however, to prove its worth to Britain in the course of two world wars.

After the debacle at Gallipoli, Malta tended and nursed thousands of wounded soldiers. During the Second World War, while great nations like France, Yugoslavia, Czechoslovakia, and Poland bowed to the might of the Nazi Panzers and cowered under the threat of the Luftwaffe, Malta, exhausted and on the brink of starvation, stood four square with the Allies despite all the ruin and destruction. Even when the swastika darkened the continent, Malta stood bravely until the wheel of Fortune turned to favour the allies. The part the Maltese played in the eventual victory was recognized by the Allied leaders such as King George VI, Prime Minister Winston Churchill, and President Franklin D. Roosevelt.[15] War historians have all honoured the Maltese for their bravery and heroism during five whole years of famine, privation, disease, and bombing. The Maltese saw their savings and property going up in smoke and, with tears in their eyes, searched for their loved ones under piles of rubble and debris.

It is natural to pride oneself on one's achievements. The Maltese, ever conscious of their smallness, often denigrated themselves but they never failed to demonstrate their valour to the foreigner. The history of the Maltese is free of treachery or cases of dereliction of duty.

But what, may one ask, is left of the past, except its memories. The heirloom of the past is not to be found only in dusty, worm-eaten volumes, because our ancestors prepared our present way of life for us. The present can never be understood and the future can never be prepared for unless we study and analyse the past.

The arrival of the Order of St John in Malta

At daybreak, on Wednesday 26 October 1530, three galleys of the Order of St John appeared on the horizon off Malta. There was a sweet breeze gently blowing from the north and the north-west. With the wind blowing from behind them, the galleys sped towards the island which the Emperor Charles V had enfeoffed to the Order of St John.

At seven or eight in the morning, two hours after sunrise, the galley *Santa Croce,* carrying the Grand Master Philip Villiers de L'Isle Adam on board, sailed into the Grand Harbour.

The other ships of the Order were already at anchor in harbour, amongst them the old carrack. A week earlier, the Order's ships had had a taste of the sudden storms that can hit the central Mediterranean in autumn. During the afternoon of Thursday 20 October, a sudden gale with torrential rains lashed the island. The storm lasted only three-quarters of an hour, but it was enough to reduce the harbour to shambles. The old carrack cut loose, was driven on to the rocky foreshore, and then drifted to the mud-flats at Marsa. The carrack was not, however, damaged at all but four ships of Maltese owners foundered.

The grand master who was still in Syracuse took the news of the escape of the old carrack as an augury of a propitious future on the island.[16] In actual fact, on this bare rock, the Order was to win its greatest honours since its foundation towards the year 1048.[17] Here the Order was to reach the zenith of her fame and to become known as the Order of Malta. The knights' galleys and their Maltese crews were to be instrumental in recapturing the Order's pristine glory after the defeat at Rhodes.

The knights had spent seven years wandering all over Europe seeking a suitable home from where they could prosecute their original purpose of fighting the Infidel.[18] When it left Rhodes, the Order had about 50 vessels.[19] When it arrived in Malta it only had three galleys left: the *Santa Croce,* the *San Filippo,* and the *San Giovanni*;[20] the old carrack *Santa Maria*; another carrack the *Sant'Anna*; the galleon of the Order; a galleot; a brigantine; and some other small vessels. Even for those days this was just a small and weak flotilla, but it was to provide the foundation of one of the finest navies in the Mediterranean. Indeed the Order started recovering its fortunes soon after its arrival in Malta.

The Order lost no time in allying itself with Charles V and his son Philip II in the Spanish campaigns against the Turks. As time went by, the Order started joining up with other Christian navies, like those of the Pope, Venice, Naples, and Genoa, in their sea-battles against the Ottoman forces.[21] The Order sent three of its galleys, the *Santa Maria della Vittoria*, the *San Giovanni*, and the *San Pietro* to fight at Lepanto, in addition to other Maltese vessels,[22] which could have been small auxiliary ships that used to accompany the galleys. It is not likely that there were large square-sailed vessels that joined the galleys.[23] There

Stern balcony of the carrack Sant Anna

were only three Maltese galleys at Lepanto in October 1571. The marquis of Pescara even disarmed the galleot he had prepared for the *corso* and gave the whole complement of slaves and armaments to the Order so that it could prepare the three galleys for Lepanto.[24]

From 1572 onwards the Order started to range all over the Mediterranean on its own, nibbling here and there at Turkish and Moorish vessels. It provided its assistance in the Sicilian and Venetian victories at Candia and the Peloponnese. However, the real strength of the Maltese galley is best seen in its unaided skirmishing.

The year 1701 marked a new development in the Order's strategy of war at sea. Till then the Order had relied on the galley for fighting the Turks. Towards the beginning of the eighteenth century, the Order imitated the other European navies and introduced square-rigged warships.[25] This period was, however, also to mark the start of the gradual decline of the Order's power until the nadir was reached with the shameful expulsion from the island in 1798.[26]

The *corso* started declining towards the end of the seventeenth century and it almost disappeared by 1748.[27] With the drying-up of these revenues, the island fell on hard times. The Order ran huge debts, there was massive unemployment, and the inactive knights themselves became listless and indolent.[28] But how far was the decline of the *corso* responsible for the decline and fall of the Order itself? Though, from the end of the eighteenth century onwards, the British and the French had started sending men-of-war to combat the Mediterranean corsair,[29] there were other earlier factors which contributed to the disappearance of corsairing.

Ecumenism was one such factor. In the hope that an agreement could be reached with the Greek Orthodox Church, the pope bade the Order not to molest Greek shipping. The knights, belonging as they did to a religious Order, had no other option but to obey the pope's bidding,[30] while the Turks and the Moors started availing themselves of Greek passports to protect themselves from the Maltese corsairs.[31]

Rome also interfered with Maltese corsairing activities in another way. Very often, whenever a Maltese galley captured some Turkish vessel off the coast of Palestine, the Ottomans retaliated by falling upon the Franciscan friars, killing every Christian they could lay their hands on, and sacking the Holy Shrines.[32] To protect these Holy Places as far as possible, Rome extended the territorial limits of the sea off Palestine[33]

An Ottoman sultan

from 10 to 50 miles in the space of 50 years from 1647 to 1697. This meant that the Maltese galleys could not attack Turkish shipping within these limits[34] and thus they were denied access to an area rich in Muslim merchant shipping.

France and Venice did their utmost to control the threat of the Maltese corsair to protect and increase their trading links with the Turks.[35] Even when the Barbary corsairs were laying waste to and ravaging whole towns and cities, France and Venice had continued to welcome Ottoman shipping in their harbours and to supply them with weapons and munitions. Paul Auphan refuses to take sides on the matter of the *'alliance impie'*, and gives the various opinions of different authors for and against France. Venice and Naples signed treaties of friendship many years after the example of France and they drew near the Ottoman empire in the eighteenth century. In 1573 Venice had agreed to a very stiff treaty with the Turks. It ceded Cyprus, paid 300,000 ducats as reparations, and agreed to a yearly financial contribution to keep Cephalonia and Zante. It also agreed not to keep more than 60 galleys.[36] Auphan treats at length about the flirtation of the French navy with that of the Turks. In 1543 both navies joined together at Marseilles. After attacking Nice and Savoy, the Turkish fleet wintered at Toulon.

England was one of the nations that used to supply the Turks with war material. Dutch vessels laden with munitions sailed regularly to the

Barbary coast. They carried masts, anchor cables, gunpowder, resin, oars, oak planks, and bronze coursiers for galleys and, at times, even sold them warships. Swedish and Dutch lead and iron were unloaded into Algerian store-rooms to be employed against Christian shipping.[37]

The Ottoman empire itself had started on its decline after Lepanto. The petty rulers of the Barbary coast waned and broke away from one another. This contributed not only to a weakening of the understanding amongst themselves but also of the potential market itself, a decline which the Maltese galleys experienced directly.[38] The Turks themselves had ironically kept the Order on its feet and fed the Maltese population. Turkey's decline enfeebled the Order and brought about the collapse of Malta's economy.

NOTES

1. G.F. Abela, *Della Descrittione di Malta* (Malta, 1647), 431 mentions the great famine of 1468; G.A. Vassallo, *Storia di Malta Raccontata in compendio* (Malta, 1845), 210, refers to the famine of 1475; see also E.R. Leopardi, 'Bandi Transactions of the Consiglio Popolare, etc, of the XV Century', *Melita Historica*, ii, No. 4 (1959), 255.
2. Lib. 223, s.v. *Tela per far le vele*.
3. Bosio, iii, 1-7.
4. Ibid., 78.
5. Bosio, iii, 89.
6. Ibid., 26, 42, 43 repeats the same idea of re-taking Rhodes. A clause in Charles V's donation states, '*In oltre s'occorresse che la Religione sopra detta ricuperasse l'Isola di Rodi ...*', ibid., 81.
7. *Istruzioni sopra gli obblighi piu principali De Cavalieri di Malta* (Malta, 1758), 28.
8. Bosio, iii, 724, 725.
9. W. Porter, *Malta and Its Knights* (London, 1871), 148, 149.
10. F. Balbi di Correggio, *The Siege of Malta 1565*, translated by H.A. Balbi (Copenhagen, 1961), 181.
11. F. Garnier, *Journal de la Bataille de Lepante* (Paris, 1965), 24.
12. A. Michaud, *Storia delle Crociate* (Milan, 1878), 347, note 64; see also Lib. 223, address to the reader, '*Al Lettore*'.
13. L. De Caro, *Storia dei Gran Maestri e Cavalieri di Malta* (Malta, 1853), i, *Prefazione*, p. ii.
14. B. Blouet, *The Story of Malta* (London, 1967), 163; W. Hardman, *A History of Malta during the period of the French and British Occupations 1798-1815* (London, 1909), 111, quotes Brit. Mus. Add. MS. 34907, f. 233. But how could that general express such a statement when the British had hardly set foot on the island?
15. George VI bestowed the George Cross on Malta in April 1942. Churchill called Malta 'The unsinkable aircraft carrier of the Mediterranean.' Roosevelt left in the island a parchment recalling the island's bravery on 7 December 1943.

16 Bosio, iii, 88, 89.
17 Lib. 413, f. 121.
18 Bosio, iii, 1-88; the author describes in detail the itinerary of the knights before their arrival in Malta.
19 Ibid., ii, 706.
20 Ibid., iii, 88.
21 E. Rossi, *Storia della Marina dell'Ordine di San Giovanni di Gerusalemme di Rodi e di Malta* (Rome-Milan, 1926), 34.
22 Dal Pozzo, i, 11.
23 J. Żarb, *Żabbar Sanctuary and the Knights of St John* (Malta, 1959), 31-4, wrongly proposes a painting as representing the gathering at Messina of the ships of the Order before proceeding to Lepanto.
24 Bosio, iii, 893.
25 Rossi, 34; Vassallo, 689.
26 Rossi, 34.
27 P. Earle, *Corsairs of Malta and Barbary* (London, 1970), 109.
28 S. Bono, *I corsari barbareschi* (Turin, 1964), 133-5; this author shows that the Order of St Stephen was passing through the same historical, social, and economic processes.
29 Earle, 265.
30 AOM 261, f. 33v; *Deliberazione che si ordini ai corsari di non molestare i Greci di Scio*, dated 3 October 1665.
31 Leopardi, 235.
32 AFH, xiv, 1921, 490.
33 AOM 264, f. 187 also mentions '*Proibizione alle navi della Religione di accostarsi ai porti di Giaffa, S. Giovanni D'Acri e Saida.*'
34 Leopardi, 227.
35 Vassallo, 696; see also L. Viviani, *Storia di Malta* (Turin, 1933), i, 325; Rossi, 38 says '*Dalla parte Cristiana, mentre la Francia s'alleava col Turco, restava Venezia, non sempre serena nella sua condotta ...*'
36 P. Auphan, *Histoire de la Méditerrannée* (Paris, 1962), 172, 186, 226.
37 Ibid., 173, 175, 178; F. Braudel, *The Mediterranean and the Mediterranean World in the age of Philip II*, Translated by S. Reynolds (London, 1973), ii, 839, note 5; Bono, 10, note 20.
38 Leopardi, 227. Earle, 100, says that privateering remained the second most important occupation of the people after agriculture. The decline of the *corso* was a very serious loss to the Maltese economy. Rossi, 86, says, '*É da notarsi il fatto che nel trentennio 1700-1730 raramente le squadre Maltesi si spingono in Levante; la loro azione e quasi circoscritta ai mari di Ponente.*' The Maltese corsairs had to turn against the Barbary corsairs; this was not an easy task and was less profitable than attacking Muslim shipping in the Levant.

A galley and a galleon by Breughel

Chapter II

SHIPS AND THEIR TERMINOLOGY

The ordinary reader's often-hazy knowledge of the names of the various types of ships and their proper terminology renders necessary a brief explanation of the terms and words used in this book.

There were two main types of vessels:
a) The lateen-rigged ships which were narrow hulled and stood quite low in the water. Such vessels had lateen sails and were the first sailing craft. Lateen-rigged vessels varied from 60 to 16 metres in length;[1]
b) The square-rigged vessels were equipped with a wide beam and had a high freeboard. These were rather large in size and fairly slow in sailing. The carrack and the galleon are examples of this type of such ships. Square-rigged vessels sometimes reached the length of 84 metres though there were others of a much smaller size, 34 or 26 metres.

Another distinguishing feature between these two types of ships lies in the use of oars. Lateen-rigged vessels could use oars to propel themselves, while the square-rigged vessels relied solely on the wind. Lateen-rigged ships were renowned for their speed and were much faster than the other type of ship. While lateen-rigged boats had two or three masts, square-rigged ones, like the carrack, had four. Each mast had its special name: the bowsprit jutted out of the bows, then, working towards the poop, came the foremast, the mainmast, the mizzen-mast, and the bonaventure.

Lateen-rigged boats used lateen sails, triangular-shaped sails on the long yard or antenna, at an angle of 45 degrees to the mast. Square-rigged vessels had two or three square sails on the foremast and the mainmast, and lateen sails on the mizzen-mast and the bonaventure.

These two types of boats also carried different types of armaments. Because lateen-rigged vessels stood low in the water and because of the oars themselves, the guns on this type of boat, from two to five in number, were situated on the bows. Square-rigged vessels stood high in the water and sometimes had up to six decks, and therefore they had their artillery distributed on both sides.

Lateen-rigged vessels had only one deck and the crew was exposed to the elements. All life, including cooking and sleeping, was spent on the open deck. On square-rigged vessels, however, there was ample room for a comfortable distribution of living space. Everybody, including the slaves, could find shelter under a deck. Since a sailing ship could always capsize in a strong wind, it always carried a ballast of stones or lead as a counterweight. Ballast was more important for square-rigged vessels because of their high structure and the strong leverage on their masts.

The principal fighting ships of the Order of St John and which made such an important contribution to the emergence of the Order as a great naval power were the carrack, the galleon, the galley, the *petacchio,* the ship-of-the-line, the frigate, and the corvette.

The Order's cargo ships were the *xprunara,* the brigantine, the tartane, the *pollacca,* the pink, and the chebec. Occasionally a fighting ship was used to carry provisions, while a cargo ship could be fitted out as a man-of-war if the need arose.

Fighting ships

In days of old all sea-going craft, including merchantmen used to carry armaments, such as arquebuses, muskets, guns, swords, cannon, or periers, to defend themselves from the corsairs who plagued the seas even up till the first decades of the nineteenth century. This threat also made it necessary for the sailor to double up as a soldier. Cargo ships hardly ever travelled in convoys but the Order always sent its fighting ships to protect its cargo vessels,[2] which explains why so few of them were ever captured by the Barbary corsairs.[3] There were times when the galleys of the Order were employed to transport provisions from Licata and Syracuse while escorting a great number of merchant ships loaded with grain, biscuit, and other commodities. One of them was the Ragusan great ship the *Drago Grande* which was loaded with all types of provisions. Occasionally the necessary licences for the provision of foodstuffs from Sicily were issued late and consequently many ships were lost owing to bad weather or as the result of the incessant attacks by the Barbary corsairs. A message explaining such hazards was carried by Commander Fra Antonio Maldonato to the court of Syracuse. Maltese-owned cargo vessels could not always depend on the Order's protection and were frequently captured by the North African corsairs.[4]

The carrack

The word 'carrack' is probably derived from the Arabic *harraka* meaning 'a fire ship'.[5] The Portuguese were the first to use the word carrack for their large ships that plied the Eastern trade routes or crossed the Atlantic to Brazil. Through Portuguese the word entered other languages where it came to refer to a particular type of vessel with a tonnage greater than 2,000 tons. The carrack was one of the main square-rigged vessels with four or five decks and with two castles, one at the bows and the other at the stern. It carried from 50 to 70 guns and could stand its own against a whole flotilla of smaller ships. The carrack, which ruled the seas in the fifteenth and sixteenth centuries, was also exceptionally sea-worthy.

Large sails were necessary to propel such a heavy ship. It normally had four masts; the first two, the foremast and the mainmast were square-rigged, while the last two were lateen-rigged.

There were differences between one carrack and another. Some, for example, carried only three masts and some were rigged in a different manner. However, the distinguishing features of the carrack were its high freeboard and the amount of guns and hand weapons it could carry.[6]

The carrack remained the largest vessel the Order of St John ever had throughout its stay on the Island; their most famous carracks being the *Santa Maria* and the *Sant'Anna*.

The Santa Maria *was formerly a Muslim mogarbina*

The *Santa Maria*

The *Santa Maria* was originally a *mogarbina* captured by the knights in 1507. This was already at least 27 years old by the time the Order came to Malta. The first carrack the knights had before coming to Malta was called the *San Giovanni Battista* which was also known as the *Gran Carracca* or the *Gran Nave*. It was this carrack that captured the *mogarbina* of the Egyptian sultan which was renamed the *Santa Maria*. The *San Giovanni Battista* is first mentioned in 1482.[7] Bosio writes that when the knights were sailing away from Rhodes to Messina with an uncertain future ahead of them, they raised just one flag at half-mast showing Our Lady holding the dead Christ in her lap. On the flag the words *AFFLICTIS TU SPES UNICA REBUS* meaning 'You are our only hope in our distress' were embroidered in gold. [8]

The *Santa Maria* was a fine and most powerful vessel. Little was actually written about it though there is an account of how the Order obtained it. On 13 September 1507 the grand carrack *San Giovanni Battista* met a Moorish *mogarbina* a vessel of more or less similar strength. The captain, the knight Gattineau, ordered all the guns of one side to fire at once. The frightening roar it made was enough to cower the Moors to surrender.[9] The knights refitted and refurbished the *mogarbina*, renamed it the *Santa Maria*, and used it to replace the *San Giovanni*

Battista. In its heyday, the *Santa Maria* proved of inestimable worth to the knights and it was the terror of the Moors. It served as the Order's headquarters during its peregrinations in search of a permanent home. It was even big enough to house the Order's mint.[10]

The ageing *Santa Maria* was laid up on its arrival in Malta because the Order had a newer and finer carrack. Many of its guns and other armaments were removed and it was left to ride at anchor in the harbour. It was used as a store[11] and to sleep the slaves taken at Modon.

The old carrack met its end quite dramatically after a young slave boy climbed aboard to steal some gunpowder. All of a sudden the whole magazine exploded and blew up the vessel. The entire upper deck of the *Santa Maria,* slaves and all, sank right in the middle of the harbour, while the rest of the hulk kept blazing away. Some of her guns started firing on their own and hit the other vessels anchored nearby. To avoid a greater catastrophe, the blazing hulk was fired upon by a large cannon from the foot of St Angelo point. Still the carrack would not sink and kept drifting for some distance till it sank off Senglea right under the small church of St Julian. Many guns, iron cannonballs, and various items of the Order's treasury were later recovered from the wreck.[12]

The *Sant'Anna*

The carrack *Sant'Anna* which replaced the *Santa Maria* was a finer, larger, and even more powerful vessel. Ironically it had been launched at Nice in 1522 on the same day the Order was finally defeated at Rhodes,[13] and the knights were therefore in no mood to celebrate.

This carrack, with its six decks, was the finest vessel the Order ever had and it was reputed to be the most beautiful ship afloat of its time. Though its two lowest decks lay below water-level, the mainmast of a galley could only reach about one metre lower than its stern. The mainmast was so thick that it took six men to gird it. It had a fine large chapel, some painted panels of which can still be seen in the musicians' gallery in the grand master's palace in Valletta.[14] Its dining room and the knights' sleeping quarters were so spacious and comfortable as to resemble similar rooms in a royal palace.[15] All round the stern galleries, there was a small garden with trees and plants where a knight could take a few hours' rest. There was a hand-operated flour mill and an

The Sant Anna – *after a painting in a private collection*

oven. Bread was freshly baked everyday – something which no other contemporary vessel could boast of.

A vessel of that size with 500 crew required several craftsmen to keep it going. It had its own forge with three blacksmiths working round the clock. It had enough food and drink on board to stay six months without having to enter harbour for provisions.

Contrary to what one would expect, the *Sant'Anna* was both fast and extremely manoeuvrable. It was ideally suited for the weak and changeable winds of the Mediterranean.

The *Sant'Anna* had 50 big guns on board and a great number of small ones distributed all round it. Its artillery was the finest available.[16] To fire those guns there was, amongst others, the Maltese bombardiers, then fast gaining a solid reputation for their skill. The *Sant'Anna* could fight 50 galleys simultaneously.[17]

This carrack was sheathed in lead below the water-level thus making the hull water-proof,[18] a revolutionary technique not even dreamt of then by other sea-faring powers. Indeed the British only started to sheathe the hulls of their ships with copper 200 years later.[19] The sides of the *Sant'Anna* were so thick that they were never pierced by a hostile cannonball.[20] Captain Windus of the British squadron stationed in India, pointed out to London Archaeological Institute on 7 February 1862, that the carrack *Sant'Anna* of the knights of Malta was the first armoured war vessel adopted to resist the projectiles of her times, thus preceding by two centuries the modern adoption of iron and steel. The *Sant'Anna*, he said, was sheathed with metal and was perfectly cannon-proof. Apparently Captain Windus either exaggerated in his description of the carrack or else he did not completely understand Bosio who only says that it was sheathed with lead to render it waterproof and not cannon-proof. If that had really been the knights' purpose they would have sheathed all the freeboard.[21] Still it is doubtful whether there was any other vessel afloat that could stand up to it, let alone sink it.

The *Sant'Anna* must have provided a wonderful sight when entering harbour. Its masts came level with the bastions, while its unfurled sails towered over and hid Fort St Angelo. Its painted sculptures[22] and a mad flurry of flags of all shapes, sizes, and colours provided an exceptional spectacle while the band playing on board proudly proclaimed yet another victorious campaign.[23]

The *Sant'Anna* had two large boats with 15 banks of oars and five smaller craft. All of these, except for one of the larger boats, were carried on board. The other large boat, probably a brigantine, was towed behind. These boats, brigantines, caiques, and skiffs, were often used to attack Turkish galleots. The brigantines were large enough to take a demi-cannon on the poop and two sakers on the bows. A similarly armed boat took part in the attack on Goletta.[24]

Nobody would have thought that this majestic ship, the terror of the Levant and the wonder of the West, was to have such a short life. In 1540, just 18 years after its launching, Grand Master Juan D'Omedes ordered the dismantling of its guns and armaments and the ship itself was left to rot away.[25]

The victorious campaigns of the *Sant'Anna* had brought great honours upon its captain, Fra Francesco de Cleremont. This had made D'Omedes envious and he sought to destroy de Cleremont by putting his ship away. Though D'Omedes ordered the building of a new carrack for another captain, in actual fact no other such vessel was ever built and two galleons were commissioned instead. All historians agree that D'Omedes was liked by nobody, neither by the Maltese nor by his fellow knights. He was a choleric and selfish old man, unscrupulous in having his way, and a real psychopath. However, the Order was then experiencing financial hardship, brought about by the confiscation of all its property in England by Henry VIII and the laying up of the *Sant'Anna* was considered as an economy measure. The vessel was also too large to enter the harbour of

Tripoli, which the Order then also held. This decision to decommission the carrack was taken in the general chapter of 1540.[26]

The galleon

Towards the beginning of the sixteenth century the European maritime powers like Spain, France, Portugal, and Venice began considering the construction of a new type of ship to replace the carrack. This came to be known as the galleon and was in actual fact an evolution of the carrack. The Order of St John built one such galleon, the *San Giovanni*, on the urgings of the other powers.[27]

The galleon resembled the carrack in many details. It had four masts, while the castles at the bows and at the poop stood very high out of the water just like the carrack's. The sides too were very strong and it had a high freeboard. The main difference was one of size; the galleon was smaller and, therefore, faster. Its sheer outline looked like a half-moon.[28]

The introduction of the galleon meant a reduction of the excessive size of the carrack without sacrificing too much of its fire power.[29] This

The galleon, after Opizio Guidotti.

does not mean that the galleon was a small vessel; in fact it could even cross the Atlantic.[30] The first battery near the water level carried 14 guns with an equal number in the battery above it. In addition to the many smaller guns, the galleon carried 30 large ones.[31]

The most important and revolutionary thing about the galleon lay in the sails. Guidotti gives the following nomenclatures for the particular sails:

Mast	Sail
bowsprit	spritsail, sprit topsail
foremast	foresail, fore topsail
mainmast	mainsail, main topsail, main topgallant
mizzen	mizzen sail, mizzen topsail
bonaventure	bonaventure, mizzen sail.[32]

It had square sails on the first two masts just like the carrack but a square sail was rigged above the lateen sail on the mizzen mast.[33] This design gave the galleon extra speed, especially since the ships had a narrower hull than cargo ships.

The galleon proved a most useful investment for the Order. Fra Opizio Guidotti described in detail the wealth and riches the *San Giovanni* brought to the island as loot. Under the captaincy of the same Guidotti, the *San Giovanni* brought home about 480 Muslim slaves in addition to other great wealth.[34] Guidotti had arrived in Malta on 30 June 1592 during the magistracy of Fra Hugh Verdalle. He was invested as a knight in August 1593 and was given command of the galley *San Giacomo* on 12 August 1603. On 24 June 1606 he assumed command of a galleon of the Order and on 22 June 1616 he was given command of the *capitana* or the flagship of the galley squadron. On 15 March 1622 he was chosen by the pope as the lieutenant general of the papal galleys. On 3 July 1635 he was nominated admiral of the Order's galleys, a position he held for two years.[35]

On 9 October 1606, while Malta was experiencing a great famine, the galleon *San Giovanni* intercepted two Turkish cargo-ships known as caramousals heavily laden with rice, bales of silk, and other expensive merchandise; 190 Turks were also captured and sold as slaves.

On 18 February 1607 the same galleon captured a caramousal laden with grain in the harbour of Salonika. It then proceeded towards Cyprus where it captured another caramousal carrying an expensive cargo of

A galleon firing a broadside

pearls and money; 116 Turks were seized including the bey himself who had to pay a very stiff ransom.[36]

On 22 March 1608, while Guidotti was on his third trip, he attacked a Turkish caramousal near the harbour of Scopoli. The crew jumped overboard and swam to land and the knights took the ship without a fight. Since the captured vessel was not in a good condition and could not be used by the Order, it was left to drift at the mercy of the waves.

On the 26th and 27th of the same month, the *San Giovanni* captured another two caramousals in the same area and it returned to Malta laden with grain and other expensive cargo, together with 178 Turkish slaves.[37]

These exploits amply demonstrate the suitability of the galleon for corsairing activities, provided it lay in good hands. Its success led to another galleon being ordered in Amsterdam which was to be named *San Giovanni* like its predecessor.[38] Commander Digut's generous contribution was not enough to cover the entire cost of its construction and the Order had to fork out the difference.[39] The galleon which could carry a cargo of 4,000 *salme*, arrived in Malta early in the morning of 26 December 1617 and Digut himself guided it into the harbour.[40]

This Dutch-built galleon became known as the 'Grand Galleon' and it gave a new profile to the Order's navy. It cost the fabulous sum of 60,000 *scudi* – indeed no expense was spared to make it the finest vessel of its time in the Mediterranean.[41]

A small galleon

The Order found it more profitable to build the galleon in Flanders though it could have used a Maltese yard or arsenal where a very large galleon had already been constructed in 1583.[42] It was to prove extremely valuable to the knights in the carrying of grain and other cargo.[43]

Whenever the Order was fortunate enough to capture Moorish vessels in good condition, it always refitted them for its own navy. This was the case with a particular Muslim small galleon which was captured on St George's day, 21 April 1543. As the knight Schilling was leading two galleys to relieve Tripoli, he spotted two Turkish galleons off Djerba. After a furious sea-battle that lasted four hours and left many Christian casualties, the two galleons surrendered. The better one was laden with the captured loot and sent to Malta, while the other one was towed to Tripoli.[44]

The galleon entered the Malta arsenal for repairs where it remained till all work was completed the following year. Fra Baldassare de Colans, known as Baumes, requested the honour of being given its command. Thanks to his hard-headedness this was, however, to bring him nothing but shame and ignominy. In fact, he was to spend a number of years in slavery and to live his days out in Malta in public ridicule.

On 7 July 1544 Baumes, while sailing towards Tripoli, was caught in a calm. Morat Aga realized that the small galleon could be only towed by its caique and prepared a galleot with 23 banks of oars and 150 musketeers. Baumes refused to open fire saying that, if the Moors were so foolhardy to keep approaching, he himself would kill them. He refused the advice of his Biscain pilot to fire his artillery, threatening to put to the sword anybody who disobeyed.

The galleot rammed the small galleon's stern which it proceeded to smash by means of the bow chaser on its rambate. The galleon, which had no guns at the stern, could not return the fire and the Moors had an easy time sniping at the Christians with their muskets. The galleon soon caught fire and the crew, having given up all hope, were all captured. The fire was extinguished and the vessel was towed towards Tagiora amidst general Moorish jubilation. This was one of the few Muslim victories over the Order.[45]

On 14 June 1564 the Order captured a large Turkish galleon called the *Sultana*. Suleiman, who had allowed the knights full military honours following the defeat at Rhodes, was so enraged that he swore to destroy the Order once and for all.[46] The Turkish galleon that could carry up to 4,000 *salme* was refitted and renamed *San Giovanni* and it was to prove most useful to the knights. On 11 May 1565 it brought 1,000 tons of grain and 400 soldiers to Malta; a timely assistance which de Valette saw as God-sent for the coming battle with the Turks. Throughout the Great Siege the galleon was kept in a very protected position under Fort St Angelo on the Vittoriosa side. The Turks, who were confident of their ultimate victory, never fired on it since they hoped to win it over in one piece. Only when they realized that victory had eluded them did they fire a few desultory and ineffective shots. The *San Giovanni* gave the Order sterling service for many years.[47]

Galleons remained in use till the seventeenth century when they started to be replaced gradually by men-of-war. The galley, however, was to prove the Order's best weapon, even better than the carrack or the galleon.[48]

The *petacchio*

Towards 1613, Soliman Rais known as 'the Maltese' was preparing a large ship to harass Christian merchantmen. Five English and two Italian slaves escaped on a Turkish ship which was sailing to Susa carrying the guns and the other weapons for Rais's ship. All alone they managed to defeat their captors and sail away with all the wealth the ship was carrying. The capture of this ship, a *petacchio*, took place at Goletta and helped in no small way to upset Muslim plans.[49]

The *petacchio* was a vessel indigenous to the Mediterranean and is rarely mentioned by North European writers. Guidotti[50] fortunately left a drawing of this vessel which first appeared on the seas early in the seventeenth century. It is not easy to determine whether it was the Christians or the Muslims who were the first to use this ship.

From afar the Order's *petacchio* looked like a small galleon but it stood lower in the water and it was not as high aft. The poop had a balcony which jutted out on the rudder and resembled the one on the carrack. The *petacchio* had a quarter deck and its poop deck was characterized by the cabin-like structure one could see on a galley. The poop area was restricted to the captain and important people. Its bows vaguely resembled that of an eighteenth-century ship-of-the-line.

A *petacchio* could only take a few small guns; the one drawn by Guidotti had three openings for guns at the side and one aft underneath the stern balcony. According to Guglielmotti, a *petacchio* carried from eight to ten guns. Early in the seventeenth century, guns were rarely mounted below the decks as it was believed then that this might weaken the whole structure of the hull and that the firing would cause the vessel to break under the strain of the gun fire.

The petacchio

Although Guglielmotti says that the *petacchio* had two masts with square sails, Guidotti shows it with three masts with a lateen sail on the mizzenmast. Strangely enough, some kind of jib sails can be seen furled round the jibboom. This made the *petacchio*'s sails look to a certain extent like those of eighteenth-century sailing ships.

The *petacchio* which barely had a tonnage of 150 was considered as the smallest of the square-rigged ships of the Christian navies and always sailed under the protection of larger craft.[51] The *petacchio* of the Order used to be accompanied by a small galleon and a tartane as it sailed to the Levant.[52]

Still a well-armed *petacchio* could more than hold its own. The Order's galleon, the curse of Muslim shipping, spent two days battling it out with a large Tunisian *petacchio* which still managed to get away. The *petacchio* with a crew of 90[53] was towing a Venetian *orca*[54] which it had to abandon.[55] Another large *petacchio* with 63 Turks on board was captured by the Order's galleys in February 1615.[56]

The Order had one or two such vessels, while private corsairs had others of their own. After a bloody encounter, two *petacchi* under the knights de Sailon and de Gerenti managed to defeat a large Turkish ship armed with 40 guns which was transporting a cargo of wood from Constantinople to Alexandria.[57] The Order kept debating till 1626 whether to sell its *petacchio* or to arm it for corsairing.[58]

This type of vessel was very popular with the Tunisian corsairs though it could also be found in the hands of Barbary and French owners. The *petacchio* was kept in the service of the Order and other Mediterranean countries up to the first decades of the eighteenth century.[59]

The Galley

The galley, an elongated and narrow vessel with just one deck and driven by means of sails and oars, is considered to be the oldest type of ship built for sailing and fighting. The Phoenicians, perhaps the most skilled navigators of antiquity, used galleys in their wide-ranging journeys. The Romans and the Carthaginians fought one another by means of galleys to win control over the Mediterranean.

In addition to their carrack and galleons, the knights also had galleys.

The Maltese galley

While the former vessels could be used both for fighting and for the carrying of cargo,[60] the galley was a fighting machine pure and simple. The real strength of the Order's navy lay in the galley. It was the equivalent of the modern destroyer – the first to seek battle and the last to disengage. Time after time, it used to sail out of harbour in the summer months in search of Muslim shipping. The galley won greater glories in fighting the Muslims than the carrack and the galleon. The historian Dal Pozzo gives a glowing description of the Maltese galley.

Commander Boisboudron, who was held in high esteem by all Muslims, spent twelve years as a slave of the Barbary corsairs. One day the general of the corsairs, Cara Hoggia, pointed out to Boisboudron his large and heavily-armed warship and asked him if the squadron of the Order together with that of Leghorn would ever dare to attack it. Boisboudron replied that the galleys of Malta always won the day whenever they encountered enemy ships. Cara Hoggia, infuriated, struck him in the face. A few years later Cara Hoggia's boasts proved vain because the Maltese galleys defeated six ships, including his 3,000 *salme* heavily-armed one with 46 guns. They were attacked on 26 August 1640 as they sheltered near the fortress of Cape Carthage preparing to attack Christian shipping. In the grand master's palace in Valletta, there is a painting that depicts this famous victory, though the date and some of the names are not exact. The inscription says: *Presa di 6 vascelli di*

A Maltese galley under a goose-wing rig

A Maltese capitana *under full rig*

Caracoggia fatta nel Porto della Goletta dal Generale Principe Langravio d'Asia alli 24 Agosto 1640. The port of Goletta is next to Cape Carthage.[61]

The galley was a much smaller vessel than either the carrack or the galleon and, like the galleys of antiquity, stood very low in the water. It was built for speed and would roll and pitch with the slightest breeze or wave. Its two masts were lateen-rigged.

The galley's masts and rigging used to be adorned with pennants, flags made of expensive, fine cloth, and gold-embroidered velvets. When the Order's finances were at a low web, it was felt necessary to limit such embellishments. On 11 October 1768 a commission of knights passed its conclusions to the grand master about the reduction of superfluous ornaments and other unimportant impediments such as chains, barrels of water and wine, and weapons.

It seems that, as time went by, many abuses crept in as regards the fitting of the galleys. So, for example, excessive thick yards rendered necessary riggings that were too thick. For this reason the commission expressly reported to the grand master that it was high time that something was done to reduce excessive baggage.[62]

According to Guglielmotti, an extra sail was added to the two main ones when a fresh breeze was blowing from astern. In the Żabbar Sanctuary Museum, there is the finest representation of a vessel under full sail[63] as follows:

1) foresail in front,
2) mainsail in the middle,
3) mizzensail at the stern,
4) another sail between the foremast and the mainmast that was hoisted when the wind was blowing from astern.[64]

There was also another type of rigging to be used in a calm or in fine weather:

1) larger than usual mainsail,[65]
2) larger than usual foresail,
3) mizzen sail that started being frequently used by the middle of the eighteenth century,
4) kind of staysails rigged between the masts.

In bad weather the following sails were used:
1) small mainsail,

2) small foresail,
3) jury sail, which was a special square sail that was only rigged in emergencies.

The galley differed from the other vessels of the time because of its oars. This meant that it did not lie at the mercy of the fickle winds; indeed, with both sails and oars, the galley could reach the speed of eight knots in the first one-and-a-half hours. De la Gravière says that the rowers could be kept rowing for 20 hours without any rest. A fully-armed galley could be rowed at 26 strokes a minute which would give it a speed of about eight knots. However, Forfeit maintains that a fully-armed galley could keep a speed of four-and-a-half knots or more for about one hour in perfectly calm seas. When the oarsmen tired, the speed would be reduced to two-and-a-quarter or one-and-a-half knots for the following hours. De la Gravière accepted Forfeit's conclusions which were based on a deep and serious study.[66]

The word 'galley' was generic name for a particular type of vessel. Indeed there were galleys of different sizes, all of which had particular names; these were the galley, the demi-galley or the half-galley, the galleot, and the great galley or *capitana*. These distinctions were absolutely not based on the number of masts carried; indeed there were numerous one-masted galleys until the sixteenth century. In 1742 there appeared in Malta the first two demi-galleys with two masts each.[67] Size and the number of banks of oars were the only features that distinguished one from the other. The great galley was the largest in size, next came the galley, then the demi-galley, and then the galleot, the smallest of them all.

The galleys themselves differed in size. Some had up to 30 banks of oars, others 28, while the common ones or *sensili* had 26 oars to starboard and 25 to port. The *capitana*, early in the seventeenth century, had 27 oars to each side with six men to each oar. Guidotti says that a *capitana* carried 360 rowers, including 40 as a reserve force which included those who worked in the various compartments of the hold. Galleys did not carry any reserve oarsmen. The 40 mentioned by Guidotti would remain ashore: '*chiurma di rispetto li quali stanno in terra e quando le galere ritornano da viaggio che hanno delli homini amalati o fiachi li lassano e pigliano li freschi*'.[68]

The length of the galley varied from 60 to 50 metres. Guglielmotti[69] says that the galley was 50 metres long while Gravière[70] gives a length of

46.777 metres, a beam of 5.847 metres, and a height of hold of 2.328 metres with every oar being 12 metres long. Quoting an anonymous treatise about ship-building,[71] he refers to an ordinary galley as having 26 banks of oars to starboard and 25 to port, the place of the missing bench being taken up by the cook and his stove. The *padrona*, or second in command, had 29 and 28 banks of oars while a royal galley or the *capitana* had 31 and 30 banks of oars and sometimes even 32 and 31. The Order's *capitana* did not always have the same number of banks of oars. The general chapter of 1574 mentions that the *capitana* had 28 banks of oars, while the other galleys had 25 on each side.[72] By 1694 the *capitana* was equipped with 30 banks of oars.[73]

Each oar had four or five oarsmen and its loom was so huge that it had to have handles to make it easy for the slaves to grasp.[74] Guidotti explains that '*nelli Remi vi sono lo sotto scritte cosse, cioé il manetiene dove voga il Vogavante, le manilie, le galaverne et la palla, il stropo*'.[75] An oar on a common galley was 11.84 metres long, while that on the royal galley or on the *padrona* was 13.83 metres long.[76]

The oar-maker, or *remolaro,* who often formed part of the galley's paid crew,[77] made the oars in a way that the loom balanced the shaft and the blade. Guidotti says that '*Il remo della Galera di 26 banchi va largo 44 palmi, cioé 30 palmi forra e 14 dentro*'.[78] To keep an oar in balance lead used to be added to the loom.[79] When four galleys capsized in harbour during a storm in 1555, 52 oars sunk and were lost '*per la granezza del piombo, essendo andati in fondo*'.[80]

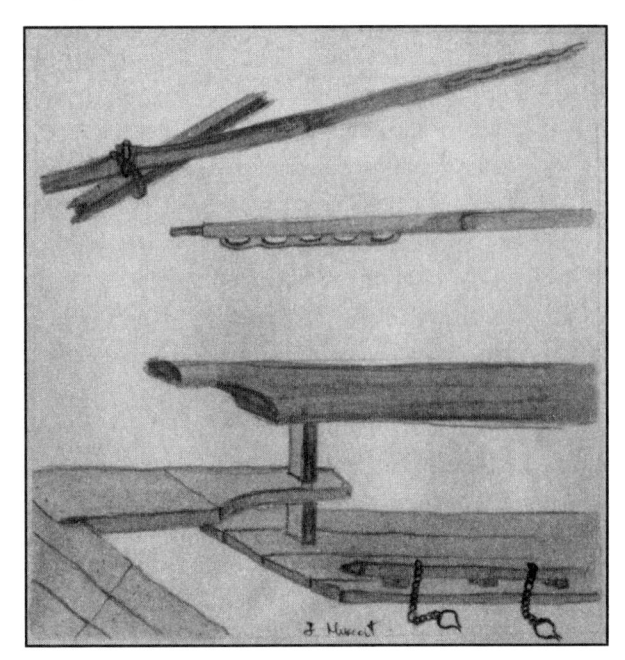

A rower's bench and oar on a galley

It seems that in 1574 there used to be, at the most, five oarsmen to each oar, as can be seen from the records of the general chapter of that year.[81] Gravière mentions that on a common galley there used to be four or five rowers for every oar, while on the *capitana* or royal galley there would be seven and sometimes eight oarsmen. He is, of course, referring to French galleys.[82] On the galleys of antiquity, each oar had one oarsman, and the rowers were placed in different banks to permit a greater number of oarsmen to work in a single vessel. The peak of this type of rowing, known as rowing *a la sensile* or *zenzile*, was reached with the five-banked vessels known as quinqueremes in Roman times. It was, however, later discovered that greater propulsion power could be obtained if three of four rowers were put to each huge oar. This type of rowing, known as *a scaloccio*,[83] also made it possible for the galley to attain greater manoeuvrability.

In pulling the oars, the rowers used to stand up and pull with all their might. A long thick board, known as the *pedana* or foot rest, lay along the whole width of the rowers' bench. The rowers stood on this *pedana* and fell with a bump on the bench, once the pull was completed.[84] For obvious reasons, the slaves covered their benches with rags or rudimentary cushions stuffed with straw or dried leaves.[85]

On the galley, everything was subordinate to the vessel's fighting needs. Because of the oars, the galley's five guns were placed at the bows.[86] This meant that the galley could only attack head on, which

Shielding the sides of a galley against enemy fire, courtesy Joe Mallia

rendered the galley itself more difficult to hit. The section from where the guns were fired and from where the soldiers used to hurl their hand-bombs was known as the rambate. Sometimes the rambate was protected all round by thick wooden planks to shelter the fighting men.[87] At Lepanto the Christian galleys were fitted with thick wooden shields all round the rambate and other similar shields or *pavesate* on the sides, precautions which were normally taken when great numbers of galleys opposed each other in battle. There were occasions when the sides of galleys were protected with huge paddings made of sails, the coats of rowers, and mattresses to neutralize the enemy's gun fire.[88]

Between the oarsmen a passage way, known as *corsia,* led from the rambate to the poop. There were two other passageways on either side between the oarsmen and the side of the galley, which were also used for fighting.[89]

Six openings or hatches on the deck and between the rowers benches were used for loading and unloading of cargoes or provisions.

At the rear of the ship there was another rambate known as *spalliera* which could also be used for fighting purposes. The captain's cabin, or as De la Gravière describes it – the tabernacle – lay in this section, which was reserved only for superiors and their guests. The post near the tabernacle was also used by the captain on special occasions, when the captain wanted to direct personally some particular manoeuvre.

The poop was reserved for the captain, the knights, important passengers, and the galley's chaplain.[90] This section was the best and finest part of the vessel, screened on its four sides and protected by an awning.[91] There were usually two of these awnings, one a little higher than the other, thus allowing a free circulation of air in between. The lower canopy was usually made of velvet and decorated with gilded frills and tassels. The upper one was less fine and expensive and was usually made of canvas. The rest of the galley, which was reserved for the Maltese sailors and the rowers, was open to the elements. On cold days, however, a canopy was erected along the main passageway to shelter the whole motor force of the galley. The *comiti* of the galleys were advised that whenever, for some reason or another, they did carry the huge canvas awning, they were to take two cotton ones to provide cover for the rowers on rainy days. *Comiti* were discouraged from rigging up spare sails instead of proper awnings as happened quite often on the galleys of the

A galley under its awning by Opizio Guidotti

Order.[92] A canvas awning was normally made up of 343 *canne* involving 56 cloths and its sides measured six *canne* and a palm while the central part was 17 *canne* and four palms.[93] If galleys cruised in rainy days, the huge awning over the rowers' benches remained in place to provide the necessary shelter.[94] Apparently this awning was left in place even when the galleys berthed, probably to screen off the squalor on board and to protect the men from the sun and the rain. A portrait of the Landgrave of Hesse at the grand master's palace, Valletta shows the awning made up of red and white stripes. The painting known as the *Piccola Barriera* which lies at the Fine Arts Museum, Valletta shows the *capitana* and other galleys with their awnings in place.

It was the poop, and the captain's cabin in particular, that made the galley look so beautiful. It was full of baroque sculpture which was gilded and painted in bright colours, statues, and high reliefs. The Order used to organize competitions to select the finest model for the galley's cabins.

Giuseppe Azzupardo was one of the unlucky competitors who asked for a reimbursement to cover at least the cost of the material he had used in his model.[95] Bosio refers to the statue of the galley *San Giovanni Battista* which was placed on top above the rear part of the cabin. Incidentally when this galley was taken by the Barbary corsairs to Algiers, the statue of the saint was tied with a chain from the feet and suspended at the main entrance to the city known as Bebazon or Bab Assan as a

Highly decorated capitana*: NLM 627*

trophy.[96] C.S. Sonnini, referring to the galleys of the Order in its decline, remarks that 'they were superbly ornamented, gold blazed on their numerous bas-reliefs and carvings on the stern'.[97] Indeed, the cabin used to cost so much in money, time, and effort that when a galley's hull was to be taken out of service, the cabin was removed and placed on a new hull.[98] In France there was the same custom of re-using old cabins on new hulls of galleys. A galley's cabin cost approximately 1/10 of the entire outlay. The cabin was not discarded, according to Gravière, not to bankrupt the state.[99]

To appreciate the decorations and sculptures on the cabin of Maltese galleys one has to examine the manuscript Lib. 627 at the National Library of Malta for the watercolours which show the magisterial galleys of the Cotoner brothers, Pinto, and Rohan and the paintings and models at the grand master's palace and at the Malta Maritime Museum, Vittoriosa. However, when the galley set out on a mission, some of these ornaments were removed to lighten the vessel and to protect them better. The Muslims, on the other hand, never really bothered to decorate their galleys. With good reason, they were ready to sacrifice everything, guns, munitions, and food for the sake of speed, which was perhaps the galley's best weapon.[100]

The area underneath the deck was divided into six principal sections. In addition to the openings for cargo already mentioned, there was a companion way that led from the poop to the first section which was reserved for the captain. In the second room slept 12 knights and the chaplain and also served to house the surgeon's instruments and some chains for the slaves. In the third section was stored the crew's food, while the bread, the ship's biscuit. and the wine were kept in the fourth store. From there wine was sold to those who could afford it, while this section also housed the ship's clerk. According to the orders of the chapter general of 1603, the clerk in charge of the tavern could not lend more than 6 *tari* a month to wine-drinkers. If he was caught lending more, he was to forfeit all the money lent. He could not even charge more than the price established by the captain. If he was caught overcharging, all the wine would be confiscated and distributed amongst the oarsmen. Wine was an important stimulant to the Mediterranean oarsmen, the equivalent of the British grog of rum in a cold climate. It gave heart to the sailor and helped to raise his morale.[101] The fifth room, called the *santabarbara* or powder magazine, was the store where gunpowder, munitions, and some extra sails were kept. The sixth and last section, situated right underneath the *rambate*, housed the ropes, sails, flags, the canopy, and the soldiers' weapons. This part was also used as the sick bay where the sick and the wounded could lie down on mattresses or on ropes and sails.[102]

De la Gravière describes the eleven rooms of the French galley:

a) the captain's berth, large enough to enable him to stretch his legs

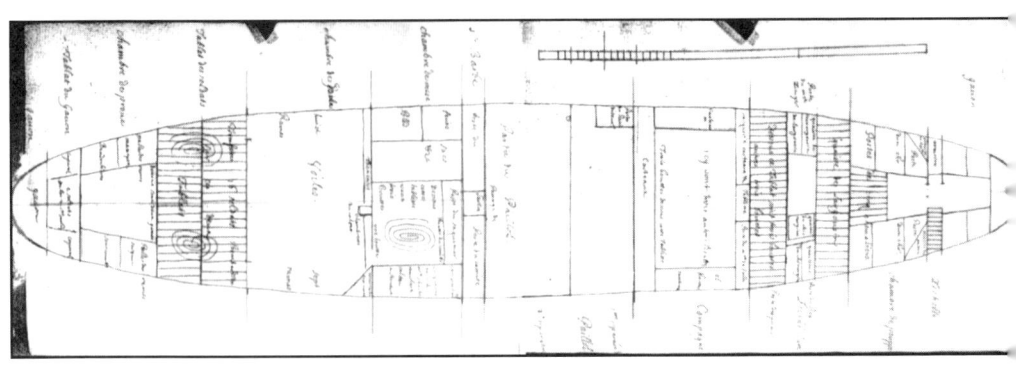

Hold plan in MMM Remarques

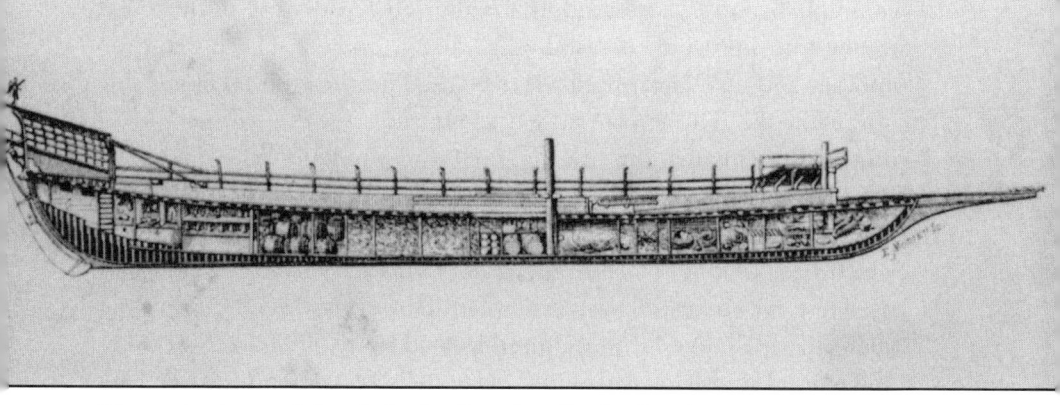

The compartments below deck of a French galley by Graviere

      comfortably and to keep a few weapons; the dining-room was, of course, in the cabin at the poop;
b) the officers' room, which was so small that it was rarely used except in case of illness or injury;
c) a store room for food and clothes;
d) a store room for wine and salted food;
e) a store room for bread and ship's biscuit;
f) the *santabarbara* or powder magazine – a store room for gunpowder, cannonballs and other munitions;
g) the tavern where the wine was sold;
h) the room where the sails were kept;
i) the room for the ropes and spare rigging, anchor cables, shrouds and all types of ropes;
j) the sick bay;
k) the small compartment at the bows which used to store coal for the ship's captain and other objects of little value.[103]

The ballast was divided among all these rooms. Unfortunately, either Guidotti or his copyist omitted to mention the weight of the galley's ballast although he says that strips, or rather sheets, of lead were used.[104] De la Gravière[105] maintains that an ordinary galley carried a ballast weighing 15 tons consisting of 500 stone-filled containers and 620 cannonballs of the 36-pounder calibre. These containers and cannonballs were distributed in all the rooms under the deck so that the weight was evenly distributed all along the keel. There were also another 240 smaller cannonballs to be used for the guns on either side of the *coursier*. There were also 12 chain shots for the *coursier* and 24 other for the smaller guns. De la Gravière also mentions the containers for the stone ballast.

In Malta there are many references to these caskets or containers which were used for ballasting galleys.[106] In addition to this, the galley used to carry about 300 barrels of water. However, when the galley was about to sail for the Levant, it used to load up to 370 barrels of water and a good supply of chains to shackle the slaves when they were put ashore to fetch and carry water and firewood. Water-barrels were kept between the rowers' benches.[107] Beneath the side passageways or *couroirs*, were kept the necessary brush-wood, the barrels of water, and the live rams.[108]

Life was normally spent on deck. Here the stove that served as the galley's kitchen was situated in place of the ninth bench from the back on the port side.[109] The stove or kitchen was a large clay-filled wooden shallow box covered with sheaths of zinc that could be dismantled. On its open fire a large metal pot was always kept filled with boiling water for the preparation of meals.[110] Large ships had a stone oven with a chimney that went through the forecastle deck.[111] At least 1,328 oven

The galley cook at work: courtesy Joe Mallia

bricks were used to construct ovens and fixed and portable stoves on ships and tartanes between 1 May 1745 and 30 April 1746.[112]

The stoves used coal and firewood. The latter was the more common fuel, although coal had long been employed by the knights.[113] At least until 1719, when Lib. 110 was written and, presumably, even later, when the slaves were shackled to go ashore to look for firewood, a green flag was hoisted at the stern bench where the helmsman stood.[114] Captains could not take more than 15 days supply of firewood on board[115] and therefore they had to go ashore from time to time to look for more fuel. The stove was extinguished at sunset.[116]

The large pot on the stove, which was used to cook the meat and the minestrone for the crew, was normally made of copper.[117] When the Order was experiencing its decline and its finances were in a mess, copper was replaced by latten or zinc.[118] According to the ordinance of 15 February 1684, no galley captain could take an oven for the baking of bread on board,[119] which proves that galleys also had ovens.

The pans and all the other cooking equipment were stored near the stove. A kindling fire was always kept nearby for lighting the stove and for firing the guns.[120] A coop with live chickens was placed on the galley's side near where the cook had his place. Every galley carried a coop for chickens.[121] French galleys carried two hen coops for the captain in addition to a chest for food and another lockable one for ice.[122] This ice box as used by the French was nothing new to the knights. The ordinance of 10 February 1684 banned the use of ice-boxes on board galleys.[123] Ice was so obviously a luxury to be reserved for the ruling classes. It is mentioned in the stories about Saladin and Richard I of England, and Don Carlos and it was also used in Turkey and other places. Braudel observes that 'in Malta, where the knights, if we are to believe them, would die if snow did not arrive from Naples, their illnesses apparently requiring this sovereign remedy, snow was, on the contrary, the height of luxury'.[124] Saladin treated his prisoners nobly;[125] he made use of ice and sent *neve in abbondanza* to Richard the Lion-Hearted. It is also said that Nero used ice to make ice-cream while Suetonius writes that Nero used to cool his bathwater with it.[126]

The chicken coops present something of a problem. An order issued on 11 March 1631 said that a galley on its way east or going either to North Africa or on the *corso* could only take one cage with one compartment, which was enough for about 50 chickens. Order No. 7 of

The stern of a Maltese galley showing the hen coop, model by Joseph Muscat

The Maltese galley by Sebille

the same date banned the carrying of more hens under the rowers' benches than the number mentioned above. A cage for 50 chickens was about two metres long, one metre high, and one metre deep. Order No. 9 of 30 October 1631 allowed the captain to carry a cage with two compartments, one on top of the other. A cage can be seen on the model of a galley exhibited at the Malta Maritime Museum. Order No. 4 of 9 March 1657 allowed the carrying on board a hen coop large enough for all the chickens required on a particular trip. However, order No. 15 of 15 February 1685 specified that a captain could only carry one cage on board whatever the duration of the voyage. If more chickens were needed, these were to be kept near or under the rowers' benches. This partly explains the sickening stench on the galleys. To contribute to the foul smells, in addition to the slaves' own ordure, there used to be four cows and four calves or six cows and 50 rams on board.[127]

The galleys of the Order were painted vermilion red but the section of the hull under water level was painted white. Guidotti always shows the galleys painted red.[128] Sebille's[129] picture shows a grey band along the waterline. There is, however, overwhelming evidence to show that the galley was only painted in two colours, red and white; in fact the Maltese galley is always represented as being red and white in colour, except for the *capitana*. In the arsenal's account there are many references to *color rosso, terra rossa, minio,* and so on.[130] Demi galleys were painted the same colour as the galleys.

The galleys used to join up as a squadron under the leadership of a head commander who would be in charge of the flotilla from the moment it sailed out of the harbour until its return. His galley, distinctively painted black,[131] was known as the *capitana*. There is a beautiful representation of a squadron of six red galleys with the black *capitana* in their midst in one of the corridors of the convent of the Franciscan Fathers in Valletta. Another picture showing a black painted *capitana* leading an attack on Alexandrian ships is to be found in the Malta Maritime Museum.

After the capture of the galleys *San Francesco* and *San Giovanni* by Bizertan galleys on 26 June 1625, the new general of the galleys of the Order, the Spaniard Ximenes, wanted the *capitana* to be painted black in imitation of the Spanish *capitana*.[132] Although Vassallo notes that Ximenes painted his *capitana* black in conformity with the Spanish practice, local people preferred to believe that the black colour was

The capitana

chosen as a sign of mourning for the galleys and crews lost at the hands of the corsairs of Bizerta. The knights continued to paint their *capitana* in black and the people in Malta continued to maintain their belief up to the days when Vassallo wrote his history in 1854.[133] Behind the *capitana* came another galley known as the *padrona* or the second in command.[134]

The number of galleys in the navy of the Order never exceeded eight. Grand Master Lascaris introduced the seventh galley in the squadron while the eighth galley was proposed early in 1685.[135] Every time a galley was lost or became too old and unfit for the sea, the Order would immediately plan to replace it. Often the grand master himself or some particular knight would contribute towards the cost of building a galley. The galley built and maintained by the grand master's own money was known as the magisterial galley.[136]

The galley squadron increased in number in the following manner:
a) three galleys – 26 October 1530; they were the *Santa Croce*, the *San Filippo*, and the *San Giovanni*;[137]
b) four galleys – the *Aquila* was added to the *San Giovanni*, the *San Michele*, and the *San Claudio*. *L'Aquila* was also known as the *Santa Fede*;[138]
c) five galleys – the need for a fifth galley is mentioned in the general chapter of 1558.[139] The five galleys were the *San Giovanni*, the *San Giacomo*, the *San Gabriello*, the *Santa Marta*, and the *Corona*.

d) six galleys – '*All'aprirsi della nuova Stagione* (1628) *trovasi la squadra della Religione accresciuta con la sesta Galera.*'[140] These were the *San Giovanni*, the *San Pietro*, the *San Carlo*, the *Santa Maria*, the *Santa Rosalia*, and the *San Antonio*.
e) seven galleys – '*Così fu istituita* (1651) *la settima Galera*'.[141] These were the *San Giovanni*, the *Santa Maria*, the *San Nicola*, the *San Pietro*, the *Santa Caterina*, the *Madonna della Grazia*, and the *San Francesco*.
f) eight galleys – in 1685.[142] These were the *San Luigi*, the *San Paolo*, the *Lascara* or magisterial galley, the *Santa Annunciata*, the *San Pietro*, the *Santa Maria*, the *San Nicola*, and the *San Gregorio*. During the tenure of Captain General Carlo Leopoldo d'Herberstein (1705-07) the number of galleys was reduced to five.[143]

There were other proposals to reduce the number of galleys in a squadron from six to five so that the money saved would be used in the construction of a ship-of-the-line. It was argued that since five galleys were found to be sufficient in the past, a similar squadron would still be enough to bring honours to the Order and to serve the needs of the Christian powers.[144]

The ships of the Order were always called after the various titles of Our Lady or saints, an example the Maltese copied in naming their seacraft. *San Giovanni* was the most popular name.[145] In 1548 the galley

The galley squadron entering harbour; private collection

Catarinetta was captured by Dragut while on its way to Malta carrying the revenues of the Order from its commanderies in Spain and Italy. Dragut also obtained a big ransom for the captured knights. De la Sengle paid for the construction of another galley called the *San Claudio*. After the loss of the *Catarinetta*, all galleys started being named after saints because some alleged that *Catarinetta* had been captured because of its profane name.[146]

Towards the beginning of the eighteenth century, the building of square-rigged ships was being actively considered. These ships were found to be less expensive to maintain, had a longer useful life-span, and did not need any oarsmen. The Order, too, started introducing such ships and the galley, which for 500 years had proved itself the principal fighting vessel of the Mediterranean, gradually became obsolete.[147]

The galley, however, continued to sail the seas till the beginning of the nineteenth century. In June 1798 Napoleon found four galleys at anchor in Malta's harbour. The *San Luigi*, which took from 19 September 1792 to 22 June 1793 to be completed, was the last galley to be built locally.[148] Two demi-galleys which the pope had ordered in Malta for his fleet were launched as late as 1796. These two half-galleys, the *San*

A galley's anchor; Malta Maritime Museum

Pietro and the *Sant'Andrea*, were constructed between 10 December 1795 and 26 August 1796. On completion these vessels were towed to Civitavecchia.[149]

The galley remained in use for light work, such as quick journeys, or to attack some small vessel, or to tow big ships out of harbour. Big ships, stranded in a calm, would ask for the assistance of galleys.[150] A painting by Giacomo Moro at the Norman House, Mdina, depicts a galley towing a square-rigged vessel in a calm.

The galley had its own particular type of anchor which never changed in the course of its history. It had four flukes, each about three feet away from the other. It was about two metres high and weighed about five *qantari*.[151] An impressively large and heavy galley's anchor together with other smaller ones can be seen in the Malta Maritime Museum. The sizes of the smaller anchors varied because they were used on lateen-rigged vessels of different sizes and for different reasons.[152] Graviere states that French galleys had four anchors, two large and two small.[153] The smaller anchors could have easily been lowered from the poop. A model of a Neapolitan galley in the National Maritime Museum in Greenwich shows an anchor being lowered from the poop.

The galley normally used to be anchored only from the bows, although occasionally a small anchor was lowered from the stern. To drop or raise, the anchor the sailors, assisted by the slaves, did not use a capstan. Instead the anchor was pulled up the hoist that lay on the *tambouret* in front of the rambate. The anchor was then tied to the ship's side by means of the ring.[154]

There was also a ladder on each side of the poop which were often left in position while sailing. Such ladders can be seen in place in various graphic representations.[155]

The galley proved itself the knights' best fighting weapon. Its mere appearance on the horizon was enough to drive every Muslim craft to the shelter of a friendly harbour.[156]

The demi-galley

In 1742 the demi-galley was introduced into the Order's squadron. In the middle of the eighteenth century, the lack of slaves had started being felt more than ever. The Order had a perennial lack of slaves. In 1685 it

A demi galley restored by Joseph Muscat; Malta Maritime Museum

was already being stated then that the recruiting of the necessary number of rowers for the galleys was proving a most difficult task. Efforts were made to search thoroughly for all the slaves of the Order, especially those detailed for various works away from the galleys or those who were relieved from forced labour. If the necessary numbers could not be found, the treasury was to recruit Maltese rowers who were to be paid for their services.[157] By 1688 the rowing force of the galleys of the Order had seriously decreased in number for various reasons. It has to be remembered that the galley squadron then consisted of eight vessels.[158] The following is a good indication of how the rowing force on a galley was divided in the last quarter of the eighteenth century:

	Capitana	Common galley	Experimental galley
convicts	110	100	100
slaves	60	45	40
buonavoglie	30	25	25
paid rowers	120	100	85
totals	**320**	**270**	**250** [159]

It was during this time that the Order started experimenting with lighter galleys to reduce the expenses on slaves, guns, and other equipment. The report of the Reverend Congregation of the Galleys sent to the grand master on 11 October 1768 refers to the chains on the oarsmen's benches, *'non stimandole necessarie, giacché in oggi la maggior parte della Ciurma vien composta di Maltesi'*, suggesting at the same time the removal of three of the seven chains on every bench.[160]

The fall in the number of captured Turkish ships had a disastrous effect on the Maltese exchequer. Poussielgue, who was the comptroller of the funds and administrator-general of the finances of the French army in Egypt, reported to Napoleon from Milan saying that, after the French Revolution, the Order lost all its revenues from France and the greater part of those normally collected from Germany and from Italy. The Order had also to provide for the upkeep of all the French knights who lost all their benefits accruing from their commanderies and to make up for the annual deficit of nearly two million francs.[161] In order to economize on slaves, the Order built the demi-galley. Guglielmotti referred to the introduction of the demi-galley in the papal squadron saying that the ministers responsible for the squadron suggested the employment of paid rowers instead of the forced labour of convicts who had mutinied on the galley *San Pietro* and were not trusted anymore on guard duties.[162] The introduction of the demi-galley was a sign of the decline of the glorious Maltese galley.

The demi-galley, which was rigged with two lateen sails,[163] was a fast craft that could overtake all other vessels.[164] It had 20 banks of oars, but

Stern of a demi galley; Malta Maritime Museum

with only one oarsman to each thwart instead of the galley's usual four or five.[165] Its oar was meant to bend on the stroke thus increasing its power.[166] Like the galley, the demi-galley was painted vermilion red above the water level and white below.[167]

Its weapons were smaller than the galley's. One large gun was placed at the bows, flanked by two smaller ones. Other weapons, known as swivel guns or *tromboncini,* could be found along the sides. It is interesting to note that the experimental galley carried the same ordnance as a demi-galley. The Order was experimenting with a smaller and lighter type of galley in order to save money. The overall reduction of dimensions resulted in a lighter type of vessel with less timber employed for its construction. Consequently, the latest type of short muzzle guns employed on the third rates of the Order and which had become so popular by the end of the eighteenth century were installed on the bows while retaining the same calibre of 24-pounders for the *coursier* and 12-pounders for the lateral guns.[168] Fully armed, it carried 200 men, 50 of them soldiers, while a galley carried about 500 men.[169]

Most of what had been said about the galley applies also to the demi-galley. It too was divided into a rambate at the bows joined by a passageway or *corsia* to the cabin at the stern. From on top, the demi-galley resembled a fishbone with the rowers' benches slanting slightly towards the poop. Its sheer outline resembled that of the galley although it had, of course, fewer oars and the rambate was somewhat smaller. Life on the demi-galley and the galley was more or less the same. It was, if anything, a little easier because most of the rowers were Maltese who had freely opted to become oarsmen.

In addition to building its own demi-galleys, the Order was commissioned to build others for the papal fleet. Guglielmotti mentions four demi-galleys, two of them forming part of the pope's fleet.[170] The Order's archives record that two demi-galleys were constructed for the pope in its shipyards. Work on these vessels, the *San Pietro* and the *Sant'Andrea,* started on 10 October 1795 and was completed on 26 August 1796. The construction was under the supervision of Giuseppe Maurin, a Maltese who had earned a great reputation for the building of ships. He had been sent to study in Toulon during Rohan's magistracy (1775-97). Back in Malta, Maurin presented his certificates, sealed and authenticated by the naval authorities of France, to the Order and he was nominated principal naval architect. His first works at the Order's

Rowers' benches on the demi galley; Malta Maritime, Museum

arsenal were the two demi-galleys for the Papal States,[171] which together cost 42,970 *scudi*.[172] The Order's accounts describe the expenditure for the construction of these two vessels and the wages received by 32 carpenters, 18 caulkers, and other workmen. Even the dues paid to the priest and to the altar boy for blessing the boats and to the musicians are recorded. The latter were paid 3 *scudi*. The knights certainly employed slaves and prisoners to reduce the cost of constructing these vessels. The accounts also refer to red lead and red powder that were probably used to paint the vessels.[173]

The number of demi-galleys in the Order's fleet cannot be ascertained. Two of them, the *Sant'Anna* and the *Sant'Ursola*, are mentioned towards 1742 as always joining the galleys in fighting the Muslim. Rossi, perhaps inadvertently, makes mention of *Santa Teresa* instead of *Sant'Ursola*. He could be mixing it with the tartane *Santa Teresa* or with a similarly-named corvette which was in service round 1743.[174]

Lieutenant Vivion in his report of 31 May 1799 to Lord Nelson mentions two demi-galleys amongst the other sea craft on the island.[175] According to Rossi, the fleet of the Order in 1796 consisted of *quattro galere, due mezzegalere, due vascelli (S. Zaccaria in efficienza e il San Giovanni in costruzione), due fregate (La S. Elizabetta in buon stato e la Santa Maria in cattive condizioni)*, while for 1742 he names two demi-galleys, the *Sant'Anna* and the *Sant'Ursola*. The absence of demi-galleys between

1742, when the demi-galleys are mentioned for the first time, and the French invasion of 1798 is hard to explain. It seems that Napoleon only took one Maltese galley with him to Egypt. The two demi-galleys mentioned as accompanying the French fleet to Egypt had been taken from Civitavecchia.

The Maltese on the French ships did not take part in the battle of Aboukir. The Maltese galley and the two demi-galleys taken from Civitavecchia which had Maltese on board were not attacked by the British forces.[176]

Guglielmotti does not mention the two Maltese demi-galleys when he discusses the last presence of these vessels in the Mediterranean at the end of the eighteenth century. He mentions the two demi-galleys of Civitavecchia, the *Santa Ferma* and the *Santa Lucia*, which had been captured by Napoleon. He also mentions another two in Sardinia, *L' Aquila* and the *Santa Barbara*, which were later taken to Genoa where they were abandoned to rot away. Guglielmotti must have overlooked the two Maltese vessels. And what, unless they had their names had been changed to the *Santa Ferma* and the *Santa Lucia*, happened to the two demi-galleys that the pope had built in Malta in 1796?[177]

As an experimental war vessel, the demi-galley was to be found in small navies, such as those of the Order and of the pope. Only such small navies retained these sailing vessels until the fleets themselves were annihilated by Napoleon. All in all, the demi-galley proved less successful than its smaller sister ship, the galleot.[178]

The galleot

The galleot was even smaller than the demi-galley. It had one lateen sail and from 14 to 20 banks of oars, each rowed by a single oarsman. Its crew consisted of about 60 sailors and soldiers. The nomenclature can be misleading. For example, when the squadrons of Bizerta and Algiers joined together, there were 16 galleots but, according to Dal Pozzo,[179] although they were so called because of their shape, they were as strong as any galley.[180] There were large galleots which could carry 200 crew. Another galleot had 18 banks of oars.[181] Muslim galleots were bigger and better armed than those of the Order or the Maltese. Galleots

The galleot

formed part of the Order's squadron, and were principally used to scout for enemy ships although it was also utilized in battle.

The galleot's small size made it ideal for private knights and some Maltese to set up as corsairs on their own. This explains why the galleot was to become the curse of the seas of the Muslims.[182] The Maltese corsair Ascanio Attard requested the permission to fly the Order's flag and sailed to harass Turkish shipping around 20 August 1687.[183] Later Censu Valera had a galleot, the *Madonna della Concezione,* which was also used to harass Moorish shipping.[184]

Together with the brigantines, the galleots of the Order were used for a long time to guard and picket the harbour area and the coast. The knight Fra Emanuel Zamora, a deputy commander, was twice commissioned by the Order to provide a galleot and a brigantine for coastal defence. The first order is dated 15 June 1693 and the second 30 July 1695.[185] On 23 July 1741 two other galleots were built which, together with a *tartana*, were meant to protect the bays round Malta which were still quite frequently raided by the Moorish corsairs. The small but fast galleots were ideal to meet this menace.[186]

Galleots also used to sail with galleys. Guidotti had a galleot in his squadron on his third corsairing mission to the Levant. On 22 March 1608 he sent it to reconnoitre near Scopoli where it found a caramousal which was later captured by the knights.[187] In 1757 two magisterial

A corsair galleot

A Muslim caramusal

galleots went to Lampedusa to keep a lookout on Turkish shipping.[188] In 1764 three galleots of the Order, the *Santa Catarina,* the *Santa Maria di Filermo*, and the *Sant'Ursola,* attacked five Tunisian ships near the Red Island of Sardinia, capturing three of them.[189] On 8 August 1765 the *Sant'Ursola* single-handedly captured another Tunisian vessel with 36 slaves on board.[190]

Many such adventures are to be found in the Order's history. The few incidents mentioned are enough to demonstrate that the small galleot played its part in the fight with the Muslim. The galleot was an ideal vessel to wait in ambush for fat Muslim merchantmen.

A galleot on the horizon could be distinguished from a galley because it stood very low in the water, had only one mast, and it did not have any rambate. The Order's and the knights' galleots were always painted red, although the Maltese owners often painted theirs black, dark green, or some other colour, the better to camouflage them.

The smaller version of the galleot had ten banks of oars rather than 14 or 20. It had a crew of about 30, half the number of the ordinary galleot.[191] One cannot be dogmatic about the relative sizes of these vessels, or even the distinctions that existed between their various types because very often such distinctions were minimal. In 1739, for example, the Order sent the ship-of-the-line *San Vincenzo* on the *corso* assisted by *una filuca, o sia galeotta ben armata.*[192] Could this *felucca* have been a galleot? The *felucca* was originally a sort of tender to the galleys but by this time it could have become large enough to sail on its own. However, the differences between a galleot and a *felucca* were slight. It was an ideal boat for the corsair, because it was fast and unobtrusive. Its crew had to serve as sailors, oarsmen, and soldiers as the need arose.[193]

The *capitana*

This was the largest of the galleys, indeed it can be called a large galley. In Italian it was called *galione*[194] – a word which resembled the other Italian word *galeone* meaning 'galleon'. It will be referred here as *galione* to distinguish it from the galleon. In days of old this difficulty did not exist because the *galione* came much after the galleon.

Like the galleys, the great galley or *galione* was propelled by means of oars and lateen sails. It was, however, larger, more beautiful, and carried

The Cotoner Capitana; *NLM 627*

heavier armaments. It had three rather than two masts and, in a good steady wind, it hoisted a third sail on the mizzenmast. Towards the beginning of the eighteenth century, the Order started increasing the size of its *capitana*[195] with the result that the need for a third mast became sorely felt.[196] Rossi insists that the Order started constructing longer galleys after 1696.[197] However, a smaller than usual experimental galley with two banks of oars fewer on each side is mentioned in the archives of the Order on 25 February 1792.[198] Guglielmotti mentions a large galley that was built of oak and ash in Civitavecchia for the knights of St John,[199] which explains the third mast on the *galione* since the first ones had only two masts. Landstrom says that the third mast was added to enable the galley to turn round faster. This is partly correct, though one must remember that oars were extremely useful to help in turning the vessel around. The third mast must have been added principally because of the heaviness of the vessel and to keep it on course.[200]

The Order of St John built three of these vessels, the first one during the magistracy of the Cotoner brothers, the second under Pinto, and the third one under Rohan.[201] All three of them were painted with a black hull as was expected for a *capitana*.

The *galione* appeared on the scene when the knights had already lost their inclination to fight and they were therefore ready, according to Sonnini, to waste their resources on empty showpieces. Sonnini

The Gran Galione; *NLM 627*

describes the Maltese galleys towards the end of the eighteenth century in these words: 'They are manned, or rather encumbered, with an incredible number of people; the admiral's galley alone carrying 800 men. They were superbly ornamented, the bas-reliefs as well as a profusion of other carved work upon the stern, were richly gilt; their enormous sails were striped blue and white, with a large red cross of Malta painted in the centre; their elegant flags waved majestically in the air; everything, in short, concurred, when they were under sail, to make them a magnificent spectacle. But their construction rendered them equally unfit for action, or to encounter stormy weather. The Order preserved them rather as a mark of its ancient splendour, than on account of their utility. This was one of those old institutions which had formerly served to render it celebrated, and now attested their weakness and decline.'[202] The very size and strength of the *galione* is an indication of the crisis the Order found itself in.[203]

Under Rohan the Order, conscious of its approaching end, took drastic economy measures because it realized that it could not live beyond its means.[204] It even removed from its vessels those sails which were not used often enough, in order to rig one or more other smaller craft. A *felucca* or a caique was often given the sails of a mothballed galley.[205]

The galley tenders

Every galley carried with it three types of smaller seacraft: the *felucca*, the caique, and the boat. The caique and the boat were normally carried on one of the side passageways of a galley while the *felucca* was towed behind.[206] The *felucca* could also be carried on board in one of the side passageways.[207] A demi-galley only carried a caique and a small boat.[208] Feluccas also accompanied the papal galleys on the pope's fishing expedition in April 1727 near the castle of Sanfelice, as described by Guglielmotti.[209] The French galleys towed their small boat behind, while the caiques were kept in their customary place on one of the side passageways or *couroirs*.[210] Each of these types had its particular duty and their sizes differed in accordance with the size of the mother galley.

There were occasions when the Order's galleys carried more than three tenders. On 4 April 1656 the council of the Order decided to reduce the number to three, on a penalty of 200 *scudi* to be paid for by the captain. However, when the need arose for an extra *felucca*, the Order readily agreed to it. On 13 April 1663 the three galleys, the *Santa Maria*, the *San Giovanni*, and the *San Luigi*, were told to share a *xprunara* amongst them, each keeping it for a month in turn. What the Order was against was a wasteful extravagance in boats.[211]

A further demand for another boat was made on 30 May 1692. The captains of the galleys were of the opinion that a fourth boat was indispensable to carry the wounded and to help in attacking the enemy on land. The council accepted this demand but ruled that no galley could have more than four tenders.[212]

Other fleets, such as the French, restricted the number of boats to two for every galley. The Order however preferred to have three, the better to cope with emergencies. In 1740, for example, some *buonavoglie* escaped on a caique[213] and a small boat was added as a precaution.

The *felucca*

The *felucca* was indispensable to carry soldiers and for other duties, such as helping people to cross from one galley to another. It was painted black so that it could steal on the enemy's coastal defences by night.[214]

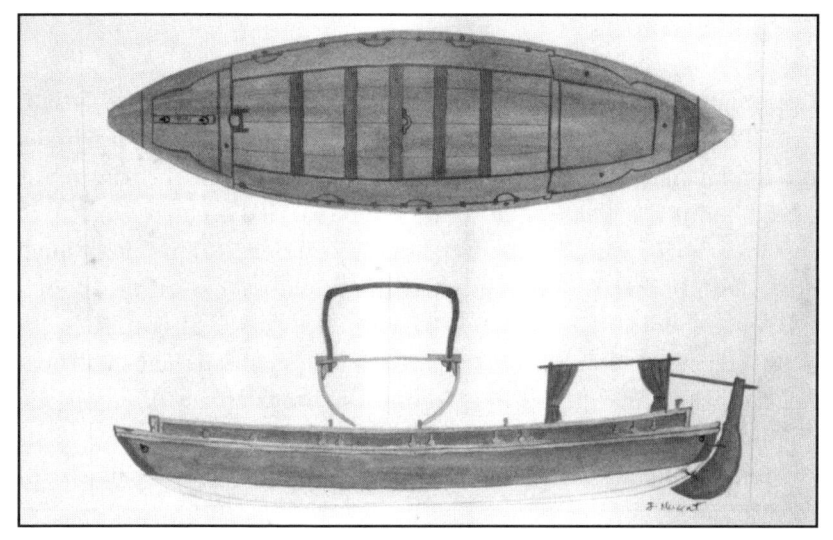

The gilded felucca

The commander-in-chief's *felucca* was painted brightly to distinguish it from the others. Apparently the *capitana* had both black and gilded *feluccas* because an ordinary galley had a flag it used to hoist as a signal to the *capitana* to send the black *felucca* over.[215] A model of such a *felucca* can be seen in the Malta Maritime Museum. The *felucca* must have presented an unforgettable sight all decked out with velvet in the harbour. The *felucca* had two masts and six rowers. A canopy of fine cloth could be erected on four supports on the poop from where the standard of the Order also flew.

The *felucca* mentioned by Guglielmotti was a double-ended open boat. It was lateen-rigged and had one mast and a jib jutting out of the bows. This long and narrow boat, which had from six to ten oars,[216] could escape from danger in a trice.

There was also a larger type of *felucca,* the size of a Gozo boat, that used to sail on its own. The *felucca* grew larger in size towards the end of the eighteenth century. This rendered a second mast necessary but it also made it possible for the *felucca* to carry some small artillery. Large *feluccas* were commonly used by Spaniards and by Turkish corsairs. It seems that the Spanish *felucca* resembled the Algerian chebec. It was a fast boat and much better armed than the smaller version which was used to carry cargo. The small guns on the Order's *feluccas* were known as *canoncini* and they do not fit any modern calibration standard.[217]

A corsair felucca

The Order too had some of these large *feluccas* which were armed for fighting[218] and also served a very useful purpose in spying on the enemy's movements and reporting to the galleys. On 5 May 1600 a *felucca* that had returned to Malta from Esgarambe informed Prior Ibernia that it had not met any hostile shipping there.[219] Another scouting trip was performed along the coasts of Branca Leone and Rochella by another *felucca* on 18 August 1620.[220] On 31 May 1643 Fra Francesco Ricasoli sailed a *capitana*'s *felucca* on a spying trip along the coasts of Sicily, Calabria, and St Mary's Rock, crossed over to Corfu and Zante, and then visited the Greek islands. Ricasoli's considerable spying odyssey included an investigation of all reports from the towns and coastal fortifications *en route*. In Zante he had to contact Giorgio Latino, then in the Order's secret service.[221]

Another *felucca* sailed towards the Levant on 8 January 1645 under Fra Victor Cerche to spy on enemy shipping. A spying mission always followed the same route and pattern: from Malta it would go to Sicily and Calabria, asking the coastal towers on the way for the latest reports. If no news was to be had there, the vessel would cross over to the Greek islands to reconnoitre the enemy's movements on his very doorstep.[222]

The caique

While the narrow-hulled *felucca* was constructed with pointed ends for reasons of speed, the caique, which was meant to carry loads, was round hulled and stood lower in the water. It had a flat stern. All sea-faring people, including the Greeks and the Turks, had caiques. However, they often differed from each other in design.[223] The caique was known as a *bastimento raso* because it had no deck.[224] It was meant to be used as a tender for the galleys and mainly used to fetch firewood and water from ashore in case of a shortage on board.[225]

The caique was also used to sound the bottom if the galley had to approach an unknown coast and to carry the shackled slaves ashore to forage for water or firewood.[226]

The caique was also used in the actual fighting. It was employed to transport the Maltese soldiers to the enemy's deck after the galley's artillery had shaken the Muslim will to fight.

The caique also performed some of the duties normally performed by the *felucca* like attacking enemy vessels at anchor or port batteries.[227] On such missions the caique was always led by a knight officer.[228] When separated from its mothership, the caique used to communicate by means of flags in daytime and by means of light in darkness.[229] The caique's sides were protected against enemy fire by a wooden screen over the gunwales, like the washboards on a modern Maltese *luzzu*.[230]

The caique also accompanied fireships on their missions to help their crews escape after lighting the fuses and setting their ships on their fiery course. On the other hand, a caique could also be used to tow a hostile fireship away from its mothership. The *Compendio d'Artiglieria* shows a reproduction of a caique being towed by a fireship.[231] It has three lateen sails and a rather tall stem at the bows, like that of a *luzzu*.[232] *Falki* or washboards can still be seen on the gunwales of the *luzzu* and the *tal-latini*[231] boats although these are falling out of favour in modern Maltese boats.[233]

The caique proved its worth during moments of calm when it could tow a ship either to catch a wind or to make it approach a becalmed enemy vessel. With the introduction of the ships-of-the-line, the duties for the caique increased as it was used to tow them out of harbour or to their berths.[234]

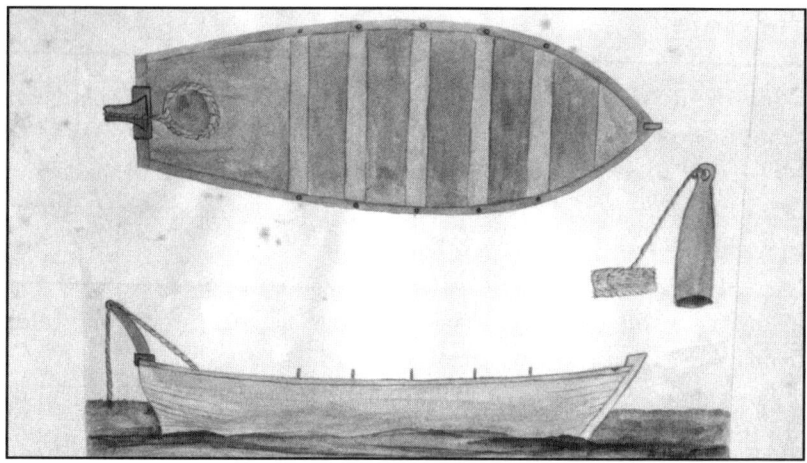

A galley's caique

The great assault caique

The fireship caique; MMM Compendio,

The great caique under sail

The caique was a fair-sized boat with a lateen sail and a fairly oversize antenna and a jib on the bows. It could also have from six to 18 oars[235] which could be used to increase the speed or when the caique was heavily laden. There were also two iron forks on which the mast could rest when it was removed. Indeed, in rough seas or with a contrary wind, the mast and the antenna used to be tied on these forks. In an emergency or to gain space, the caique could be dismantled and stored. Such a dismantled caique was known as a *caicco in fagotto*.[236]

There was a far larger type of caique as well which was used whenever the knights wanted to launch a sea-borne attack. For this purpose it had two passageways, one on each side, from where the soldiers could fight while its gunwales were built high to serve as protective screens. A small gun and some periers were placed on the bows. Such a caique was too large to be carried on board the galley and was normally towed behind.[237]

The *fregatina*

The boat or *fregatina*, the smallest of the tenders, was used whenever the galley lay in harbour or in some sheltered cove. It was used for light tendering work and was therefore kept moored alongside the ship.

The fregatina

The small boat was double ended and it could be propelled by both sail and oars.[238] Originally it had a lateen sail but, in the eighteenth century, it was discovered that two square sails and a jib gave increased speed and were moreover far easier to hoist and to lower.[239] Occasionally, as can be seen in some old pictures, the poop had a red velvet canopy.[240]

The boat could also be used an as emergency lifeboat though only a few of the 500 crew on a galley could hope to find a place on it. The caique could take about 125 persons[241] at most and the *felucca* a few more. The boat could take about 20 individuals. The pick of the crew would therefore be saved, while the slaves would remain chained to their places. Bosio described the horrible scene that occurred in the night between 23 and 24 October 1555 when four galleys capsized in the harbour after they were hit by a hurricane. The miserable spectacle that presented itself after the disaster showed the four galleys turned upside down with their keels above the sea level. Hundreds of slaves, still chained to their benches, were drowned and the scene recalled the great deluge as narrated in the Bible.[242]

Ceremonial barges

The ceremonial brigantine was of the same class as the galley but was never used for war. This small vessel, which was built for the exclusive use of the grand master, was equipped with two lateen- rigged masts and nine oars on each side. The cabin at the far end of the *corsia* was all gilded baroque sculpture on an olive green background.[243] The grand master used it to cross from Cospicua to Valletta and perhaps from Malta to Gozo. It is rather difficult to name a particular occasion when the grand master went to Gozo on his brigantine. All existent references point to the grand master using a galley to cross over to take possession of the smaller island.[244] In his cabin the grand master could relax on woollen cushions amidst red velvet hangings.

The knights always referred to this vessel as the magisterial gondola[245] though it had absolutely nothing to do with its Venetian namesake. It is not known how the name originated but it is relevant to remember that the ceremonial boat of the king of Spain was also known as a gondola.[246] There were, of course, close links between the Order and Spain.

Since this vessel could not carry provisions it could not sail far. It could possibly make it as far as Messina where the galley squadron used to assemble before embarking on the *corso*.[247] If a grand master ever sailed far in the gondola, he would have to be closely guarded by the galleys

The ceremonial brigantine

but then grand masters very rarely left Malta. Grand Master Verdalle left for Rome on 11 November 1587, risking a winter storm.[248] On that occasion he sailed in the *capitana*. Six years earlier, in September 1581, La Cassiere had gone to Rome to answer accusations against him on the galleys *San Pietro* and *San Giovanni*.[249] This is, however, extremely improbable because such a vessel could never properly defend itself and it had such a low freeboard that it could only sail in perfectly calm waters.

On the other hand, it should be remembered that *xprunari* and brigantines, which were not any larger that the gondola, could reach almost any harbour in the Mediterranean. It is very probable that the gondola was used only for ceremonial occasions as in official receptions of important visitors or during the possession of the general of the galleys.[250]

The gondola was seen at its finest during the possession of Grand Master Manoel de Vilhena at Vittoriosa in 1722.[251] On that occasion the rowers were Muslims, the better to show the domination of the Order over the Infidel. It was, perhaps, for the same reason that the Order occasionally used to put a carved Moor's head at the end of the spur on the galleys.[252] A mast cap was also known as *testa di moro* or 'Moor's head'.[253] Even the pink stern of the gondola's cabin used to rest on the backs of two sculptured Moors, one at either side of the vessel.

The magisterial gondola

Besides the ceremonial brigantine, Grand Master Alof de Wignacourt had his gondola which remained in service at least up to 1705.[254] There is a contemporary fine model of the gondola at the Malta Maritime Museum.[255]

As in the case of the Order, most seafaring nations used to have ceremonial craft with which to show their greatness. Venice had its Bucentaur, England had Prince Frederick's boat, and Portugal had the Royal Brigantine.[256] The same can be said for Spain, France, and the Netherlands.

The ship-of-the-line

Late in the seventeenth century a new type of ship called square-rigged vessels or ships-of-the-line started being built by the European sea-faring nations. The Order of St John too followed suit and in 1701 Grand Master Ramon Perellos decided in favour of such a vessel.[257] The considerable shortage of slaves then being experienced was a determining factor for the introduction of these vessels. Furthermore they had a life-expectancy of at least 24 years, compared to the eight years of the galley.[258] They were extremely sea-worthy and could stand up to winter sailing conditions as well as carry a good number of guns.

The ship-of-the-line; courtesy Francis Galea Naudi

The stern galleries of the San Gioacchino; *Malta Maritime Museum*

The stern balcony of the San Gioacchino; *Malta Maritime, Museum*

The introduction of these vessels was to coincide, for various reasons, with the decline of the Order as a maritime power.[259]

There were many different sizes of square-rigged warships. The largest, or the first rate, carried between 100 and 120 guns and were to be found amongst the British, the French, the Dutch, and the Spanish[260] who also had smaller version, or second rate, that carried between 80 and 100 guns.[261] Such vessels were better suited for the Atlantic Ocean rather than for the Mediterranean. This partly explains why the Order never felt it had to build large vessels of this type. Another reason was that the Barbary corsairs only had small and fast vessels themselves.

The third rate of such vessels was a 900-ton version that carried 56 to 60 guns.[262] The Order had such thirds like the *San Antonio* which had 56 guns and the *San Giovanni* which was launched in 1768 and was derelict but still whole in 1798 when Napoleon seized Malta.[263]

Yet another square-rigged warship in the Order's employ was the *San Zaccaria* which was smaller than the *San Giovanni*.

Although small, all these vessels could sail even during the winter months. Indeed, on 28 October 1768, the *San Zaccaria* sailed out into the Atlantic in search of corsairs.[264]

The *San Giovanni*, the second such vessel to bear this name, could have been one of the finest square-rigged warships the Order ever had. It had just been launched early in 1798 when it was seized by Napoleon.

After constructing various types of small vessels for the Order and carrying many modifications and repairing many ships, Maurin undertook the construction of the 64-gun ship *San Giovanni* which was to prove to be the finest and the most elegant warship of the Order that was ever built in Malta since the times of Perellos.

The *San Giovanni* was launched early in 1798 amidst the joy of the crowds in festive mood who attended the ceremony. Grand Master Hompesch himself, surrounded by all the high ranking officers of the Order, was present for the occasion. There were thousands of small boats near the shipyard where the *San Giovanni* was ready to slip into the waters. The ship was launched amidst the shouting, singing, and the playing of music by the thousands of people in attendance wishing the best of luck for the majestic huge hull perforated to take 64 guns.[265]

These vessels looked very much like carracks since they had a high freeboard and from four to six decks. However, while the carrack's mizzen mast and the bonaventure were lateen-rigged, these vessels' mizzen mast had a square sail hoisted above the lateen one. The carrack's castles were also much higher than these ships. While the carrack's rounded, tubby hull resembled a giant walnut, ships-of-the-line had a straighter and narrower beam. A ship-of-the-line also stood much lower in the water than either the carrack or the galleon.

Unfortunately these vessels came about too late in the Order's history. Yet the ship squadron too contributed its part to the Order's naval glories. Its exploits are immortalized in the paintings along the top corridors of the grand master's palace in Valletta. Two beautiful models of these third rates are on view in the Malta Maritime Museum and an excellent model of the *San Gioacchino* can be seen in the Żabbar Sanctuary Museum.

The frigate

By the first decades of the eighteenth century, the nomenclature of the lateen-rigged frigate referred to the larger, speedier, and better-armed vessel.[266] Frigates of this sort were frequently involved in the sea battles between the British and the French. Such vessels started to accompany the ship-of-the-line formations in battle.

The French had a great reputation for the construction of such vessels. It was to Toulon, in fact, that the Order sent the famous young Maltese naval architect Giuseppe Maurin to specialize in shipbuilding.

The eighteenth-century frigate was completely different from its fourteenth-century lateen-rigged counterpart. It did not have a high freeboard and it had only two decks. Its guns which could number up to 20 were carried on the main deck. The number of guns on an eighteenth-century frigate varied from country to country. Guglielmotti states that the frigate could have 8, 12, 24, 32, or even 60 guns.[267] Dal Pozzo mentions four frigates with 24, 22, 12, and 8 guns respectively that belonged to Maltese corsairs in 1668. However, before the eighteenth-century, all vessels that were not large or tall enough to be called galleons were known as frigates.[268] Quite frequently the upper or main deck was not covered at all and the guns could therefore be seen on both sides.

The Order had always wanted a small and fast but well-armed vessel that could catch up and fight with the Barbary corsairs which were renowned for their speed. The frigate met these demands and was more economical to run than either a large galley or a ship-of-the-line.[269] At this time economy was a very important factor to the hard-pressed Order.

The Order's frigates included the *Santa Elizabetta,* the *Santa Maria,* and *La Santissima Vergine del Pilar.*[270] This latter ship accompanied a

The frigate

The Maltese small warship

ship-of-the-line the *San Zaccaria* on a corsairing mission in October 1778.[271] The *Santa Elizabetta* and the *Santa Maria* joined the Spanish squadron and saw action at Algiers early in December 1783.[272] The *Santa Elizabetta* was still being used by the Order in April 1798.[273] Its sistership, the *Santa Maria*, had, however, become too old by 1796. Since it would have been too costly to repair it, it was decided to auction it together with all its equipment.[274]

Another smaller type of frigate, known as a light frigate, could be seen in Maltese waters. This fast warlike vessel had one deck and carried from 16 to 24 guns.[275] Though it looked very much like the other frigate, an experienced eye could tell the difference immediately.

There was an even smaller version which seems to have been unique to Malta. This had one deck, a foremast, and a mainmast together with a jibboom at the bows and could carry 4, 6, or 8 guns.[276]

The corvette

The corvette was smaller than the frigate. The Order had already constructed corvettes even before they became popular with the other European navies. In 1773 the Order's first corvette replaced the obsolete ship-of-the-line the *San Giovanni*.

The corvette was a fast vessel meant to catch up with the speedy Barbary corsairs. It was furthermore much more economical to build and to maintain than any square-rigged vessel. Between 1733 and 1734 the Order decided to build two corvettes, the *Santa Teresa* and the *San Francesco di Paola*,[277] one of which was paid for by Grand Master Manoel de Vilhena himself.[278]

Early in 1733, a few weeks after its launching, the *Santa Teresa* under the knight Combreux sailed on a corsairing mission near Palermo. It later went on to Genoa to collect cargo for the Order.[279] In 1734 it sailed out on a *corso* with another corvette, the *San Francesco di Paola*, under Lapparelli.[280] On 1 October 1734 it joined the *San Antonio*, the *San Giovanni*, and the *San Vincenzo* on another *corso* mission.[281] A report of 15 September 1735 stated that the *Santa Teresa* could not catch up with the ships of the Barbary coast.[282]

On 18 April 1740, the *Santa Teresa* and the *San Francesco di Paola* sailed together towards Trieste to scout for enemy shipping. They returned on 9 May 1740 with five or six of their crews sick with tertian fever and the rest suffering from dysentery.[283]

Because of the poor showing in action of the *Santa Teresa* in 1734, the Order did not build another corvette until 1783 when Grand Master Rohan himself paid for one to be constructed.[284] A year later another corvette, the *Santa Maria della Neve*, was built.[285] In 1785 these two corvettes sailed on a 50-day reconnaissance mission together with two galleys under the general leadership of the knight Ruspoli. Their journey took them to Sicily, Sardinia, and Italy.[286]

The corvette resembled a cross between the frigate and the square-rigged brigantine. Its three masts were square-rigged and, since it had a low freeboard, it could also be propelled by oars in emergencies. It never had more than 12 oars on either side,[287] and carried from 20 to 30 guns. It was a very versatile vessel that could be used for fighting, for carrying cargo, and for scouting missions. It appears that the corvettes of the Order only had 12 guns. At least, when in 1730 the *Santa Teresa* was being armed, an order was issued for two galleys to sail to Gozo to bring back to Malta 12 guns which were thought to be enough for the corvette under construction. A gun pontoon was loaded with 12 heavier guns to be installed on the fortifications of Gozo for the defence of that island.[288]

When the only deck of a corvette was not covered, the guns used to be laid out in the open as on the English corvettes. The Order's corvettes

The corvette

resembled closely those of the French navy which had their guns placed below deck. Guglielmotti maintains that the corvette was more or less identical with a small frigate, the only difference being in the oars. According to this author, the corvette was *'in sostanza piccola fregata'*.[289]

The *palandra*

In addition to the guns, the knight had another piece of ordnance – the mortar. To carry these mortars and to withstand their strong recoils, an unusual vessel with a more or less flat bottom was constructed out of strong heavy wood. This vessel was known as the *bombarda* or *palandra* or bomb-ketch, a vessel which started forming part of the fleets in the second half of the sixteenth century.

The *palandra* had no deck; instead the mortars were placed directly on a strong platform on the bottom.[290] It had only two masts, one in the middle and the other towards the stern. This kept the forecastle or the bow section unencumbered for firing the mortars. At one time the *palandra* used to carry a large mortar on the bows and a smaller one at the stern. The larger mortar fired bombs with a diameter of 40 cm.[291]

There were only a few such ships. In sea-battles where bomb-ketches were used, there are references only to one or two such vessels. The

The mortar ship

The mortar mounted on a bombard; model by Joseph Muscat

Venetian fleet that attacked Sfax in 1786 consisted of four ships-of-the-line, a frigate, a galleas, and two bomb-vessels.[292] The *palandra* was far more useful in attacking coastal batteries and fortifications, as when the carrack *Sant'Anna* attacked Goletta on the North African coast in 1535. In 1685, when Venice was still involved in the war at Candia, French ships employed a *palandra* constructed in Venice to fire bombs with two mortars. It was placed in front of the point of the fortifications of the city with the sea beneath it; it proved very efficacious since previously the shots from the ships had done little damage to the enemy buildings and personnel.[293]

Few wanted to sail on the *palandra* of their own free will; the recoil of the mortars and the ear-splitting report made life extremely unpleasant. Furthermore its flat bottom made it most unsteady.

Since the *palandra* had no deck, the bombs were stored under the platform on which the mortar rested. Though the *palandra* always sailed accompanied by other ships, it carried means to defend itself in case of attack by hostile craft such as *feluccas* or caiques.

The *palandra* never held a place of honour amongst the navies and it took very little part in sea-battles. It is not certain whether the Order had any such ships. Whenever a *palandra* is mentioned in the Order's records, it always formed part of someone else's navy, though the knights used to be trained in its handling.

The fireship

The fireship changed little over the centuries.[294] Fireships were also used in olden times to set hostile fleets on fire. When Genseric sent his Vandal corsairs to ravage the Peloponnese in 467, Byzace the Byzantine leader prepared a fleet to defend his territories. Genseric became frightened and sought to make peace. However, the Vandal leader secretly prepared a fleet and burnt the Byzantine ships in Carthage harbour by means of fireships. These is the first documented use of fireships which could be found in all fleets. The English used eight against the Spanish armada in 1588, while the Dutch employed them successfully against the English in 1653.[295]

The number of such ships was increased according to the demand.[296] The English had only one fireship in 1675, while in 1688 they had 26.

They did not use any fireships against Napoleon. In 1697 the Venetians had two fireships in a fleet of 25 ships, 20 galleys, six galeasses, and 15 galleots. The Turkish fleet which faced it consisted of two fireships, 26 large ships, and 16 galleots.[297] In 1698 the Venetians had three fireships in a squadron of 25 large ships-of-the-line.[298]

The fireship was never used on a large scale in the Mediterranean. It is not known whether the Order had any; it certainly never had any built specifically for this purpose but, when it felt the need for one, it made use of an old brigantine or a tartane.[299]

It was then believed that the larger the fireship the more difficult it would be for the enemy to board and put out the fire. Sometimes a large ship of 60 guns was prepared as a fireship. It was laden with gunpowder with the real guns on board being replaced by wooden replicas[300] so that it would still look like its sisterships. The English used to prepare a sixth rate as a fireship.[301] At other times the fireship would simply be an old derelict ship for which no further use could be found.[302]

During the battle, the fireship used to be steered with a few sailors on board towards an enemy ship with which it entangle by means of the many hooks and grappling irons it had on its spars.[303] A skilful captain would give time for his crew to escape before lighting the fuse and fleeing himself. One cannot overemphasize enough the responsibility carried by the fireship captain. There were incidents when captains of fireships overloaded their vessels with gunpowder causing them to break up too quickly thereby overturning parts of the freeboard over and taking down with them the accompanying caiques and drowning most of the crew.[304]

The crew of the fireship varied according to its size. A large vessel needed 50 or 60 hands, but when the ship was about to enter battle only a few sailors remained on board. Such a large crew was required because a fireship full of gunpowder had to be handled with the utmost care and attention.[305]

The fireship could be steered on to its target in different ways. The crew could jam the rudder in the right direction, light the fuse, and then escape on the caique the fireship had in tow.[306] At other times a wooden plank was fixed to the rudder. Two ropes were tied to the plank and these were then used by two caiques to direct the burning fireship on its course. This reduced the danger of the crew being burnt themselves and also enabled them to use the fireship itself to protect them from the enemy's musketry fire.[307]

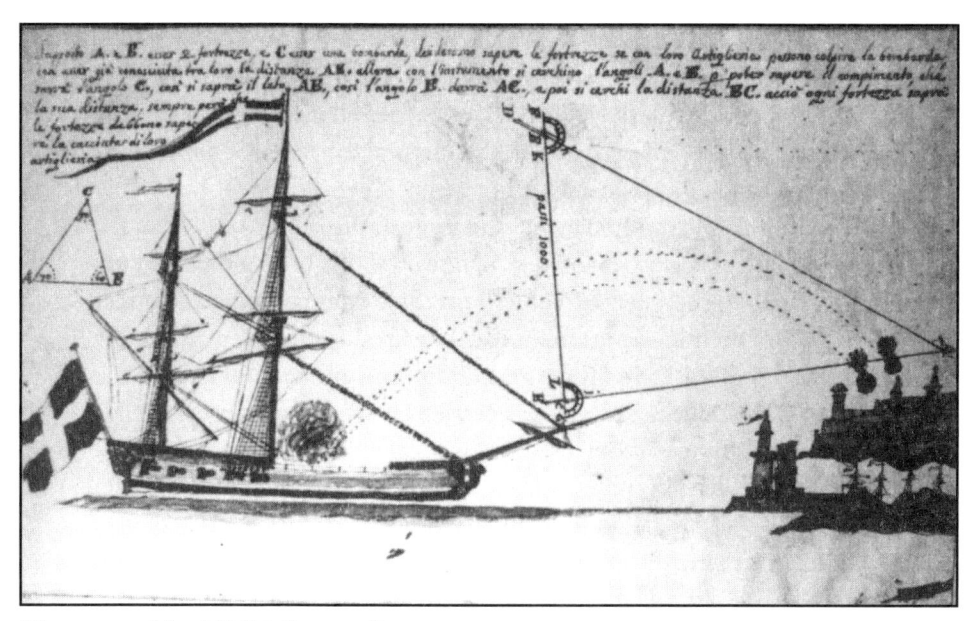

The mortar ship; MMM Compendio

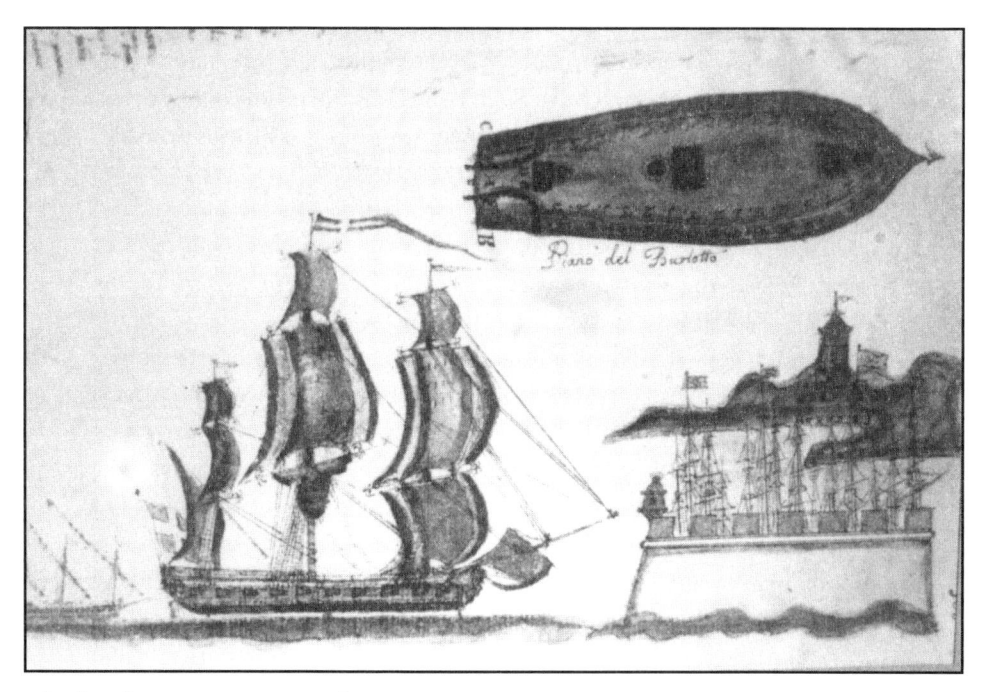

The fire ship; MMM Compendio,

It was extremely expensive to fill a fireship with gunpowder and as such a fireship was only employed where it could damage a number of enemy ships, particularly when they were moored in harbour. A fireship could also be steered right into the thickest of the battle towards some damaged stationary enemy ship when it would explode with a devastating roar. Another tactic was to use a fireship to disperse the enemy sailing in a close formation. Quite often the best-laid plans went astray. In 1646 the fleets of Venice and the Order combined to attack the Turks in their own port in Canea. The fireships they sent, however, got entangled with a submerged chain and burnt themselves out innocuously.[308] Since the fireship exploded before it caught fire it needed not only skill to steer it but a readiness to take risks.[309]

The hospital ship

The Greeks and the Romans had a type of fairly large vessel called the *grippo* that was used to transport spices and medicinal herbs from India. In time a *grippo* came to mean 'a hospital ship' for the nations round the Mediterranean sea-board, probably because of the fragrance of the herbs and spices one could smell on it. Such a ship was purposely constructed quite large and with a wide beam so that it would roll as little as possible.

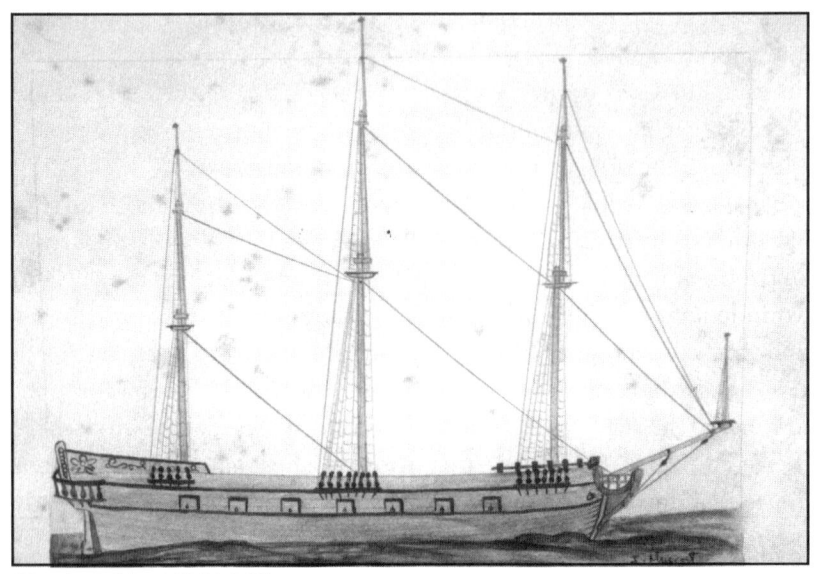

Hospital ship; NLM 223

Almost all available space was taken up with beds.[310] Today '*grippo*' means a type of boat used to carry spices in Eastern waters.[311]

The Order of St John had been founded by a group of merchants from Amalfi to look after the sick and the pilgrims.[312] By 1048 they had been granted permission by the Caliph Abu Tamin Bomensor to build a hospital and a convent in the Holy Land. The Benedictines took up the running of the convent[313] while the hospital, which was dedicated to St John, had the Blessed Gerald as its first rector. When the Christians conquered Jerusalem, Gerald and his companions took the vows of poverty, chastity, and obedience and became a religious Order. Their primary aim was to look after the sick and the pilgrims in their hospitals and this earned them the name of Hospitallers. Brother Gerald died in 1120 and was succeeded by Raymond de Puis as rector, who wanted the brothers to be trained as warriors to defend the Holy Places as knights.[314] Pope Paschal II granted de Puis's wish.[315] For many years, the knights had the finest medical service in Europe and one therefore could expect to find a hospital ship accompanying the Order's navy.

It cannot be ascertained whether a ship was specifically built for this purpose, although this possibility cannot be excluded. However, every time that a squadron of more than ten vessels went on the *corso*, or whenever the galleys of the Order left to attack enemy territory, a ship for the sick and wounded was always prepared. There is a great deal of information about a pink that served as a hospital ship. Below decks it looked like a fully-equipped hospital with beds, surgical instruments, doctors, nurses, orderlies, and a chaplain.[316] Though the Order could use any other cargo ship for this purpose, it actually preferred the pink[317] which could later return to its original mercantile use.[318]

Paul Cassar maintains that the Order never possessed a hospital ship like other countries such as England and Venice but refers to the carrack *Santa Maria* which was temporarily fitted as a hospital for the sick and wounded after the loss of Rhodes.[319] It cannot be said that the Order built ships to serve specifically as hospitals, but in 1669, after the fall of Candia, as the galleys were sailing back to Malta, they had a great number of the sick crew members. First they stopped at Messina where they made use of the palace of that priory as a hospital and later another one at Standia, utilizing the hull of an unserviceable galley. Apparently the other galley squadrons followed suit, as many members of the various crews died because of the contagious disease.[320]

The council's ordinance of 17 November 1691 repeated once more (it had first been issued on 4 April 1651) that no galley squadron could carry more than the prescribed number of boats but, when necessary, by the galleys, the land forces, the wounded, and the sick were to be provided with the necessary transport over and above the number of boats normally carried.[321] The ordinance was referring to the assault on Candia by the forces of Venice, the papal squadron, and the Order.[322]

The English had hospital ships under James I, while the French used old galleys to house the sick. Before it came to Malta, the Order used a galleon[323] for the victims of the plague they encountered at Messina. Even the carrack *Santa Maria* got infected and the knights had to make a hasty departure.[324] According to Bosio, the Order had a hospital ship that accompanied the fleet during the assault on Djerba in 1560.[325]

The galleys of the Order were always ready to make a common cause with anybody who was fighting the Muslims. They joined the Spanish fleet every time it attacked the North African coast. They played their part in the 25-year-long war over Candia.[326] Names such as Patras, Modon, and Lepanto ring out the honours of the Order's galleys and of the other humble craft that accompanied them. All this means that the galley squadron of the Order often needed a hospital ship.

Though each galley had a place under the rambate where it could tend its sick and injured, this only could accommodate about 30 at the most. It was, therefore, imperative that a hospital ship or a converted tartane, brigantine, or old galley should follow the fleet when high casualties were expected.[327]

NOTES

1   B. Landstrom, *The Ship* (London, 1961), 127; P. Auphan, *Histoire de la Méditerranée* (Paris, 1962), 28 says, '*Pelages et Pheniciens, hommes du Nord et hommes du Sud confronterent leurs techniques. Sans qu'on sache tres bien la part que revient a chacun d'eux, de leur conjugaison naquit l'instrument qui allait regenter la Méditerranée pendant plusiers millenaires: la galere.*'

2   AOM 271, f. 20: '*Partirete subito che il tempo ve lo permettera con le tre Galere Sensiglie, ed una tartana da carico per Augusta, ad oggetto d'imbarcare i biscotti ed altre provisione, che ivi si trovano per servigio delle nostre Squadre.*' A great number of similar commands can be seen in the archives of the Order.

3   P. Earle, *Corsairs of Malta and Barbary* (London, 1970), 53, 54 states that many cargo

ships used to fall victims to the Barbary corsairs.
4   Dal Pozzo, i, 65, 116; see also J. Muscat, 'The Warships of the Order of St John' in S. Fiorini (ed.), *Proceedings of History Week 1994* (Malta, 1996), 77-113
5   A. Guglielmotti, *Vocabolario marino e militare* (Rome, 1889), s.v. *Caracca;* see also E. Brockman, *Last Bastion* (London, 1961), 164. The word 'carrack' is derived from the Italian *carricare* – 'to load, or take in cargo'. G. Darmanin Demajo, 'The Grand Harbour of Malta and its surroundings in 1530', *Daily Malta Chronicle*, 7 January 1926, 5 carries other useful information.
6   Guglielmotti, s.v. *Caracca*; E. Rossi, *Storia della Marina dell'Ordine di S. Giovanni di Gerusalemme di Rodi e di Malta* (Rome-Milan, 1926), 108.
7   M.U. Ubaldini, *La marina del Sovrano Militare Ordine di San Giovanni di Gerusalemme di Rodi e di Malta* (Rome, 1970), 59.
8   Bosio, iii, 8, 15; the *Santa Maria* carried to Malta a large number of knights and many other natives of Rhodes who decided to follow the Order, together with their belongings. While the *Santa Maria* was in Messina the plague, then raging in the city, infected the ship itself where fortunately little harm was caused.
9   Bosio, ii, 591.
10 Bosio, iii, 5.
11 Ibid., 98.
12 Ibid., 108; see also J. Muscat, *The Carrack of the Order* (Malta, 2000), 10-5.
13 Ibid., 22. There were so many fires and so much smoke in the yard where the *Sant' Anna* was being built, that nobody working on the ship was affected by the plague then rampant in the city; see ibid., 149.
14 Ibid., 150; see also E.W. Schermerhorn, *Malta of the Knights* (Surrey, 1929), 113.
15 P.J. Taurisano, *Antologia del Mare. Dalle opere del P. Guglielmotti* (Florence, 1913), 198.
16 Bosio, iii, 150.
17 Ibid., 114.
18 Ibid., 150
19 F.C. Bowen, *From Carrack to Clipper* (London, 1948), 20.
20 Bosio, iii, 150;
21 The Byzantines used lead sheathing to protect the hulls against shipworm and rot, see H. Frost, *Under the Mediterranean* (London, 1963), 234, 235.
22 Schermerhorn, 113.
23 Bosio, iii, 150.
24 Ibid., 148.
25 Ibid., 197.
26 Ibid., 254. See also Muscat, *The Carrack*, 15-28.
27 All that remains of this galleon is a picture by Guidotti, which greatly resembles the two engravings by C.J. Visscher of the *Golden Lion* and the *Whitebear*; see E. Keble Chatterton, *Old Ship Prints*. Second impression (London 1967), 61, 62. As for the name *San Giovanni Bonaventura*, see Lib. 413, f. 14: '*come il Religioso in Christo a noi charissimo fra Opizio Guidotti Cavaliere della Ven. Lin. d'Italia, essendo stato da Noi eletto per Capitano del Gran Galione della Sacra Religione nominato San Giovanni bonnaventura.*' It is sometimes referred to as *San Giovanni* and sometimes as *Bonaventura*.
28 Guglielmotti, s.v. *Galeone*.
29 Lib. 413, f. 228 gives all the details about the galleon's armaments: '*Artiglieria esistente a bordo del Galeone di Malta quando ne era Comandante il Guidotti.*'
30 Guglielmotti, s.v. *Galera*.
31 Ibid., s.v. *Galeone;* Guidotti, NLM, Lib. 413, f.228, however, gives more detailed information about the galleon's armaments.
32 NLM, Lib. 413, f. 224.
33 Guglielmotti, s.v. *Galeone*; Lib. 413, f. 225 lists the following: main sail, foresail, bonnet for the mainsail, bonnet for the foresail, main topsail, fore topsail, spritsail, sprit

topsail, main topgallant, mizzen sail, bonadventure mizzen sail. Ibid., f. 224 omits the bonnets for the mainsail and foresail together with the mizzen topsail. The bonnet was an extra sail attached to the fore and main sails used when there was a good wind blowing aft.

34   Ibid., f. 7; the author does not speak about himself out of vanity. Guidotti had earned a wide renown and a deep respect for his sea-faring activities.
35   Rossi, 112, 113.
36   A lateen-rigged frigate assisted the galleon in this last-mentioned *corso* cruise. They returned to Malta on 15 May 1607; Lib. 413, f. 14.
37   Ibid., f. 68; this time the galleon was accompanied by a galleot. The two of them sailed away on 27 February 1608 and came back on 13 April 1608; see also ibid., f. 77.
38   AOM 1759, f. 363.
39   Lib. 273, f. 2.
40   Lib. 413, f. 168. It is interesting to note that the name Digut is a corruption and stands for Commander Fra Filippo de Gouttes; see Dal Pozzo, i, 635.
41   Dal Pozzo, i, 634.
42   Rossi, 53.
43   Dal Pozzo, i, 243.
44   Bosio, iii, 219.
45   Ibid., 233, 234.
46   Ibid., 471 *et seq*.
47   Ibid., 510, 511.
48   J. Muscat, *Il-Flotta ta' l-Ordni ta' San Ġwann* (Malta, 2000), 97-105.
49   Dal Pozzo, i, 586, 587. The account of how the seven slaves armed only with three axes and some knives took over the *petacchio* makes unbelievable reading. See also J. Aquilina, *Maltese-English Dictionary* (Malta, 1987) who renders the nomenclature in Maltese as *pittiċċ*.
50   See picture in Lib. 413, f. 236.
51   Guglielmotti, s.v. *Petacchio*.
52   AOM 1768, f. 79.
53   Guglielmotti, s.v. *Petacchio*, mentions in a note the engraving by Callot of what is described as *Petacchio di Tunisi, di 800 salme*. This shows that the Tunisians used to have large *petacchi*.
54   The *orca* or *urca* was a cargo ship used by the Muslims, the Venetians, and other mainly Eastern nationalities; see ibid., s.v. *Orca*.
55   Dal Pozzo, i, 548.
56   Ibid., 603.
57   Ibid., ii, 41.
58   In AOM 1759, f. 365 and AOM 256, f. 64v there is the order: '*Che si venda il petacchio*.'
59   AGPV 39, bill of lading dated *A di 20 Aprile 1680 Venezia*; AOM 1771, f. 103v; NAM Cons. 8, *Pro aliis Carolus Borg et Vincentii Arnaud*. See also Muscat, *Il-Flotta*, 105-8.
60   Lib. 223, s.v. *Caracca*; Guglielmotti, s.v. *Galeone*.
61   Dal Pozzo, ii, 48, 50.
62   AOM 272, f. 158v.
63   Guglielmotti, *Vocabolario*, s.v. *Galera*; see also Żarb, 19, votive painting 19.
64   AOM, 1934A, f. 18.
65   Lib. 223, s.v. *Marabutino*.
66   J. Gravière, *Les Derniers Jours de la Marine a Rame* (Paris, 1885), 79, 233.
67   Guglielmotti, *Vocabolario* s.v. *Mezzagalera*. There was a one-masted galleot but as Dal Pozzo, ii, 27 says, when referring to the vessels of Bizerta, that there were cases when '*Galeotte cosi chiamate, se ben di corpo, e di forze pari all'altre Galere ...*' Though galleys normally had two masts, up to the end of the sixteenth century, there were

many examples with just one mast. In the eighteenth century, however, a third mast was often used, especially in Malta.

68 Lib. 413, f. 177, 185.
69 Guglielmotti, *Vocabolario*, s.v. *Galera*.
70 Gravière, *Les Derniers*, 4.
71 Ibid., 196.
72 Dal Pozzo, i, 99.
73 AOM 1759, f. 463.
74 *Histoire de la Marine* (Paris, 1934), 153; Graviere, 191.
75 Lib. 413, f. 177.
76 Gravière, *Les Derniers* 190; Lib. 413, f. 177 refers to an oar of a common galley which was 44 palms long (one palm was $10^5/_{16}$ inches).
77 AOM 1759, f. 353 and Lib. 413, f. 179.
78 Ibid., f. 186.
79 Gravière, *Les Derniers*, 190.
80 Bosio, iii, 367.
81 Dal Pozzo, i, 99: '*Nella Capitana, ch'era di banchi 28 vi fossero 250 Remiganti, armandosi il quartiero di poppa a cinque per banco e il resto a quattro, e nell'altre non più di 200 non essendo che di 25 banchi.*' But see also Lib. 413, f. 185: '*Vanno armate di chiurma a cinque homini per bango ... e la Capitana e armata a 6 per banco ...*'.
82 Gravière, *Les Derniers*, 191.
83 Guglielmotti, *Vocabolario*, s.v. *Galera*.
84 Gravière, *Les Derniers*, 185; see also A. Guglielmotti, *Storia della Marina Pontificia* (Rome 1886-93), i, 175.
85 Ibid.
86 Gugliemotti, *Vocabolario* s.v. *Galera;* Gravière, 194.
87 R. Morton Nance, *Sailing-Ship Models*. Revised edition (London 1949), 60, plate 73. There is a reconstructed model of a galley by Joseph Muscat in the Malta Maritime Museum where the rambate can be clearly seen. See also Gravière, 153, 154. Lib. 413, f. 204 mentions '*Qualita di legname per le diverse parti di una Galera - Rambata che si arbora - di pioppo.*'
88 Dal Pozzo, i, 20; ii, 238.
89 Guglielmotti, *Vocabolario*, s.v. *Galera*; Lib. 413, 178: '*et le Balestriere sonno certe tavole dalle Bande dove dormano li Marinari et dove si stia quando si combatte, le Rambate dove sta sotto l'artiglieria il piu' onorato locho ...;.* The rambate on the bows of the galley was the place of honour during sea-battles with the Muslims.
90 Guglielmotti, *Vocabolario*, s.v. *Galera*
91 *Histoire de la Marine*, 151. In Lib. 413, f. 182, there is '*e 60 (canne - qasba) per il Tendalle e parasoli*'.
92 AOM 1759 f. 461.
93 Lib. 413, f. 182.
94 Dal Pozzo, ii, 80, 81.
95 AOM 648, ff. 313, 314.
96 Bosio, iii, 860.
97 T. Zammit, *Malta - The Islands and their History* (Malta, 1971), 224, 225.
98 AOM 260 f. 45, '*Ordine che si levi la poppa della Capitana vecchia per la nuova*' and ibid., f.171v says '*si levi la poppa dalla Capitana vecchia 8 -11-1663*'.
99 Gravière, *Les Derniers*, 169-71.
100 H.J. Hansen, *Art and the Seafarer* (London, 1968), 121; S. Bono, *I Corsari Barbareschi* (Turin, 1964), 78.
101 AOM 1759, f. 384.
102 NLM, Lib. 413, f. 182; for a diagram of the sections of the hold of a Maltese galley, see MMM, 'Remarques', ff. 146, 148.

103 Gravière, *Les Derniers,* 178-80.
104 NLM, Lib. 413, f. 179.
105 Gravière, *Les Derniers,* 183.
106 AOM 1899 f. 80; AOM 271 f. 170v.
107 Lib. 413, f. 179; Dal Pozzo, ii, 81: *'per alleggerirsi la Galera Santa Maria butto' a mare tre barili d'acqua per banco, e gli altri impedimenti di sopra coperta ...'*
108 Gravière, *Les Derniers,* 148.
109 Lib. 413, f. 177.
110 Gravière, *Les Derniers,* 172.
111 Lib. 223, s.v. *Cucina*
112 AOM 1899, ff. 68, 176.
113 AOM 1759, f. 454.
114 Lib. 110, f. 6, no. 18.
115 AOM 1759, f. 451.
116 Lib, 110, f. 19, no. 80.
117 Lib. 223, s.v. *Caldara dell'equipaggio.*
118 AOM 1877, f. 130.
119 AOM 1759, f. 451.
120 The 'Libro della Marina', Lib. 318, f. 182, refers to square-rigged ships rather than galleys, but the use of a lighted match or a kindling light in a barrel must have been common to both types of ships. See also Taurisano, 235. Where Guglielmotti mentions that more than 200 matches could be lit at one go during an emergency.
121 Lib. 413 f. 177; AOM 187, ff. 124, 128; Lib. 223, s.v. *Gallinaro.*
122 Gravière, *Les Derniers,* 171.
123 AOM 1759, f. 451: *'Non possa il Venerando Generale e Capitani in qualunque viaggio portar casse per conservar neve ...'.*
124 Braudel, 29.
125 De Caro, 86.
126 Suetonius, *The Twelve Caesars* (London), 223.
127 AOM 1759, f. 451.
128 Guidotti, *passim.*
129 *Histoire de la Marine, passim.*
130 AOM 1923, ff. 62, 69.
131 Lib. 223, s.v. *Capitana: cosi chiamasi la Galera sopra la quale s'imbarca il Generale, o un comandante che abbia sotto il di lui comando molte Galere.* Gravière, *Les Derniers,* 116, *'La Capitane etait toujours peinte en noir; les six autres recevaint une au plusieurs couches de peinture rouge.'* The author was referring to the Maltese galleys.
132 Dal Pozzo, i, 744.
133 G.A. Vassallo, *Storia di Malta Raccontata in Compendio* (Malta, 1854), 657.
134 Schermerhorn, 241.
135 AOM 1759, f. 332, *'Accrescimento di Galere nella Squadra, dovuta alla settima Galera fondata dal Gran Mastro Lascaris con tutto il disporto per il suo armamento.'* A gun from Lascaris's galley can be seen at the entrance to the Palace Armoury in Valletta. Dal Pozzo, ii, 545, *'il lor parera era, che non più si servissero di vascelli: ma s'armasse l'ottava Galera, la quale sarebbe stata e di piu profitto all'Armata ...'.* AOM, 262, f. 233: *'Si disarmi l'ottava galera 22-11-1685'* and in AOM 262, f. 242v: *'Elezione di Capitano per l'ottava galera 28-12-1685'.*
136 Rossi, 47, *'alla fine di aprile con tre galere, di cui due mantenute dal Gran Maestro e percio dette magistrale'.*
137 Bosio, iii, 88.
138 Ibid., 99.
139 Ibid., 402.
140 Dal Pozzo, i, 767.

141 Ibid., ii, 193.
142 Ibid., ii, 545.
143 AOM 265, f. 129: *Ordine che la squadra delle galere si riduca al numero di 5.*
144 AOM 273, f. 3; AOM 1763, f. 2.
145 AOM 6450 and AOM 6451 give an endless list of such names.
146 Rossi, 39-40.
147 Ibid., 108.
148 AOM 1922, f. 11, '*Costruzione (della) Galera s. Luigi ... principiata il 19 Settembre 1792 e terminata il 22 Giugno 1793*'.
149 AOM 1923, ff. 94-137.
150 Lib. 413, f. 50; AOM 1773, ff. 4, 96 show how galleys used to help ships out of the harbour till their sails caught the wind.
151 Lib. 223, s.v. *Rizzone;* Guglielmotti, *Storia*, VIII, 185; *Histoire de la Marine*, 150.
152 Lib. 413, f. 179: '*Et piú porta quattro ferri da darre fondo dui in operra et dui di rispetto: pesano l'uno Cantara cinque.*'
153 Gravière, *Les Derniers*, 155; see also MMM, MS. 'Segni della Capitana', f. 2. Four anchors are referred to here as in Gravière.
154 Gravière, *Les Derniers*, 156.
155 Lib. 627 shows the Rohan galley with the stern ladder in place; the Cotoner and Pinto's galleys are without it.
156 For more information see J. Muscat, *The Maltese Galley* (Malta, 2000).
157 Dal Pozzo, ii, 546.
158 Ibid., 676.
159 AOM 274, f. 221.
160 AOM 272, f.158v.
161 W. Hardman, *A History of Malta during the period of the French and British Occupations 1798-1815* (London, 1909), 27.
162 Guglielmotti, *Storia*, ix, 291.
163 See the *ex-voto* dedicated to the Holy Crucifix in Senglea church which is a vow made by the captain of the galley *San Nicola*, dated 1745. This is one of the few extant pictorial representations of the half-galleys *Sant'Anna* and *Sant'Orsola*.
164 Guglielmotti, *Storia*, viii, 275; id., *Vocabolario*, s.v. *Mezzagalera*.
165 This explains why this type of rowing on the demigalley was known as *a sensile*.
166 Guglielmotti, *Vocabolario*, s.v. *Mezzagalera* mentions *remi lunghissimi e sottili ed elastici di faggio*.
167 See model of a demi galley at the Malta Maritime Museum, Vittoriosa. It should be noted that this unique, contemporary model shows 14 banks of oars on each side.
168 AOM 1934A, f.15
169 Gugliemotti, *Vocabolario*, s.v. *Mezzagalera*.
170 Id., *Storia*, viii, 275.
171 *L'Arte*, No. 24, 7 November 1863.
172 AOM 1923, ff. 144, 145: balance for two half-galleys: 42,979 *scudi*, 3 *tari*, 13 *grani*.
173 Ibid., ff.48-144.
174 Rossi, 87, 151; but see also AOM 269, f. 234v.
175 Hardman, 213.
176 Ibid., 102.
177 Guglielmotti, *Storia*, viii, 275.
178 Muscat, *Il-Flotta*, 73-6.
179 Dal Pozzo, ii 27; see also Guglielmotti, *Vocabolario*, s.v. *Galeotta*.
180 Dal Pozzo, ii, 544.
181 Ibid., 671.
182 AOM 274, f. 26.
183 AOM 1767, f. 313.

184 Ibid., f. 369; AOM 263, f. 101v; Valera armed his vessel on 25 September 1691.
185 AOM 264, ff. 10, 77v; AOM 1767, ff. 405, 420.
186 AOM 269, f. 198.
187 Lib. 413, f. 68.
188 AOM 271, f. 72v.
189 AOM 272 ff. 3v, 8.
190 Rossi, 89.
191 Guglielmotti, *Vocabolario*, s.v. *Galeotta*.
192 AOM 269, f. 158v.
193 Guglielmotti, *Vocabolario*, s.v. *Galeotta*.
194 Lib. 627; the author of this unpaginated MS. refers to the galley of Grand Master Cottoner as *Gran Galera* but, when he refers to those of Grand Master Pinto and Grand Master Rohan, he uses the nomenclature *galione*.
195 Bowen, 29.
196 At Tal-Ħerba Sanctuary, Birkirkara there are two *ex-voto* paintings showing a common galley for 1779 and a *capitana* for 1793 both equipped with three masts; see Prins, A.H.J. Prins, *In Peril on the Sea* (Malta, 1989), plates 33, 34 and N. Vella Apap, *L-Istorja tas-Santwarju tal-Madonna tal-Ħerba* (Malta, 2000), 127.
197 Rossi, 105.
198 AOM 274, f. 209v: '*Hanno osservato i commissarij, che senza pregudicar punto il servigio puó diminuirsi il numero delle persone al medmo. addatte specialmente dopo essersi adottata la costruzione di Galera minore di quelle che si sono fin ora usate di due Banchi per parte, ...*'.
199 Guglielmotti, *Storia*, VIII, 275.
200 Landstrom, 141.
201 Representations of these vessels are to be seen in Lib, 627 '*Fascicolo a Colori*'.
202 While C.S. Sonnini, *Travels in Upper and Lower Egypt* (London, 1800), 50, 51, mentions a striped blue-and-white sail, Schermerhorn, 215, says that the Order frequently used a red-and-white sail, Lib. 627 shows a striped white-and-blue sail with an eight-pointed white Maltese cross on a red background.
203 Muscat, *Il-Flotta*, 69-73.
204 AOM 1934A, f. 2 remarks that '*Le Service de la Religion n'est plus maintenans qu'une affaire de Calcul, ...*'.
205 Ibid., f. 16 asks for an inventory of all the galleys up to 1 May 1792 and ibid., f. 18 it explains that economies should be made, even on sails.
206 See the beautiful watercolour in the Cathedral Museum Mdina.
207 AOM 271, f. 20.
208 AOM 1923, ff. 18, 63, 64.
209 Guglielmotti, *Storia*, IX, 82.
210 Gravière, *Les Derniers*, 173.
211 J. Muscat, *The Dgħajsa and other Traditional Boats* (Malta, 1999), 44 refers to the occasions when *dgħajjes* or *barche del passo* accompanied the galley squadron; see also J. Muscat, 'The Dgħajsa - In Memoriam', *The Mariner's Mirror*, lxxvii, no. 4, 389-405.
212 AOM 1759, f. 426.
213 AOM 269, f. 160.
214 MMM, MS Segni della Capitana, f. 3, no. 45: '*La Felugha nera vadi abbordo della Capitana* and ibid. f.7, no. 23: *Chiamare la Felugha nera, abbordo della Capitana.*'
215 MMM, MS 'Segni delle Galere Sensil'; see also MMM, MS 'Segni della Capitana', f. 3, No. 44: '*La Felugha d'orata torni abbordo della Capitana*'.
216 Guglielmotti, *Vocabolario*, s.v. *Feluca*.
217 AOM 1773, f. 70v; Guglielmotti, *Vocabolario*, s.v. *Feluca*.
218 AOM 1773, f. 70v: '*due filuche Corsare*' are also mentioned.

219 AOM 1768, f. 6: '*tomamos lengua de una feluga que abia niuguna nueba de Vaxeles de enemigos*'.
220 AOM 1768, f. 73; every time the *felucca* unfailingly reports news of the enemy's movements.
221 AOM 1766, f. 53.
222 Ibid., f. 170.
223 Guglielmotti, *Vocabolario*, s.v. *Caicco*.
224 Lib. 223, s.v. *Bastimento raso*.
225 Ibid., s.v. *Caicco*.
226 Ibid., s.v. *Caicco a fare l'acqua, i viveri, le legna*.
227 Dal Pozzo, ii, 35, 36, 66 gives precise details on the activities of the caique in the face of the enemy. It was a very risky business that did not always end successfully.
228 Lib. 223, s.v. *Caicco armato in guerra*.
229 MMM, MS. 'Segni della Capitana - Di giorno', 51, 53; 'Di notte', 18; 'Di nebbia', 37, 38. These signals were regularly changed. The captain of the *capitana* used to impart new signals to the other captains before every mission.
230 J. Muscat, 'The Dgħajsa and the Luzzu'. *Treasures of Malta,* iii, No. 3, 37-41.
231 'Compendio', f. 100; see also Lib. 223, s.v. *Caicco impagliettato*; ibid., s.v. *Brulotto*
232 Muscat, *The Dgħajsa*, 127-33.
233 At present the majority of Maltese traditional boats are equipped with a *falkaviva* or fixed washboards, as commonly referred to by fishermen but C. Pulè, *Qxur, Biċċiet, u Opri tal-Bahar* (Malta, 2000), *passim* refers to it as *falka morta*.
234 AOM 1774, f. 56.
235 Lib. 223, s.v. *Caicco*.
236 Ibid., s.v. *Forchette del Caicco*; ibid., s.v. *Caicco in fagotto*.
237 Ibid. s.v. *Caicchi doppi*.
238 Lib. 223, s.v. *Fregatina*.
239 Ibid. s.v. *Fregatina gelosa*.
240 AOM 1899, f. 96.
241 Dal Pozzo, ii, 89 insists that '*vi si stivarono dentro con estremo pericolo 125 huomini*'. This was just an exceptional occurrence.
242 Bosio, iii, 367. For more information about the Maltese *fregatina* see Muscat, *The Dgħajsa*, 100-4.
243 A contemporary model of the ceremonial brigantine can be seen in the Malta Maratime Museum.
244 Lib. 726, f. 180; Dal Pozzo, i, 492, 532 says that the grand master used the *capitana* escorted by the other galleys to cross over to Gozo. Manoel Vilhena had sailed to Gozo on the *capitana*, see ibid., ff. 185, 186.
245 Lib. 1222, f. 69.
246 Lib. 726, f. 94.
247 Guglielmotti, *Storia*, VIII, 165: '*in una spiaggia deserta presso il Faro di Messina: luogo assegnato al convegno dei Maltesi*'.
248 Dal Pozzo, i, 297.
249 Ibid., 195.
250 Muscat, *Il-Flotta,* 183-4.
251 Lib. 726 ff. 185, 186.
252 See a watercolour with the representation of a galley at the Cathedral Museum, Mdina.
253 Lib. 318 diagram facing f. 8, item 67; Lib. 223, s.v. *Testa di Moro*.
254 The Wignacourt gondola appears in a painting exhibited at the Maritime Museum in Paris showing the maiden voyage of the Order's ships-of-the-line squadron leaving the Grand Harbour.
255 Muscat, *Il-Flotta,* 181-2.

256 A beautiful model of Prince Frederick's barge can be seen in the Maritime Museum, Greenwich. One perfect example of the Portuguese Royal Brigantine is to be found in the Museu de Marinha, Lisbon.
257 Rossi, 32.
258 Ibid., 86; Ubaldini, 488.
259 J. Muscat, The *Maltese Vaxxell* (Malta, 2000).
260 Lib. 223, s.v. *Vascello di Primo Rango*.
261 Ibid., s.v. *Vascello di Secondo Rango*.
262 Ibid., s.v. *Vascello di Terzo Rango*.
263 Hardman, 133 mentions 'Two ships-of-the-line and three frigates. The *Guillaume Tell* is much damaged but may put to sea. The *San Giovanni* formerly a Maltese 64, ready for sea; very old and in a bad state and badly manned.'
264 AOM 272, f. 154: '*Partirete subito che il tempo ve lo permettero assieme colla Nave San Zaccarhia, e farete rotta per lo stretto di Gibilterra: Indi passarete all'altro Mare a fare il corso contro i legni barbareschi che ivi fanno danni infiniti ai Bastimenti Cristiani.*
265 *L' Arte no.24, 7 November 1863*.'
266 Guglielmotti, *Vocabolario*, s.v. *Fregata*.
267 Ibid., s.v. *Fregata*.
268 Lib. 223 s.v. *Fregata*.
269 AOM 273, f. 20.
270 AOM 1839, f. 304.
271 AOM 273, f. 180v.
272 AOM 1839, f. 304.
273 AOM 276, f. 35v.
274 AOM 275, f. 9. For more information see Muscat, *Il-Flotta*, 108, 131.
275 Lib. 223, s.v. *Fregata leggera*.
276 Ibid., s.v. *Vascellotto a cascia*.
277 Rossi, 154.
278 AOM 269, f. 9v.
279 Ibid., f. 26.
280 Ibid., f. 36.
281 Ibid., f. 33v.
282 Ibid., f. 48v: '*corvetta Sta. Teresa non sia riuscito vassello Leggiero ed agile al corso, conforme aspettava*'.
283 AOM 269, f. 161v: '*cinque, o sei convalescenti di febbre Terzana, e dissenteria*'.
284 AOM 1839, f. 299; this and all subsequent accounts all refer to the *corvetta di Sua Eminenza*.
285 AOM 1840, ff. 38-68.
286 AOM 274, f. 53.
287 Hansen, 543; Landstrom, 179.
288 AOM 269, f. 12.
289 Guglielmotti, *Vocabolario*, s.v. *Corvetta*. see also Muscat, *Il-Flotta*, 135 *et seq*.
290 Lib. 223, s.v. *Palandra*; Dal Pozzo, ii, 566.
291 Compendio, f. 101.
292 AOM 274, f. 70v; Dal Pozzo, ii, 500 says that the Venetian fleet, which was a very large one, had six *palandre per bombe*.
293 Ibid., 566; for the operations of the carrack *Sant'Anna* at Goletta, see Bosio, iii, 145. The carrack was not provided with mortars but its huge guns caused terrific damage to the fortress.
294 Compendio, f. 100; see also Francois de Malthe, *Traite des Feux* (Paris, 1640), 45.
295 Auphan, 89.
296 Lib. 223, s.v. *Brulotto*.
297 AOM 1771 f. 111.

298 Dal Pozzo, ii, 137.
299 AOM 260 f.107; Dal Pozzo, ii, 137.
300 Lib. 223, s.v. *Cannoni Finti: Sono Cannoni di legno fatti al tornio, se gli da il Colore di bronzo, accioche siano creduti tali, e per che ingannino piu facilmente il nemico.*
301 Ibid., s.v. *Brulotto.*
302 Guglielmotti, *Vocabolario*, s.v. *Brulotto: talvolta si componeva con la carcassa di alcun vecchio bastimento.*
303 A picture of a fireship can be seen in the Compendio, f. 100. The hooks can also be clearly distinguished. See also Lib. 223, s.v. *Brulotto* and *Rizzone di Brulotto.*
304 Ibid., s.v. *Capitano di Brulotto*; see also Lib. 318, ii, f. 151.
305 Lib. 223, s.v. *Brulotto.*
306 Compendio, f. 100.
307 Francois de Malthe, 49, 50.
308 Lib, 223, s.v. *Brulotto.*
309 Guglielmotti, *Vocabolario*, s.v. *Brulotto*. For further information as to how the fireship used to be loaded with gunpowder see Lib 223 s.v. *Brulotto*; Lib. 318, ii, ff. 148, 149; Compendio, f. 100. Francois de Malthe, 46, gives useful information as well.
310 Guglielmotti, *Vocabolario*, s.v. *Grippo.*
311 R. de Vertot, *Histoire des Chevaliers* (Paris, 1726), ii, 382 says this was a small and fast craft. Ibid., iii, 274 refers to *grippi* or brigantines and reports the same idea in ibid., iv, 12,13. Braudel, 296 mentions the *grippi, marani*, or *marciliani* that sail in the Adriatic. Bosio, ii, 229 and 237 mentions two cases when a *grippo* was armed for fighting. This shows how difficult it can be to be absolutely certain about the various nomenclatures attributed to various types of ships.
312 Engel, *Histoire*, 15, 16.
313 F. Balbi di Correggio, *The Siege of Malta*. Translated from the Spanish by Major H. A. Balbi (Copenhagen, 1961), 16.
314 Engel, *Histoire*, 25.
315 *Regula Hospitalariorum Et Militiae Ordinis Sancti Ionnis Baptistae Hierofolimitani* (Rome, 1556), ff. 1, 1v.
316 Lib. 223, s.v. *Pinco* and *Spedale*; see also Guglielmotti, *Vocabolario*, s.v. *Ospedale*. For the surgical instruments, see Lib. 1222, f. 26: *Ustencils Du Chirurgien*. AOM 1761, f. 285 mentions: '*Il Rosmarino, che s'imbarca l'impieghino in profumare il luogo dell'Infermi il più spesso li sará permesso. Atteso il gran calore del luogo, ove si tiene la Cassa de rimedji spesso faccino la rivista de medemi accio non deteriorino.*' For the duties of the *chirurgo*, see AOM 1761, f. 283; for the *barberotto*, see AOM 1761, f. 245. Such personnel were to be found on every warship of the Order.
317 Lib. 223, s.v. *Capitano di Fluta o sia Pinco.*
318 Ibid.
319 P. Cassar, *Medical History of Malta* (London, 1964), 124.
320 Dal Pozzo, ii, 383.
321 AOM 1759, f. 426.
322 Ubaldini, 459.
323 Bosio, iii, 15: '*Accomodando gl'infermi sopra il Galeone del Priore di San Gilio Fra Preianni de Bidoux, il quale serviva come di Spedale in quell'Armata.*'
324 Ibid.: '*Intanto crescendo tuttavia gagliardamente la peste nella Citta di Messina; fra pochi giorni s'appicco ancora nella Carracca.*'
325 Ibid., 431.
326 See Valiero, *passim*, for the part played by the Order in the war of Candia.
327 For more information see the unpublished paper by J. Muscat, 'Maltese Galleys - Medical and Sanitary Aspects', read at the 'Maritime History Conference - Health and the Sea', Exeter, October 1996.

Chapter III

MERCHANT SHIPS

The Maltese, since time immemorial, have depended on imported food supplies as the islands produced just one-third of the annual provisions necessary for their survival. Consequently the inhabitants had to turn to the sea as fishermen, corsairs, or sailors on merchant ships to supplement the lack of available food. Maltese *padroni* managed with success their mercantile activities. Especially during the period of the Order's stay, the Maltese reaped the greatest benefits from their work as the knights left all mercantile activities in their hands.[1]

There were many typologies of merchant ships but Maltese masters showed a preference for the *xprunara,* the brigantine, and the *tartana* although other types were employed, perhaps with less frequency than the three mentioned ones.[2] The civil arsenal located behind Senglea catered especially for the construction of *tartane* and other merchant ships.[3]

In the eighteenth century, local mercantile activities replaced corsairing at a steady pace. By 1750 *la guerre de course* was held to be an anachronistic activity and local private *padroni* increased the numbers of their vessels and their relative hold capacities.[4] While the majority of the Maltese merchant ships were employed in the carrying trade, transporting grain, meat, and shipbuilding materials, there were also those which accompanied the galley squadron of the Order transporting ship-biscuit and munitions.[5]

The Maltese masters of merchant ships had to face two main hazards at sea: Muslim corsairs and inclement weather conditions. The *Consolato di Mare* was a civil court instituted by the Order of St John for the benefit of all parties employed in the mercantile activity and to settle matters arising from the normal and abnormal procedures of that activity.[6]

The *xprunara*

Just as the history of the galley is really the history of the knights of Malta, so the history of the *xprunara* is the history of the Maltese sailors. Its direct descendant, the *tal-latini* boat, was, until a few years ago, seen everyday carrying food and other cargo between the two islands under full sail and oars just as the *xprunara* of old sailed to Corfu or to Leghorn.[7] The *tal-latini* or Gozo boat was in fact called the *speronara del Gozo*. As the Gozo channel was frequented by the Barbary corsairs, the crew and passengers used to pray for protection from God as such vessels never carried any defensive arms.[8]

The *xprunara* was painted in bright green and blue and looked exactly like the modern *luzzu*. The only difference is that while the modern boat is motor-driven, the *xprunara* had two sails, a lateen one and a jib at the bows, and oars for moments of calm or for further speed when escaping from corsairs.

In addition to its colours and its sails, the *xprunara* could be distinguished from other craft by its high forestem and the beak-like spur on the bows, with the eyes on both sides of them. The projecting cut-water could still be seen on the *tal-latini* a few years after the First World War.[9]

The sculpted or painted eyes or *oculi* on either side of the bows can still be seen on the *luzzijiet*.[10] Their origin is lost in antiquity and probably

Early 16th century xprunara

derives from the sailors' wish to protect themselves against a vengeful and harmful deity. By painting an eye on the vessel, the sailors invoked the benevolent gods to watch over them.

The name '*xprunara*' is of Sicilian origin which is derived from '*sperone*' which was a spur that jutted out of the bows and to which the jib was tied.

As well as transporting its cargo, the *xprunara* served the Order as a reconnaissance vessel and to carry news and information.[11] C.E. Engel mentions the case of Gabriel de la Richoidie who asked Rome for a pardon hoping that His Grace the Grand Master would be good enough to send a *speronara* to bring it back. He was ready to pay all expenses, if necessary.[12] The *xprunara* was a swift rowing boat, used when there was an urgent message to carry. Amongst many other incidents, one can mention the case when a *xprunara*, often called the *barca Maltese*, carried instructions from the commander in chief in Favignana to Fra Vincenzo Montalto the captain of the magisterial galley *San Giuseppe*, to sail with two galleys to Capobuono in North Africa.[13] On 10 August 1733 a *xprunara* was sent to Corfu, right under the enemy's nose, to report on the war preparations taking place.[14] It also carried out similar duties between the English ships and the Maltese when Malta rose up against the French in 1799.[15] The French took particular care not to let the *xprunari* be used against their interests. Admiral Villeneuve, informed the minister of the navy and the colonies that he had to arm a *felucca*

Maltese xprunara *under lateen rig*

The 1740 xprunara

with a crew of 30 to control the movements of the *xprunari*. He even managed to seize one laden with oil and cheese.[16]

The *xprunara* also played an important role inside the harbour. It assisted the caiques to tow sailing ships out to sea.[17] At one time the Order built and armed two *xprunari* to protect the coast and the harbour.[18] In the accounts of the Order there are many references to the money spent to maintain the *xprunari* that were used to guard the coasts. Sometimes they are referred to them as simply *barche di guardia*, sometimes as *le speronare di guardia*.[19]

The *xprunara* also came in useful for a quick voyage. It could be chartered by the rich for such a purpose; in fact a small cabin or shelter was often rigged at the stern[20] to protect paying passengers from the elements.

Because of it small size, being only 10 or 12 metres in length, the *xprunara* was normally restricted to central Mediterranean waters. It sailed regularly as far as Sicily and occasionally as far as Leghorn, Lisbon, Naples, and Rome. It was a *xprunara* that brought over the news of the plague that infected Venice in 1793. This information enabled the Order to take the necessary precautions against ships coming from that city.[21] The *xprunari* continued to ply between Malta and foreign shores even in the nineteenth century.[22]

The *xprunara*'s only defence against attack was its speed. One typical incident took place in the Bay of Gabes when a Barbary *londra* met a

Maltese *xprunara* captained by Luigi D'Anville. Three Maltese were injured but the boat managed to get away.[23] *Londras* were mostly employed by the Turks in the Black Sea to keep a watch over the Cossacks. Smaller than galleys, they could be used to transport cargo but were mainly used for fighting and corsairing.[24]

Sometimes the *xprunara* would run out of luck. On 10 May 1796 Barbary corsairs gave chase to a Christian pink which sought shelter in the bay of Mazzarelli in Sicily. The Muslims sent two caiques that attacked the pink and carried away two *xprunari* that happened to be there. One of these *xprunari* belonged to Pietru Saliba.[25]

The French appropriated all available *xprunari*. They were used to convey news to Napoleon in Egypt[26] and to fetch meat from Tripoli.[27] Since they were such small craft they could pass unobserved through the British blockade.[28]

The lateen-rigged brigantine

The brigantine was another vessel that could be found sailing round Malta even before the arrival of the knights. Such a vessel could not have been very large, since it was commonly found in the hands of private Maltese corsairs.

The brigantine was slightly larger than the *xprunara* and was more or less the same size as a galleot.[29] It looked like a galley without a deck but had a central *corsia* running along between the benches of the rowers. Like the galley, it had a pointed bow from which the anchor could be dropped and raised. It had a lateen sail and a jib together with 12 or 14 banks of oars to provide for moments of calm.[30] It was used by many Maltese corsairs to harass Muslim shipping[31] and it even formed part of the Order's navy. Dal Pozzo mentions two brigantines that accompanied the four galleys of the Order. Later on he states that six galleys, each accompanied by a brigantine of the Order, were armed to face the galleots of Bizerta on 8 August 1640: '*e s'allestirono sei Brigantini comandati ciascuno da un Cavaliero, dovendo ogni Galera, oltre il proprio Caichio haverne uno*'.[32]

The brigantine was first and foremost a cargo ship but, as was the case with such ships then, it had a fair amount of weaponry on board to defend itself. It had to be able to look after itself if it was to sail up to

Messina and then continue to the Italian, French, and Spanish coasts as far as Lisbon. It used to have two guns at the bows and occasionally another one at the stern. However, its best means of defence were muskets and periers.

These vessels were responsible for most of the great mercantile activity of Maltese *padroni* and they brought into the country great sums of money. Their owners normally started their activities in Sicily loading great quantities of bales of satin at Messina. From there they used to continue all along the coast of Italy trumping all the way to France and from there to Spain where they normally found the best markets for their cargoes. They normally stopped in small places to do business wherever possible. During the seventeenth century there were hardly any masters of such small vessels who dared to pass through the Straits of Gibraltar but a century later they continued all the way up to Lisbon, where they found an excellent market for the fine cotton articles manufactured in Malta. If at one time similar articles used to be regarded as rarities in Lisbon, by the middle of the eighteenth century that city was supplied with great quantities of cotton articles through the great mercantile activities undertaken by Maltese owners on their brigantines.[33]

Such passages throw light on the life of the Maltese common sailor under the Order. In addition to the great number of brigantines in the employ of the Order, there were many private Maltese ship-owners who employed a great number of local sailors on their own vessels. Having delivered their cargo, many vessels could try their hand at a little corsairing activity on the return trip.

In the seventeenth and eighteenth centuries, Maltese cotton was much sought after and fetched a high price in Portugal. This explains the frequent voyages of the brigantines to Lisbon. In Portuguese, the word '*maltes*' meaning 'a native of Malta' has come to mean 'a double dealer, a thief, and a traitor', probably as a result of the shady activities of these traders.

The brigantine is regularly mentioned in the annals of Maltese history. It was a brigantine that brought about a worsening of relations between the Order and England and Holland. On 14 September 1741 France had requested the Order to arm locally four brigantines or two large ships for the coming winter. These vessels were to be crewed with Maltese sailors, fly the French flag, and attack Tunisian corsairs only. Two of

MERCHANT SHIPS

Early 16th century brigantine

A 1680 brigantine

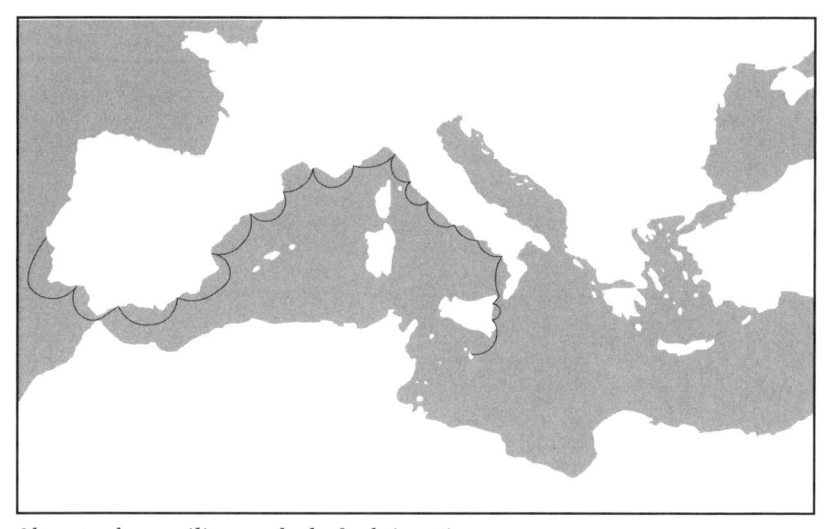

Shore to shore sailing method of a brigantine

these brigantines attacked the first two ships they met, one of which happened to be English and the other Dutch.

Grand Master Pinto wrote to the Order's ambassador in France, the Balí Emanuel Bocage, to explain things to England and the Netherlands. The king of France agreed to stop supplying weapons to the Maltese brigantines flying the French flag and the captured Dutch ship had to sail to Malta from where it had to go to Tunis by way of Leghorn. According to the law of neutrality, no corsair could attack neutral shipping or harm the natives of neutral countries, such as England and the Netherlands were then. Still, in the absence of other shipping, the corsairs had to earn their living somehow.[34]

As well as the *xprunara*, the Order also used the swift brigantine to protect the Maltese coasts from the corsairs. A brigantine or a *xprunara* was always kept ready for emergencies,[35] such as pursuing runaway slaves and sending messages abroad or to the galleys at sea. It was also used to reconnoitre the seas around the island.[36]

The brigantine suffered a similar fate as the frigate. Its size and shape remained unchanged for hundreds of years till the nineteenth century, that is a lateen-rigged boat that could be helped along by oars. It was used by all the Mediterranean navies primarily because it was inexpensive to build and to run. A new type of brigantine, however, appeared towards the end of the eighteenth century. It originated in

MERCHANT SHIPS

An early type of square-rigged brigantine

Northern Europe and resembled a square-sail ship with only two masts and with a flying jib or two on the jibboom. It was the first vessel to use a spanker boom, for it changed a little the shape of the mizzen sail. In time the square-rigged brigantines grew in size and the number of masts and sails increased.

The Maltese brigantine of the British period gained a universal reputation because of the far-flung voyages it undertook. Such brigantines sailed regularly on the Black Sea and the Argentine routes and regularly visited all the Mediterranean seaports.[37]

The lateen-rigged frigate

In the fifteenth century a type of sailing ship known as a *fregata* or frigate was very popular with the Mediterranean naval powers. Even the Turks had many such vessels.

They were used to fetch victuals and munitions for the galleys, especially when these latter were deployed near trouble spots away from their bases. These frigates were cargo ships, more or less the same size as a galleot, with a fairly high freeboard and used both a lateen sail and oars for propulsion. They became obsolete because they were too heavy.[38]

Early sixteenth-century lateen-rigged frigate

In a fairly large *ex-voto* painting (votive picture)[39] at the Żabbar Sanctuary Museum there is probably the finest depiction of a seventeenth-century frigate. Guidotti too left a clear description of the frigate of his time.[40] It looked roughly like a galley without a cabin at the stern. It had two lateen sails and eight oars at either side. The oars passed through holes in the sides which were rather higher than a galley's.

According to Dal Pozzo, the frigate was a fairly common sight in the Grand Harbour. It sailed out with the galleys and carried passengers and urgent messages[41] even in stormy seas. The Codex Vilhena refers to the frigate with the *felucca* and the brigantine as being small oar-driven vessels which had to be guarded at all times by at least two guards because slaves could use them to escape from the island.[42]

Another frigate, the *fregata del passo,* (of the passage) was used to carry messages, news, and instructions and plied regularly between Malta and Gozo.[43] In the eighteenth century this frigate lost much of its importance and was replaced by a more suitable vessel. However, the only connection with this later vessel was to be its nomenclature – the square-rigged frigate.[44]

The tartane

Like the brigantine, the tartane too spent its time hugging the Western European coastline as it made its way to Lisbon.[45]

The Order, preoccupied solely with building vessels of war to fight the Muslim, had to rely on the tartane to transport its food and weapons when the galley squadron sailed away on the *corso*. Until the end of the Order's stay in Malta, the harbour used to be full with Maltese and foreign-owned tartanes. When the French took the island, they expropriated them all and used them in their Egyptian campaigns.

The Order had its own tartanes which it sometimes armed for fighting.[46] The Maltese, having realized the indispensability of the tartanes to the Order, started overcharging for their hire. In 1688 the Order retaliated by building a large tartane to meet all its needs.[47] It kept building its own tartanes until its last days in Malta.

The Maltese tartane was a fairly large vessel and could carry a load of up to 800 *cantari*. It was very reliable and was a much sought-after cargo ship.

The Maltese tartane had peculiar rigging. Its three masts were usually lateen-rigged but, with a strong wind, square sails would be set up. From the foremast to the jibboom a fairly large flying jib was rigged; the tartane usually had a lateen sail on each of its three masts.[48] The Italian tartane

A seventeenth-century tartane

seems to have had one mast. Guglielmotti describes it as being a small one-masted vessel employed for transport and for fishing.[49]

Some tartanes were equipped with oars which were operated in emergencies. Oars could be used because, in spite of its large size, the tartane had a fairly low freeboard.

The tartane was widest midships where the mainmast was fixed. The rather wide beam of the tartane gave it increased stability. Its ends were pointed but the deck extended aft.[50] Its bows were equipped with a special type of *sperone* like those of the galley and the brigantine known as *battalotto* with the jibboom being tied to it.[51]

Below deck was one large hold and therefore life had to be spent in the open air on deck, where the stove could also be found.[52] At night a canopy gave some shelter to the sailors and passengers lying on blankets. The tartane provided the cheapest means of travel. The seventeenth-century tartane, at least, had only one deck and there was no covered cabin at the stern poop and it was therefore completely open. This explains the necessity of erecting a shelter aft.[53]

Unlike the *xprunara*, which was ideal for a quick voyage, the tartane only sailed when there was a need for it, and it always ventured protected by some galley or other fighting ship.[54] One could have had to wait a long time before a tartane sailed out of harbour.

The tartane's wide beam[55] made it slow-moving and the ideal prey for Muslim corsairs unless it happened to be specially armed. Moreover,

A 1750 Maltese tartane

it usually carried expensive cargoes of grain, meat, wood, or ship biscuit,[56] which made a desirable prey.

When armed for war, the 18 or so guns and a number of periers were placed on the deck,[57] where the roughly 150 sailors and soldiers had to spend their time.[58] The hold was reserved for the weapons, the munitions, and the provisions. The great eighteenth-century Maltese tartane was equipped with a stern cabin which was partly decorated with gilded sculpture.[59]

A clear picture of the tartane's task can be had by imagining these large slow-moving vessels trying to keep up with the slim and fast galleys as the Order's squadron sailed on the *corso*.[60] It may be difficult today to understand the daily hard work of the Maltese sailor as he toiled to keep the tartane sailing. With his crew of ten, the Maltese owner of a tartane could convey any cargo to any harbour in the Mediterranean in any weather.

The Order organized protection for its tartanes from the menace of the Muslim corsairs but the private owner had to lay his trust in God and hope for the best.[61]

The pink

This section deals with the Mediterranean pink, rather than its Dutch, English, or Swedish counterparts. It is not known for certain when the Order started using it, but the Muslims were already employing pinks in the middle of the sixteenth century. It was probably through the assistance of English, Dutch, and Swedish renegades that the Barbary corsairs adopted the North European pink for their purposes.

The square-rigged Barbary pink had a flat and wide bottom and could be used for corsairing even during the winter months. It carried from 10 to 24 guns, a crew of about 200, and was primarily armed in Tunis, Algiers, or Tripoli.[62]

A particular pink which was captured during the famous attack of the Maltese galleys on Caracoggia on 24 August 1640 was armed with 20 guns and could carry up to 2,000 *salme*.[63] The French had even larger pinks that could carry between 3,000 and 3,600 *salme*.

Having captured another pink off Rhodes on 28 August 1644,[64] the Order started thinking of building its own, primarily to be able to chase

The Maltese pink

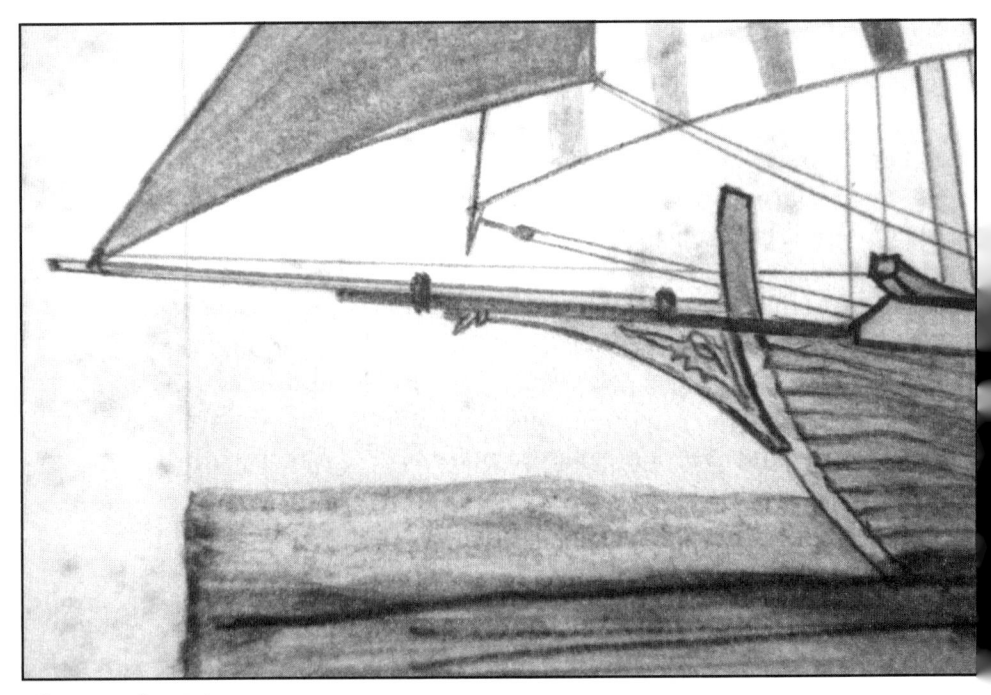

The spur of a pink

the Muslim in winter. However, many years were to pass before De Redin took practical steps to see what could actually be done for winter corsairing activities and this grand master died before his plans could be carried out. An order in council actually provided for the building of two ships with a burthen of 2,500 *salme* each to be armed against the Muslim enemy since 'these vessels would provide a better service to the Order than the galleys themselves, at least during the winter season'.[65]

The Italian pink was a fairly large three-masted lateen-rigged vessel. The foremast was inclined forward and the bows were provided with a *battalotto* or *sperone* which was made up of a grated framework like a chebec's.[66] The pink looked very much like the tartane, except that it had a poop which was often beautifully decorated while the early seventeenth-century tartane had none. Like the tartane, the pink hugged the coast on its voyages.[67]

The Italians also used a smaller pink of barely 1,000 *salme*, with three lateen-rigged masts and which was frequently used along the coasts of Calabria and Sicily to carry small loads.[68] This is being said for accuracy's sake because some old pictures do not seem to agree with this description.

The pink as employed in Malta in the seventeenth and eighteenth centuries seems to have been square-rigged.[69] The guns placed near the rather high stern rested on special wooden platforms so that the gun carriages could be levelled off with the surface of the sea.[70] The North European pink looked like the Dutch fluyt, a square-rigged vessel which carried up to 12 guns which was, however, mostly used to carry cargo.[71]

At one time the Order had three pinks: the *Concezione Immacolata e le Anime del Purgatorio*, the *Santissimo Crocifisso*, and the *San Giovanni*.[72] The crew of the *Santissimo Crocifisso* consisted of a captain; a clerk or bursar; a doctor; a first-class guard; bombardiers; nurses; first-, second-, and third-class sailors; guards; and soldiers. This was a first-rate corsairing crew for a pink.[73]

Private Maltese shipowners too adopted the pink,[74] as they did with all the vessels that had proved their worth in the Order's hand, with the exception of the carrack and the galley.

The *pollacca*

The word '*pollacca*' is derived from the Italian '*polaccone*' which means 'a great jib'.[75] This vessel therefore got its name because its foremast was rigged up with a lateen sail giving the impression that it was flying a great jib sail. This lateen sail on the foremast of the *pollacca* distinguished it from all craft.

Often the *pollacca* was mistaken for a tartane[76] although the former was always larger and faster.[77] The *pollacca*'s bows were more concave than the tartane's so that it could cut the water better. Also the *pollacca* was square-rigged except for the foremast, while the tartane had lateen sails. Guglielmotti[78] describes the *pollacca* as having three masts and square sails. Earle,[79] however, shows a *pollacca* with a large lateen sail on the foremast. On the other hand Landstrom,[80] while agreeing on this detail, shows two square sails on the mainmast, while Earle shows three. Vessels, of course, change from one country to another and even from one time to another.

Two interesting votive paintings can be seen in the Żabbar Sanctuary Museum. One shows a French *pollacca* or *polacre* with square sails on all three masts and the other shows a *pollacca* of the Order with a great jib sail at the bows, three square sails on the mainmast, and another square sail on top of a lateen one on the mizzenmast.

The masts of the *pollacca* used to be made out of a single tree trunk; this made them comparatively shorter and stouter than those of other vessels. The difference can be clearly seen in the large picture of the carrack in the Żabbar Sanctuary Museum where the single-piece type of mast is shown.

When rigged with square sails, these pole-type masts made good use of even the slightest breeze and, moreover, they needed less work and time to handle than other types of rig.

The sheer of the *pollacca* resembled that of the tartane. The stern, however, had little or no decoration and only a little gilded mouldings round the windows of the captain's quarters. The Order's flag always flew at the stern.

The seventeenth-century *pollacca* had three or four openings for guns,[81] while the other armaments, such as periers or large muskets, were kept on deck. In later centuries the number of guns was increased. The first *pollaccas* mentioned were the French ones which were captured

MERCHANT SHIPS

A pollacca *from Marseilles*

A Maltese pollacca

by the Turks towards 1634.[82] The *pollacca* the knights captured at Goletta in 1640 carried only six guns,[83] which means that it was not very heavily armed; the Order's *pollaccas* had the smallest guns, calibre 6 or 4. A 1751 bill of accounts for the Order's *pollaccas* shows that by then the guns had increased to eight on either side.

The armed *pollacca* could also join in fighting. In the middle of the eighteenth century, the Order had two such vessels: the *Santa Teresa* and *L'Immacolata Concezione*.[84] Like the tartanes, they were used to carry provisions for the galleys and to ply between Malta and Sicily.[85]

The *pollacca* earned a good reputation all over the Mediterranean. It was used by the Turks just as often as by the French or by the Greeks or by the Maltese.[86] Its rigging and sail plan proved so successful that by 1750 the French, the Spaniards, and the Algerians had adopted this system for their chebecs.[87]

The Maltese too followed suit. They realized the value of the *pollacca* as an all-year-round ship, but since it was larger and cost more than a tartane to build, they actually owned only a few. The Maltese *pollacca* kept plying the trade route to Tunis until the very eve of the French invasion of Malta.[88] A wise captain of a Maltese *pollacca* would wait for the protection of some warship of the Order if there were news of movements of the Barbary corsairs.[89] This was not always the case; whenever they found that little profit was to be had in carrying cargo, the Maltese adopted their *pollaccas* for corsairing instead.

The chebec

The chebec first appeared in the Mediterranean towards 1633 as a small cargo carrier sailing in Alexandrian waters; it could carry about 40 people.[90] By 1653 it had increased in size and had been adopted by the Turks.[91] In 1674 the galleys of the Order started meeting such craft regularly, then apparently still more used to carry merchandise than for fighting.[92] The North African corsairs, especially the Algerians, transformed the chebec into a terrifying weapon.

By the end of the seventeenth century, trade between the Eastern Mediterranean countries had decreased appreciably and with it the Order's strength as a naval power. On the other hand, the fighting and

MERCHANT SHIPS

double-dealing between the Christian nations increased. The Algerians were quick to avail themselves of this situation and their chebecs soon drove terror all over the Mediterranean.

The chebec was the ideal corsairing ship, bristling with weaponry and carrying some of the blood-thirstiest miscreants of the Barbary coast.[93] Algiers remained for long the capital of the corsairs in spite of the many attempts to bring it to heel. Algiers was such a bothersome corsairs' nest that in 1809 the French consul wrote to those countries as England, Spain, Sweden, Denmark, the Netherlands, and the United States who furnished it with all its corsairing needs, so that they could take steps to bring its corsairs under control.[94] The Algerian chebec remained a real menace even after 1816 when the European nations made a concerted bombardment of the city. The Algerian corsairs robbed every ship that came their way. France, which was supposed to have been granted certain rights by Algiers, had 26 of its merchantmen seized between 1817 and 1827. This helped to bring matters to a head and, on 5 July 1830, France occupied Algiers and ended this menace once and for all.

Almost all seafaring nations like Spain, Russia, France, and Sweden had chebecs of their own. The Order built two chebecs to guard the harbour in place of two *xprunari* for the congregation of the Order was of the opinion that they were cheaper to maintain.[95]

The two chebecs, the *San Pietro* and the *San Paolo*, could always be seen together guarding the harbour and the coasts all year round,

The chebec

107

The chebec under sails and oars

The small chebec

The pollacca-*chebec*

carrying cargo between Sicily and Malta, and even fighting the Muslim.[96] Balì d'Avernes de Bocage, the minister of the king of France, came to Malta in 1741 to arm a chebec for the *corso*.[97] The other chebec of the Order, the *Santo Spirito*, normally sailed on its own.[98]

The chebec was renowned for its speed. A large ship-of-the-line, the 56-gun *San Antonio*, pursued an Algerian chebec for a whole day and still it got away.[99] The chebec had three things which made it so fast: large sails, 18 oars, and the special type of flare on the bows which were arched inwards the better to cut through the water. Oars could be used in dire emergency,[100] even though Guglielmotti[101] does not mention them.

The crafty Algerians preferred to leave their corsairing for the winter months when the merchantmen did not have any protection.[102] Therefore the chebec had to be built with a fairly-wide beam to stand up to the winter conditions.[103] The deck at the bows and at the stern which jutted out of the boat consisted of grated framework which offered the least resistance to the waves which could pass through without any danger to the vessel.

The chebec carried 24 small guns. The *Indiscret*, a French chebec, also had a good number of smaller weapons at either side of the poop and other swivel guns pointing to the bows. Such a vessel could not face a fully-armed warship; instead it preyed only on cargo ships. The sturdy chebec, which could carry a load of up to 300 tons, was sometimes also used to carry cargo.

Frightening as the chebec could be in battle, it provided a beautiful sight as regards its design and its colours. Its three masts were rigged with red-and-white striped lateen sails; its arrowlike beak head ended in some carved animal's head.[104] The sides of the three decks at the stern were painted in bright different colours.[105]

The chebec was still popular in Malta in 1814, which was actually its Algerian heyday; two chebecs, one French and the other Neapolitan, were in fact sold by auction in the Grand Harbour.[106]

In the second half of the eighteenth century, the chebec was given a new type of rigging. While the foremast retained its lateen sail, the other two masts were rigged with square sails. This made it look like a *pollacca* and it was in fact called a *pollacca*-chebec. Although Earle[107] says that the *pollacca*-chebec was used by the corsairs of Malta and of the Barbary coast, no reference has been found as yet in Malta to such a type of boat in local use. Something vaguely similar can be seen in the Żabbar Sanctuary Museum in a votive picture, though it is rather difficult to be quite certain about it. Most probably it was the Moroccans and the French who started using this new type of vessel.[108]

NOTES

1. AOM 1759 ff. 371, 372v; but ibid., f. 501 says that no captain was to refuse embarkation on his galley any merchandise belonging to the Order.
2. For more details see: J. Muscat, 'Maltese 18th Century Merchant Ships' in A. Fehri, *L'Homme et La Mer* (Sfax, 2001), 105-30.
3. NLM, Plan 156.
4. NAM LIB for the years 1743-47 is a series of arrival booklets which provide exhaustive details about the mercantile activities of that period.
5. AOM 1770, f. 228; AOM 1771, ff. 80v, 117; AOM 261 ff.144, 149.
6. For more details see, Muscat, 'Maltese 18th-Century Merchant Ships', 105-30.
7. AOM 269 f. 18; AOM 274, f. 223.
8. G.A. Vassallo, *Storia di Malta Raccontata in Compendio*, Malta 1854,386.
9. B. Landstrom, *The Ship* (London, 1961), 34 admits that he would have been unable to explain the projection of the bow stem of the Greek cargo boats if he had not seen the Sicilian fishing boats or the Maltese *xprunari*.
10. Muscat, The Dghajsa and The Luzzu, *Treasures of Malta*, iii. 1997 No.3, 37-41.
11. AOM 269, f. 252v; A. Guglielmotti, *Vocabolario marino e militare* (Milan, 1967), s.v. *Speronara*.
12. C.E. Engel, *Knights of Malta* (London 1963), 148.
13. AOM 269, f. 200.
14. Ibid., f. 18.
15. W. Hardman, *A History of Malta during the Period of the French and British Occupations 1798-1814* (London, 1909), 110.
16. Ibid., 170
17. AOM 1773, f. 70: 'con il Rimburchio de caichi, e le Speronare di Guardia'.
18. *Leggi e Costituzioni Prammaticali* (Malta, 1724), 76, V; 77, VI; AOM 1773, f. 70.
19. AOM 274, f. 124; AOM 1773, ff. 70, 81v.
20. *L' Arte*, No. 23, 7 March 1864.
21. AOM 274, f. 223.
22. See *Malta Government Gazette*, 4 February 1829.
23. AOM 271, f. 256v.
24. Guglielmotti, *Vocabolario*, s.v. *Londra*.
25. AOM 277, f. 9v.
26. Hardman, Introduction, p. xxix, 99; ibid., 292, 'who was to leave in a *speronara*, the smallness of which it was thought might escape the vigilance of the blockaders ... *m'a demande l'expedition d'un esperonare (barque du pays) avec un officier pour faire parvenir les duplicata des despatches dont il avait charge le Guillaume Tell.*'
27. Ibid., 104.
28. For more details see J. Muscat, *The Xprunara* (Malta, 2000), *passim* and id., *The Xprunara* (Malta, 1997), 123-49.

29 AOM 272, f. 9v. Very often the nomenclatures was confused, especially when referring to small vessels of the same size: *'depredato un Brigantino o sia Galeotta'*.
30 Lib. 223, s.v. *Brigantino*, mentions *venti remi*, probably meaning 10 on each side. Guglielmotti, *Vocabolario*, s.v. *Brigantino*. See also Dal Pozzo, ii, 671, *'e due Brigantini di 10 (banchi)'*.
31 Lib. 223, s.v., *'Brigantino: che si arma in corso'*; see also Bosio, iii, 840.
32 Dal Pozzo, ii, 49.
33 Lib. 223, s.v. *Brigantino*.
34 AOM 269. f. 206v.
35 *Leggi*, 76 V, 77 VI; see also AOM 261, f. 9: *'si tenga armato anche d'inverno il brigantino'*. Dal Pozzo, ii, 407 says *'Brigantino del Porto'*.
36 Ibid., 48.
37 J. Muscat, 'The Maltese Brigantine' in C. Vassallo (ed.), *Consolati di Mare and Chambers of Commerce. Proceedings of a Conference held at the Foundation of International Studies* (Malta, 2000), 199-214.
38 Lib. 223, s.v. *Fregata*.
39 A. Cuschieri and J. Muscat, 'Maritime Votive Paintings in Maltese Churches', *Melita Historica*, x, No. 2 (1989), 121-44; see also J. Muscat, 'Maritime ex-voto Paintings', *Treasures of Malta*, iv, No.3, 13-8.
40 Lib. 413, f. 236 shows a picture of a frigate.
41 Dal Pozzo, ii, 41; Guglielmotti, *Storia*, iv, 386.
42 *Leggi*, 78, XXV.
43 Dal Pozzo, i, 78.
44 J. Muscat, *Il-Flotta ta' l-Ordini ta' San Ġwann* (Malta, 2000), 167-69.
45 Lib. 223, s.v. *Tartana*.
46 AOM 269, f. 297.
47 Dal Pozzo, ii, 676.
48 Lib. 223 s.v. *Tartana*.
49 Guglielmotti, *Vocabolario*, s.v. *Tartana;* S. Bono, *I corsari barbareschi,* (Turin, 1964) 130, note 112.
50 Guglielmotti, *Vocabolario*, s.v. *Tartana* gives a good description of the vessel.
51 AOM 1899, f. 87: *'Per un sperone della Tartana S. Teresa.'*
52 Ibid., f. 68: *'fugoni volanti delle Navi e Tartane'*.
53 *Histoire de la Marine,* 154; see also the engraving by Manglard at the Cathedral Museum, Mdina.
54 AOM 269, ff. 8, 50, 158v, *'che partono due Galere con una Tartana per le solite provisioni dalla Sicilia'*. There are such orders repeated in various places of the same document. Ibid., f. 161v mentions *'La nave S. Vincenzo ... che la medesima nave resti in Canale* [the stretch of sea between Malta and Sicily] *sino al ritorno delle Tartane che si aspettano dalla Sicilia'*.
55 Guglielmotti, *Vocabolario*, s.v. *Tartana* says that its hull was *'gonfio nella mezzania'*. A cargo ship used to be long three times its width, while the length of a fast lateen-rigged galley type was six times its width.
56 AOM 269, ff. 60, 84v, 161v mention *'frumento, carne da Susa, legname di costruzione'*.
57 Lib. 223, s.v. *Tartana*, *'armate fino a dieciotto cannoni, e quantita di Petrieri'*.
58 AOM 269, f. 165v.
59 See watercolour annotated as 'Tartana di Malta' exhibited at the Malta Maritime Museum.
60 Dal Pozzo, ii, 286, 301, 315 always mentions the tartanes as carrying the provisions for the galleys; see also AOM 269, f. 8v.
61 Muscat, *Il-Flotta*, 149-52.
62 Guglielmotti, *Vocabolario*, s.v. *Pinco Barbaresco*.
63 AOM 1769, f. 7.

64 AOM 1769, ff. 93-6.
65 Dal Pozzo, ii, 275.
66 Guglielmotti, *Vocabolario*, s.v. *Pinco*.
67 Lib. 223 s.v. *Fluta o Pinco*, '*sono Piccoli bastimenti simili alle Tartane, senz'altra differenza che questi hanno le poppe*'.
68 Guglielmotti, *Vocabolario*, s.v. *Pinco*.
69 Lib. 223, s.v. *Fluta o Pinco*.
70 Ibid., s.v. *Piatte forme per cannoni*.
71 Muscat, *Il-Flotta*, 163-4.
72 AOM 1869, ff. 286v, 567, 663.
73 AOM 1860, f. 664.
74 AOM 1774, f. 56.
75 Guglielmotti, *Vocabolario*, s.v. *Polacca*: '*Donde venne questo nome? Di Polonia non certamente. A me sembra la stessa radice di Polaccone*'.
76 AOM 270, f. 104.
77 Guglielmotti, *Vocabolario*, s.v. *Polacca*, mentions that the *polacca* could carry up to 500 tons, much more than the 800 *cantari* the tartane could transport.
78 Guglielmotti, *Vocabolario*, s.v. *Polacca*.
79 Earle, 65.
80 Landstrom, 171.
81 Ibid. shows only three openings on either side.
82 Dal Pozzo, i, 815.
83 AOM 1769, ff. 5-8.
84 AOM 270, ff. 97, 176.
85 AOM 271, f. 89; but see also Dal Pozzo, ii, 136, 137.
86 AOM 272, ff. 75, 83; AOM 274 f. 26; AOM 277 ff. 3v, 4, 6.
87 Muscat, *Il-Flotta*, 164-7.
88 AOM 277, f. 3.
89 AOM 1773, f. 89.
90 M.U. Ubaldini, *La Marina del Sovran Militare Ordine di San Giovanni di Gerusalemme di Rodi e di Malta (Rome, 1970)*
91 A. Valiero, *Historia della Guerra di Candia* (Venice, 1679), 304.
92 Dal Pozzo, ii, 439.
93 Guglielmotti, *Vocabolario*, s.v. *Sciabecco*: '*Lo Sciabecco era usato dai barbareschi per la pirateria*'.
94 Auphan, 234, note 1.
95 AOM 270, f. 263.
96 Ibid., f. 263v; AOM 269 f. 24v; AOM 272 f. 69.
97 AOM 269, ff. 206v, 207v.
98 AOM 1860, f. 6.
99 AOM 1774, f. 25.
100 Ibid.: '*egli* [the chebec] *si aiutava con i remi, mentre aveva meno vento di noi*'.
101 Guglielmotti, *Vocabolario*, s.v. *Sciabecco*.
102 Ibid.
103 Ibid. mentions '*grosso il scafo reggente al mare*'.
104 Ibid.
105 H.J. Hansen, *Art and the Seafarer* (London, 1968), 27 shows a beautifully painted 18th-century Catalan chebec with white and blue or white-and-pink striped sails.
106 *Gazzetta del Governo di Malta*, No. 13, 19 January 1814, 50.
107 Earle, 255.
108 B. Landstrom, *The Ship* (London, 1961), 181; Muscat, *Il-Flotta*, 160-2.

Chapter IV

THE SEARCH FOR MUSLIM SHIPS

Malta being so small and arid, the inhabitants of old had been forced to find some means of earning a living other than agriculture. Well before the arrival of the knights, they had resorted to corsairing, a profitable but dangerous activity. According to G.A. Vassallo, there were corsairs prior to the arrival of the knights but their activities, when compared with those of later centuries, were almost insignificant. The naval operations and assaults on Modon, Coron, and Patras, together with those of June 1534, when the galleys of the Order swept the Barbary coast, heralded a golden era for corsairsing activities by Maltese corsairs.[1] When Caruana referred to the operations by Henry Count of Malta against the Venetians in 1205, he mentioned the Maltese islands for

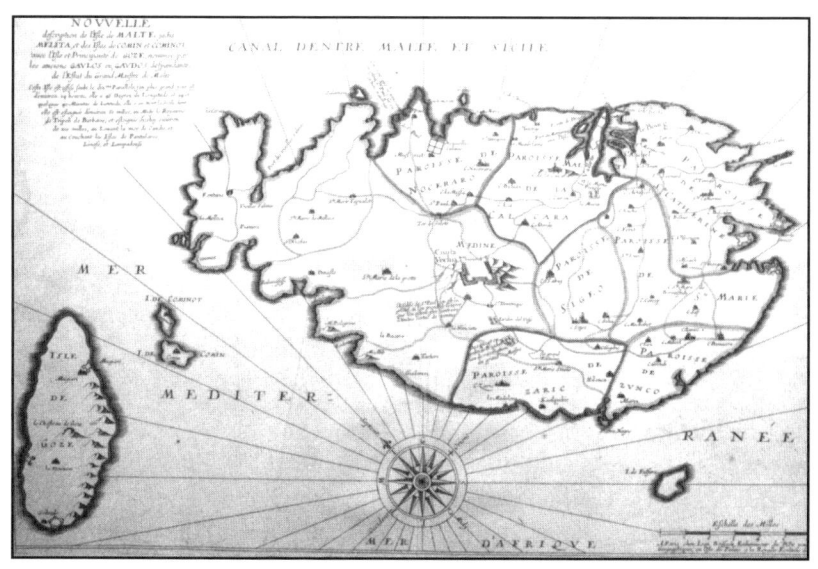

The Maltese Islands; Malta Maritime Museum

their strategic importance in the middle of the Mediterranean Sea and their natural harbours which offered safe anchorages. But he also referred to the Maltese sailors for their expertise and who were excellent corsairs, too.[2]

The skill and bravery of the Maltese corsair attracted many a noble foreigner to the island to fight the Muslim and make a good profit in the process. Even when they were still at Rhodes, the knights had requested the help of a Maltese corsair, Michele di Malta.[3] The Order hired Michele to protect the seas round Rhodes from the Muslim threat. Michele, however, started harassing Christian shipping as well and things came to a head when he set upon a galley that belonged to the knight Castelvi. The Order then prepared a galley to destroy him and finally caught up with him as he was on his way home to Malta laden with loot. Michele was killed in the sea-battle in 1467.[4]

The Maltese and the galleys of the Order

Although in 1530 the knights found the Maltese already well-trained in seamanship and the skills of navigation, it was under the Order that the Maltese corsair was to earn an international notoriety. Malta soon became a source of envy for such important naval powers such as Venice, France, and Rome. Attracted by the bravery of the Maltese and their skill in the building of boats, many came to the island to set up a vessel for corsairing. Even when the Order's fortunes recovered and its fleet was greatly increased, the Maltese continued in their chosen vocation of corsaring. The Maltese, both on the Order's ships and on their own vessels, were the terror of the East.

The *corso* in Malta can be divided into three types:
a) the official or state *corso* run by the Order and generally directed at Turkish and Barbary coast shipping;
b) the *corso* run by private knights mostly during the seventeenth century and principally raiding Muslim shipping;
c) the *corso* organized and run by private local Maltese armateurs.

The Maltese sailors and soldiers were, however, at their finest on the Order's galleys. Evidence of this are the repeated requests of other nations, such as Rome, Spain, and France,[5] to the Order to rid the

The Birgu Galley Arsenal; courtesy Marquis Anthony DeSain

La Piccola Barriera; Malta Maritime Museum

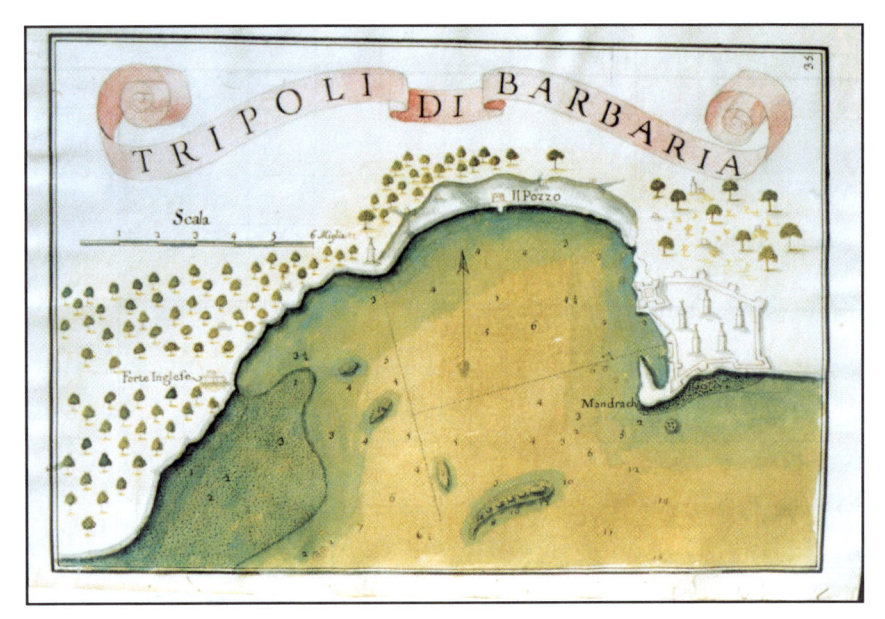

The harbour of Tripoli; NLM 317

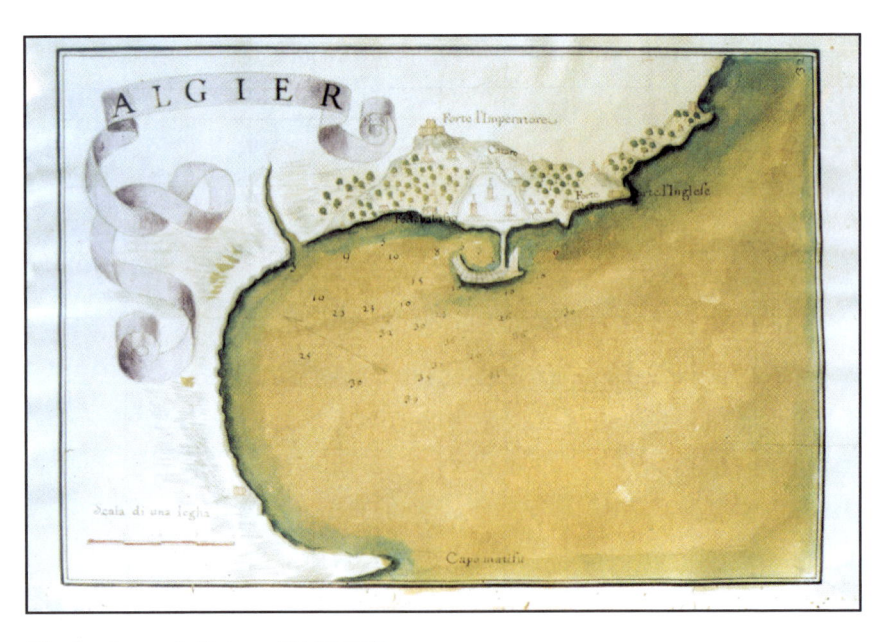

The harbour of Algiers; NLM 317

Third rate of the Order; courtesy Francis Galea Naudi

Maltese Tartana; Malta Maritime Museum

*Left: Stern of a model of (
Museum*

*Top: Stern of a model of t
Maritime Museum*

*Right: Bows of a model of
Museum*

; Malta Maritime

court's gondola; Malta

lley; Malta Maritime

The three galleys of the Order which took part at the battle of Lepanto; detail, from the painting Madonna della Flotta by Antonello Riccio; Malta Maritime Museum

A galley of the Order; NLM 413

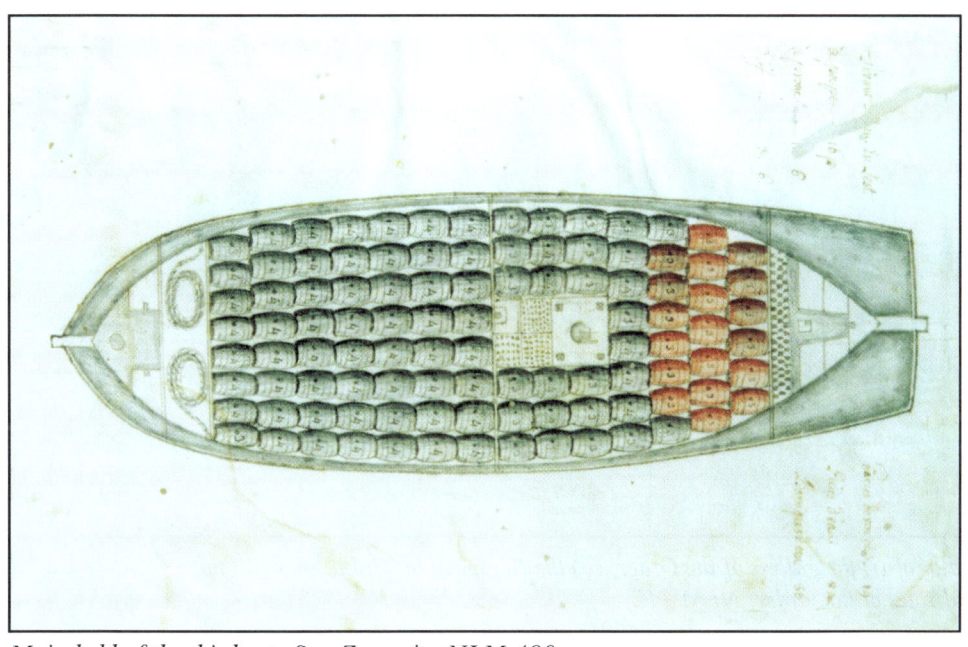

Main hold of the third rate San Zaccaria; NLM 480

Soldier of (i) the galleys of the Order, (ii) the Regiment of Malta, and (iii) the third rates of the Order; NLM 112

Mediterranean of the Muslim threat. It was their ships, sometimes smaller than those they bravely attacked, that contributed to the Order's finest moments. But the ships would have been nothing on their own without the skills and the courage of the Maltese sailors and fighting-men.

It can justifiably be said that the Maltese raised the galley in the estimation of the rest of Europe and made it the scourge of the Muslim. It was not the galley which rendered the Maltese famous but the other way round. The Maltese bombardiers used to be quite careful not to sink the enemy ship in order not to lose the cargo, though if the enemy ship proved particularly stubborn they would not think twice about sinking it.[6] Although Maltese bombardiers were notorious for their expertise yet foreign ones would be brought over from time to time. On 12 December 1657 France was requested to send some bombardiers.[7] Dal Pozzo[8] refers to the bravery of the Maltese soldiers and sailors *'facendo prove mirabili'* in an encounter against three Tripolitan vessels which took place on 13 June 1636. Though the knights never admitted it, the European nations came to refer to the galleys as being Maltese.

The training of the Maltese for fighting on the galleys

Grand Master Emanuel Pinto founded two schools, one for young people and the other for older persons to prepare future sailors. In the first school the youngsters were taught arithmetic, reading, and writing and served as apprentices on the galleys. In the second school, the students were also taught the art of sailing and navigation. Tuition used to take place on the galleys moored at Vittoriosa.[9]

Originally the school was run by a group of knights who were responsible for square-rigged ships. Pinto set it up as an official school in January 1742. In 1769 the same grand master founded a university of studies where, in 1779. Grand Master Emanuel de Rohan introduced instruction in arithmetic and navigation. From the accounts of the expenditure for the teaching of seamen it appears that Pinto's second school had its seat within the university in the Jesuit's college in Valletta.[10]

The students were very carefully instructed and many families sought to have their children accepted in this school. A student placed first in

Grand masters of the Order; NLM 627

A pilot of the Order; Malta Maritime Museum

the examination in the first school got five *scudi*. The best student in the school of navigation got ten *scudi*.[11]

Knights too used to be given instruction in seamanship. No knight could be promoted unless he had passed through the second school. He had also to learn the gunnery exercises and the handling of ships, including the study of astronomy, winds, and instruments.[12] Because of the different languages the knights spoke and because of the rivalry between the different nationalities, the days of instruction were divided as follows. The French and German knights attended on Mondays, Wednesdays, and Fridays, while the Italian and Spanish knights attended on Tuesdays, Thursdays, and Saturdays. Instruction lasted from eight till eleven in the morning and the instructor could not proceed unless everybody had mastered a particular lesson. This is indicative of the seriousness of the institution.[13]

The printing press of the Order which was set up on 25 May 1644 in the grand master's palace helped to foster education in this field.[14] A number of books, many of them written by Maltese seamen, were published for use in this school. The Maltese Giovanni Pagnini was the author of *Il Trionfo in Mare*,[15] *Costruzione delle Radici Quadrate e Cube*, and *Trattato della Trigonometria Piana con un Breve Saggio della Geometria Pratica*,[16] while another Maltese, Michele Angelo Farrugia, wrote *Varie Osservazioni di Porti*.[17] The art of sailing, steering, and chart-making was known as hydrography.[18] There is ample room for further research on this subject. It is interesting to learn the curriculum, of the Maltese student in these schools. Some of the books and manuscripts used were:

'Trattato Pratico della Manovra dei Vascelli';
'Dizionario della Marina';
'Libro della Marina';
'Portolano';
'Portolano del Mediterraneo' by Giuseppe Pace;
'Trattato di Navigazione' by Carlo Imbroll.[19]

Apparently some of these books and the necessary equipment were bought from shops in Malta itself as can be seen from a bill paid to Giuseppe Pace in the name of his late brother Silvestro who had sold some books and teaching equipment to this school.[20]

Maltese seamen figured amongst this school's instructors. Famous Maltese pilots were invited to pass their lore to the students.[21] Many were the Maltese pilots who gained a solid reputation. These included:-

a) Zaccaria Rispolo who was dismissed by the Order but, on the strength of his vast experience, became the royal pilot of the Sicilian squadron. He wrote a portulan of the Mediterranean which is still in manuscript form;[22]
b) Narducci, a royal pilot, who was a man of great experience and ability. On 28 August 1644 he was hit in the shoulder during a fight with a Turkish galleon and died of his injuries in Malta;[23]
c) Giovanni Uzzino who served the Order for a long time and was then allowed by the general of the galleys, Prior Bichi, to become a pilot in the papal squadron;[24]
d) Paolo d'Avola, Bartolomeo Casha, and Antonio Baldacchino who all made a name for themselves as pilots;[25]
e) After the fiasco of the Spanish and the Order's assault on Algiers in 1541, some galleys managed to escape the storm that battered the expedition and returned to Malta thanks to the courage and skill of the Maltese pilots and sailors. This was the opinion of the historians of the Order.[26] However, the Order occasionally experienced shortages of pilots and had to ask for some from France.[27]

It is to be expected that the sailors of old were expert weather observers, dependent as they were on the whims of the skies. A Maltese

Model of a third rate restored by Joseph Muscat

proverb says: 'A wakeful moon, sleeping sailors and a sleeping moon, wakeful sailors.' The seaman's skill showed itself in the choice of sail to make the utmost of the prevailing wind.

The pilot had to know every rock, every reef, and every cove in the Mediterranean. He had to know what kind of seabed he could expect in a particular place. For this purpose there were written special portulans or charts for pilots that noted all important navigational details. These charts can still be seen and consulted.

At school, the student furthered his theoretical knowledge by familiarizing himself with various models of ships. Pasquale Montagna was paid by the treasury of the Order the sum of 50 *scudi* as payment for a model of *un piccolo vascello armato* bought for use in the Nautical School for the benefit of the *Illustrissimi Cavalieri*.[28] It is probable that the models found at the Malta Maritime Museum and in other places are some of the many that were in use in this school. These models were most carefully and skilfully constructed and they are a mine of information to the serious student of ships and navigation.

The Maltese student was enrolled at eight years of age and left school around the age of twenty. On finishing school, the student hoped for a good position in the Order's navy though very often he was disappointed for the better jobs were always given to the Order's faithful servants. This often caused many to turn away in disgust from a career on the ships. This resulted in a great wastage of money and a commission of knights was chosen to investigate the matter. The commission advised a drastic reduction of the intake and that instruction should be limited to those who showed good leadership qualities. This interesting excerpt gives an indication of the social aspects of life in Malta at that time.[29]

Like all other dominators, the knights sought to promote their own interest first and foremost. The good postings were given to the foreigner while the locals were good only to bear the brunt of the fighting. The knights had to wait until 'the Maltese nation hopefully matured in wisdom so that it could take on responsible positions.' In the absence of a sufficient foreign workforce, soldiers and sailors were recruited from the local male population but not the bombardiers.[30]

These schools were set up in 1742 when the activity of the Order on the sea had already declined considerably and time could now be 'wasted' on theoretical knowledge.

Ambassador of France at the Grand Vizir's divan

The Maltese galleys: a school for foreigners

In 1530 nobody could have foretold the honours and glory the Order was to win during its stay on Malta. Nobody could have foretold that the Order's navy would be able to go to the very lion's den and sail victoriously as far as the Dardanelles.

Very often the Maltese galleys served as training ground for many foreigners, some of whom were to achieve a great reputation. The squadron of the Order's galleys became a sort of international school of navigation.[31] Dal Pozzo[32] insisted that the galleys of the Order should be always kept at their very best. Many of the officers of the Holy League who assisted Don John of Austria and Marc'Antonio Colonna were knights who had passed through this school of the Order.

France benefited greatly from all this. Most of the corsairs on the Order's galleys were French citizens and they got the greater share of the loot. France also obtained a valuable nucleus of trained officers and men. At one time, Engel calls the Order's navy as an international school but at another, Malta is only called the kindergarten or nursery (*pepiniere*) of the Royal French Navy. At least Engel admits that a considerable number of illustrious French naval officers started their career on the Order's ships.[33] It was on the galleys of the knights that were trained the likes of Pregeant de Bidoux, Valbelle, De Grasse, D'Hocquicourt,

Tourville, Suffren, and many others. Referring to the effect of the training of the French knights, Dal Pozzo says that most of the corsair ships of the Order during the seventeenth century were French and the booty taken from Muslim ships enriched the subjects of the French king. Moreover, while employed on the Maltese *corso*, the subjects of the French crown gained valuable naval experience and from such a school France managed to train captains and sailors of great reputation and valour.[34]

Even Russia came to know and value the glory of the Maltese galleys. Indeed Catherine II sent her naval officers to train on them during Pinto's magistracy. The Russians left a good impression during their period of service. A letter from Catherine II renders thanks to the grand master for all his efforts on behalf of her officers and for having treated them as if they were knights of the Order.[35]

The Maltese and the Muslim corsairs

The coming of the knights helped the Maltese to further their corsairing activities. About 1660 there were 30 corsairs in Malta each with his own ship or ships, all crewed by experienced men ready for fighting. Long before the Order settled in Malta the *corso* was practised by the inhabitants.[36] It was for this reason that the *Università* asked to be granted

Scene depicting Tripoli and its harbour

Catherine II

Patriarch of the Maronites

permission to arm its own galleys for the *corso*. Apart from the utility of such an activity, the *corso* against the Muslims helped to clear the North African coast of corsairs and at the same time ensured to keep them away from local shores.[37] The danger from the intrusion of the Barbary corsairs was always there as Malta was so close to their strongholds in North Africa. On the other hand, the Maltese never feared their attacks although they never had the sufficient numbers of warships to oppose them as they wanted to do. Yet the Maltese islands were too exposed to the frequent attacks from the Barbary corsairs who 'periodically burned and pillaged the villages and carried off large numbers of the inhabitants into slavery'.[38]

Amongst the most notorious corsairs there were Pawlu Micciolo and Martinu Mula.[39] In 1570 reference is made to Captain Daniel. Other Maltese corsairs included Captain Fugazza and Enrico Mancuso[40] and in 1669, Ascanio Attard is quoted as sailing the sea in search of ships to plunder. Even knights were attracted to corsairing; these included D'Escrainville, Coulonga, Cardena, Hoquincourt, and the Temericourt brothers.[41]

Corsairing was an extremely important and popular source of revenue. Indeed there were many protests in 1689 when the Order directed all the corsairs to disband. Many corsairs did not want to listen and many procrastinated to the very end.[42]

In a similar situation the knights too had not been quick to follow a similar injunction from Rome, in spite of the fact that as a religious Order the Hospitallers were in duty bound to obey the Pope. The case had risen in 1623 when four Muslim holy men had been captured by the knights. In retaliation, the Muslims set upon the Franciscan friars who looked after the Holy Places and threatened to expel them. On 20 October 1623 Pope Urban VIII asked for the release of the Muslim priests but the grand master refused to listen. On 5 December Fra James of Vendosme, the guardian father of the convent of Nazareth, came to inform Grand Master Antoine De Paule that, unless the priests were freed within three months, all the Franciscans would be imprisoned for the rest of their lives and the Holy Places themselves destroyed. Still the Order would not listen and the holy men were only released after the Franciscans paid a stiff ransom.

The Order's campaigns against the Muslims were inspired more by a desire for profit than by any fervour for the Christian Faith.

This can be inferred from the answer the Order gave Cardinal Barberini.

In 1636 the Greek Orthodox patriarch of Jerusalem and Constantinople successfully bribed the Muslim chiefs to expel the Franciscans from the Holy Places and to give his co-religionists full control. In retaliation the cardinals in Rome decided to ask the Christian nations to launch a new crusade for the recovery of these shrines.

The Order was not pleased at all. Instead it plainly told Cardinal Barberini that it did not want to see the launching of this crusade but asked for permission to seize Greek shipping in the belief that this would put pressure for the return of the Holy Places. After all the Order had been much annoyed with the order that Rome had passed on to Christian ships, namely that Greek shipping was not to be molested, in the hope that an understanding could be reached with the Greek Orthodox Church.

Calahorra, commenting on those vicissitudes, criticized harshly the knights who never heeded neither the prayers of the Franciscan friars nor the special recommendations pronounced by the Holy See. The Holy Land, governed by the Muslims, had to reimburse the Christian knights a great sum of money for the release of the four Muslims. There were other instances when the Holy Land had to suffer the consequences of the attacks by Maltese corsairs on Muslim ships. This is a very strong indictment of the Order, but Calahorra may be excused owing to the circumstances that prevailed in the Holy Land. Referring to the *corso* as piracy is something rarely found in other authors. Venice was also expected to use her naval influence over the Turks in relation to the Holy Land. Cardinal Barberini wrote a letter from Rome dated 16 January 1638 to Cardinal Cornaro of Venice in relation with the loss of some of the Holy Places and about the necessary means to be adopted by the senate of Venice to recover those places.

The cardinal, amongst other suggestions, mentioned twelve steps to be taken in such a contingency, one of which was intended to refuse all representations by the Greeks when they claimed restitution of ships and property taken by corsairs, until they returned the Holy Places to the Catholic Church. But there were other more stringent measures to be adopted against the Greeks:

1) Corsair galleys and warships were to attack Greek ships and property on land also and to enslave them as if they were Muslims;

2) Corsair galleys and warship were to patrol the normal routes taken by Greek vessels near Egypt and Asia to take them as prizes or to sink them if necessary;
3) The Cossacks were to do the same operations in the Black Sea against all shipping supplying Constantinople with bread as that city depended on such provisions;
4) Corsair warships were to be financed up to 8,000 or 10,000 *scudi* or to be given to the Cossacks so that they would be able to interfere with their ships in the traffic to Constantinople in the Black Sea.
5) To disrupt all commercial activities with the Turks.

The Franciscan Girolamo Colubovich, writing in 1634, also suggested certain measures to induce the Greeks to return the Holy Places, if not by means of money than through the adoption of stringent measures. One measure was that proposed by Cardinal Barberini which required that when the Greeks claimed damages by Christian corsairs, they were to be treated as Turks, until such time when they decided to return the Holy Places. All Christian merchants were to boycott all transactions with the Turks to disrupt the circulation of money in the Ottoman empire.[43]

The *corso*

The *corso* used to mean the hunt for the Muslim ships. Every knight had the statutory duty to fight the Muslim wherever he could be found. Throughout the Order's stay, Malta was in a state of continuous war with the Muslim world.[44] Cantu refers to a mystic and austere rule which in a certain way imposed on the knights who joined the Order a perpetual exile from their country. It obliged them also to an incessant war against the Muslim, obliging them to accept battle even when they were outnumbered by three to one.[45] This explains why so many foreigners used to come to the island to set up as corsairs flying the flag of the Order. It was, however, dangerous to set up as a corsair without the grand master's and the council's licence. In 1574 Fra Giovanni Battista Mastrillo prepared a galleot for the *corso* without waiting for the official permission and was condemned to forfeit his vessel to the Order's treasury.[46] Quite often the European nations used to ask the knights to clear the Mediterranean of the Muslim threat.

The Order had well paid spies all over the Muslim world. These informed the knights of the movements of enemy shipping, especially cargo ships.[47] Most of these spies were Venetians although there was a good number of Greek Orthodox citizens. Most probably these were those same spies who kept the grand master informed of what the Turkish sultan thought about Malta.[48]

As soon as they arrived on the island, the knights started making preparations for the *corso*. The *corso* was perhaps the main reason for the Order's decision to stay in Malta. It reached its apex in the latter half of the seventeenth century under the Grand Masters Lascaris, Nicholas and Rafael Cotoner, and Carafa. It is calculated that about half of the able-bodied male population of Malta was employed on the sea between 1650 and 1750.[49] By 1660, there were most probably 30 corsairs operating from Malta.[50] Under Carafa, however, the *corso*'s sudden collapse spelt it the beginning of the end for the Order, for the absence of its revenue was sorely felt by the exchequer.

The decline of the *corso* was felt elsewhere as well. Algiers had only 25 corsairing vessels in 1725, compared with at least 70 in 1630. There were times when many European powers were prepared to pay protection money to the bey of Algiers for their shipping to be left alone. Even the Jews started looking for some other income to replace the profits from the investments in sponsoring *corso* activities. France had a yearly trade with Algiers of a million francs and five or six million francs with Tunisia. This, however, paled into insignificance compared with the 60 or 70 million francs worth of trade with the Eastern territories and France with good reason looked upon the Ottoman empire as its best colony.[51] Engel's main concern was to praise the knights, especially those of French nationality, and she speaks somewhat disparagingly of the Maltese. But when the *corso* declined, French knights who could not dispose of the necessary money to arm their own corsair ships served on Maltese ones making a virtue out of dire necessity. *Il fallait bien faire feu de tout bois*.[52] The decline of Turkey therefore left very wide repercussions.

Literally everything depended on the Muslim. The ships of the Order had to spend the entire year at sea, and the Order built ships that could withstand winter conditions. More than any other vessel, the galley

Grand masters of the Order; NLM 627

Muslim minister and mufti

A Jew and an Armenian

Naval battle: NLM 413

Galley squadron of the Order attacking a Muslim galleon: NLM 413

enriched the Order and Malta at the expense of the Muslim.[53] The galley was the knights' most prized possession and even when the other navies introduced square-rigged ships the Order still felt that its galleys could not be beaten. After all what really mattered were the skill of the sailors and the courage of the soldiers.

The hunt for the Muslim was often left in the hands of a squadron of five or six galleys. The squadron of the Order sought to control the galleys of Turkey and those of the Barbary coast thus allowing Christian shipping to sail unhindered. At the same time the knights and the Maltese could go about their corsairing activities with little danger of being intercepted by hostile ships. Even if the squadron included large square-rigged warships, like the *petacchio* and the pink, the galleys were still expected to lead since they had to bear the brunt of the fighting. The congregation of the galleys retained its primacy even after the introduction of the squadron of the ship-of-the-line under Perellos.[54] As well as being superbly prepared for battle and carrying a crew of perfectly-trained Maltese hands, the galleys were extremely fast and manoeuvrable. During the actual fighting the oars gave it the ability to respond to the fluctuating needs of battle or, if need be, to make a speedy retreat.

When firing on the enemy, the galleys used to keep away from one another to avoid tragic situations like what happened during the attack on the Turkish galleon when a son of Sultan Ibraim was captured on 28 September 1644. Captain Neuchese ordered all the galleys to open fire and a shot from the galley *Santa Maria* killed eight men on a friendly galley.[55] This explains why the Book of Signals says that when the galleys start shooting they were to remain in a proportional distance from one another to avoid accidents.[56] When attacking, it was not uncommon for the galleys to approach three on each side of the enemy and to open fire simultaneously.[57] When the *Benghen* was captured on 8 September 1700, it was surrounded by four galleys.[58]

The galleys used to fall upon their victims in a crescent formation;[59] if such a simultaneous show of force was not needed, they attacked one after the other. The *capitana* or flagship led the way followed by the *padrona* or second in command and then the other galleys, according to their captain's seniority.[60] Occasionally the galleys surrounded a ship and opened fire simultaneously.[61] As soon as the flagship hoisted the red-and-yellow striped flag that signified the commencement of the attack, the guns came into action.

During the actual fighting the rowers, who were chained to the floorboards by their ankles, could squat underneath their benches. The deck, however, remained a most dangerous and unsheltered place to be during a bombardment. This naturally applied to all members of the crew; so the oars were raised on the galley's side and blankets and old sails were woven between them to serve as some sort of protection before the fighting started. This was mostly done during battles in which many galleys were involved; Lepanto in 1571 was the last classical example.[62]

As soon as the enemy appeared suitably subdued and their crews had descended below deck for shelter, the caiques transported the soldiers over for the bloody hand-to-hand fighting that invariably followed.

The Maltese soldiers wore bright red uniforms, at least during the eighteenth century,[63] designed to make them accustomed to the sight of blood so that they would not panic during the battle.

Red was a popular colour with the Order. The galleys, half galleys, and inner sides of the large warships were all painted red. But the uniform of the Maltese soldiers employed in the Candia campaign had been changed to green in 1686. The Maltese battalion became known as the Green One on that occasion.[64]

Sometimes it happened that during a battle a vessel sank carrying friends and foes down with it. At the beginning of the eighteenth century the *capitana* commanded by the Balì Spinola suddenly broke up and sank as it was attacking a Turkish vessel. Of the 22 knights and 500 sailors and soldiers on board, only Spinola and a few others survived.[65]

The hand-to-hand fighting on the Turkish decks used to be extremely bloody and fearful. The poorly-paid Maltese soldier wanted to jump overboard and swim to the hostile ship because this entitled him to claim an extra reward for being the first to board the enemy vessel. There was a severe punishment for those who tried to swim over to the enemy vessel without waiting for the caique which had to transport the fighting men *en masse*.[66]

On the whole, Maltese sailors and soldiers were poorly rewarded by the Order. There was indeed a pension payable to the widow or to those who were injured in action; this was, however, a mere pittance. The case of Grazio Delia who lost a leg in battle is a typical illustration. After 27 years' faithful service, he was given just 20 *scudi* once on 29 December 1738.[67] The knights used to give a lot of alms. In 1587, for example, just before he left for Rome, Grand Master Verdalle left instructions for the distribution of alms to the poor Rhodiots and Maltese and especially to the orphans and to the widows, and those who lost their fathers and their husbands in active service on the galleys of the Order.[68]

The first person to board the enemy's deck got an extra 50 *scudi*, the second one 30, the third 20, and the fourth 15. The one who lowered the enemy's standard and handed it to the captain got 12 *scudi*. The man who spotted an enemy ship by day got five *scudi* and ten *scudi* if by night. If any of these services were performed by a knight the remuneration was doubled.[69] The Barbary corsairs had a similar system of rewards. The first one to sight a Christian vessel or to board it would get a monetary reward or, more often, one of the captured slaves. He could claim his reward before the division of the spoils.[70]

Anyone could take and carry off whatever one fancied from above the enemy's decks. One could even take the clothes off the enemy's back![71] Nobody, however, not even the captain, could touch whatever lay below decks. Stiff penalties were reserved for those who broke this order.[72]

The grand master received one-tenth of the profits of all the loot from the *corso*.[73] Everybody on board, except the slaves, had a right for a share of the profits. This share varied according to the relative posts of responsibility on board.[74]

The Maltese galley – always victorious

In the annals of the Order one meets victory after victory of the Maltese galleys over Turkish ships. This might lead one to suppose that those victories were made up and invented, but this was a subject about which there could be no misrepresentation. The Order could not deceive the Maltese into believing in non-existent victories because the Maltese themselves actually participated and witnessed the events with their own eyes.

The *corso* also served to feed the entire nation and a lack of prey immediately resulted in dearth and famine. Malta suffered from perennial famines and the shortage of grain resulted in widespread privation and hunger.[75] These were greatly alleviated with the regular income of the *corso*, especially when grain ships were taken as prizes.

A Muslim saica after Opizio Guidotti

There was also a great pique and animosity among the various langues of the Order. Each nationality kept a watchful guard over the others and was ever ready to diminish the others in order to increase its own glory.[76] This was quite apparent in the way the langues temporarily united not to leave the admiralty of the fleet an Italian monopoly. Such animosity was most felt when there were members of different langues on the same galley.

How, therefore, can one explain the repeated defeats of the Muslim, especially when he had vessels that were just as battleworthy, designed by the Venetians and built by the Greeks? The Muslims practically had the same types of vessels as the knights; indeed very often the knights copied the ships they captured. It is certainly strange to realize that the Turks were taught the art of navigation by the Christians themselves.[77] The Muslim's error lay in that they did not protect their cargo ships with their fighting vessels enough. The Order always protected its cargo ships and those it chartered extremely well on their voyages to and from Sicily. On the other hand, the unprotected tartanes that belonged to private Maltese owners often fell victims to the Barbary corsairs. Indeed, the caramousal or the *germa*, the humble Turkish cargo carrier, provided the majority of the victims of the Maltese galleys. They certainly could not stand up to this fighting machine. Still some of the Turkish ships and those of the Barbary coast in particular, were so well built that often

A galley soldier by Joseph Muscat

the knights designed their own vessels like them. The chebec, the pink, the *petacchio*, and the *pollacca* all appeared in Malta a long time after they had been in use by the Turks and the Barbary corsairs.

Of course the galleys also captured enemy fighting ships such as the foist, the *salettina*, the *maona*, and the *saettia*.[78] This was, however, not as common as the capture of cargo ships.

Turkish fighting ships were sturdily built and well equipped for battle. However, they suffered from a perpetual shortage of men. On the whole, the Turkish fleet administration was less able than that of the Barbary coasts.[79] Auphan gives details of the maladministration in the Ottoman fleet and the endemic corruption it suffered from which is, perhaps, the main explanation of their weakness.[80] The Maltese galleys naturally turned this to their advantage. When attacking a Turkish fighting vessel, the galleys approached on both sides in order to divide the enemy. So divided, the Turks could never hope of coping with the fearful assault that followed.

Back in Malta, the return of the galley squadron was most eagerly expected. All those who could afford it had invested a lot of money in the *corso* and now looked eagerly forward to reaping their profits.[81] The Ursuline sisters started taking a share of the prizes that were carried to Malta with the obligation of praying God for the propagation of the Holy Catholic Faith '*e per l'armi e prospero stato della Religione*'.[82] Even the Barbary corsairs used to give 1 per cent of their profits to their marabouts (Muslim holy men) in their mosques.[83] The poor womenfolk waited expectantly for the return of their loved ones. Each homecoming brought with it the usual admixture of happiness and woe, fortunes made and lives lost.

When news of the loss of two galleys which had been seized by seven Turkish galleys from Candia on 10 August 1583 reached Malta, the Order was horrified. All of a sudden a lot of shouting and crying of the people in Valletta was heard for the galleys of the Order which had been taken by the Turks. But later the magisterial galley, which had been given up for lost with the other two galleys, entered harbour.[84] After the fiasco of Zoara in 1552, Grand Master Juan D'Omedes received the bad news while he was at Fort St Angelo. He was heard sighing and raising his hands in prayer recommending the souls of the innocent knights to God. Vassallo remarks that on that occasion the grand master never recommended the souls of the many Italian and Maltese soldiers who died there and whose bones are still buried in the sands of Zoara.[85]

Signals

Ships signalled to one another by means of flags of different shapes and colours, lanterns, rockets, fires, and the firing of guns. Bells, trumpets, drums, and petards and arquebusses were also used. A concerted shout by the crew or the lowering of a sail were sometimes used by one ship to salute another.[86]

The signals used by the Order remained unchanged for a long time. The signals as given by Guidotti, writing about his life between 1592 and 1637, are in agreement with Lib. 110, a manuscript of 1719, and with two other eighteenth-century manuscripts to be found in the Malta Maritime Museum. Ship signals used on Italian vessels are similar to the ones used by the Order.[87] A signal book of Pinto's time (*c.* 1750), to be found in a private collection in Malta, agrees with the foregoing system of signals. Another manuscript in the Franciscan Minor convent in Valletta agrees with the system of signals as put down in Lib. 110, though it contains some interesting additions.[88] Even the signals of the papal galleys as described by Guglielmotti are in agreement. These leads

THE SEARCH FOR MUSLIM SHIPS

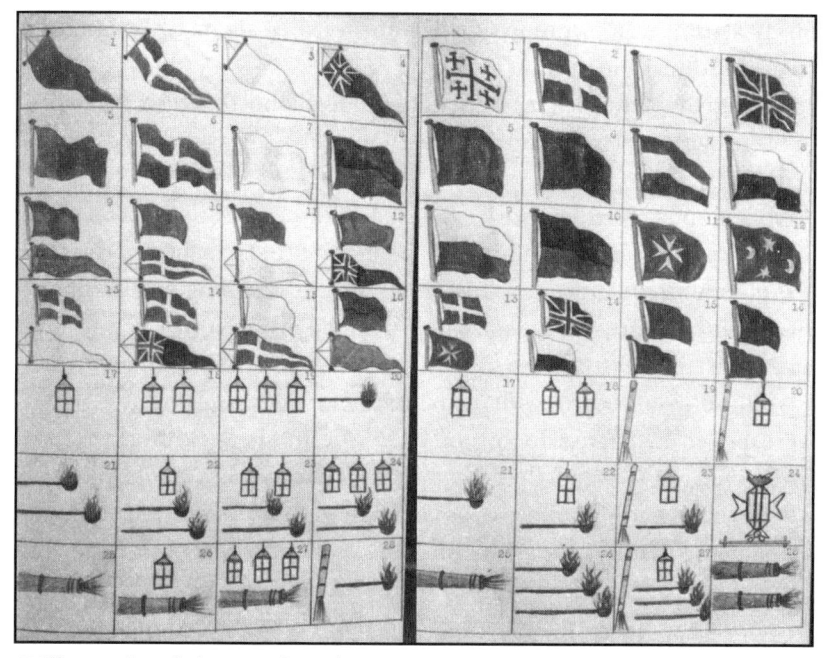

Different signals in use after 1720

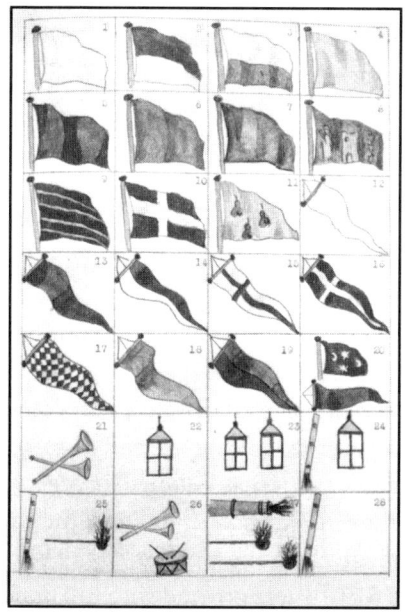

Signals by the capitana *to the rest of the squadron*

one to assume that common signals were in use by all the Christian fleets in the Mediterranean.

The signals of the *capitana* were different from those of the other galleys in the squadron. To communicate with the *capitana* a vessel used specific signals.[89]

On a ship, a stern lanthorn was used to indicate the captain's status and for communication. Three lanthorns on the stern and another one on the mainmast indicated that an admiral of the fleet was on board. Just three lanthorns on the stern indicated the presence of a vice-admiral or the general of the galley squadron.

At sunset, a lanthorn was lit on the stern of every vessel.[90] These signals were, however, far from foolproof. In 1661, Captain Ricasoli on a *padrona* had joined the Venetian fleet to attack the Turkish navy. While following a light which he thought was the Venetian *capitana*'s lanthorn, it turned out that he was following a Turkish galley. Fortunately, Ricasoli managed to get away.[91]

Specific signals applied when a ship wanted to greet another one. If the vessel encountered on the seas belonged to a monarchy, the crew greeted it with shouts of 'Long live the king!' If it was a vessel of a republic, the crew greeted it with shouts in favour of the republic's patron saint. If the ship belonged to the Order, it was greeted by shouts of 'Long live St John!', the Order's patron saint.[92] The shouts of joy were followed by the firing of guns.

A greeting could also be given by means of flags and the lowering of a sail. As a salute, the flags were lowered or kept from flapping. A ship that carried no guns saluted another ship by lowering the topsails either completely to the tops or at half-mast.[93] However, the firing of the guns was the most common salute. A ship fired three, five, seven, or nine rounds of gunfire, either with or without cannonballs. The galleys of the Order always fired an even number of rounds: four, six, eight, or ten.[94]

A salute with gun fire followed closely a set protocol. The number of rounds fired is always recorded in books and documents, since it showed the degree of respect shown. In addition to being a means of expressing joy, the firing of guns showed etiquette both on the part of a ship's captain and on the part of a welcoming port or city.[95] When Prince Philibert visited Valletta in 1619, he was greeted with full honours. He replied by firing six rounds from his royal galley. This he did to show his great respect since he only used to fire four rounds for other cities.[96]

Instead of guns, chambers of breech loaders or *mascoli* were used for everyday saluting to economize on gun powder. It was Damiano Garcia who, on 10 July 1651, suggested to the Order to use chambers instead of guns for everyday greetings since this would halve the consumption of gunpowder. On 30 January 1652 the galley *San Nicola* tried it out and proved Garcia right. For his good sense, Garcia received a decent reward from the Order. Six galleys made use of 72 *rotoli* of gunpowder for signalling. Garcia showed that 36 *rotoli* could suffice. The *capitana* carried four chambers for saluting and the other galleys two.[97] In 1795 the Order forbade the firing of guns or chambers as greetings because the exchequer was almost bankrupt. The Order always felt the need to economize on gunpowder. Towards 1605, when in Malta there was a number of armed vessels for corsairing, there was a great shortage of provisions, both of foodstuffs and munitions.[98]

To call the soldiers and sailors quickly to the galleys, the cavalier of St James in Valletta fired three gun shots and raised three flags. The signal was repeated at Mdina in the same manner for the sake of the nearby villages.[99] During the night three lanterns replaced the flags.

On hearing the signals from St James or Mdina, the village church rang for half-an-hour and a flag was raised on the church steeple. At night a lantern took the place of the flag.[100] On hearing the signal the

Signals hoisted by the village churches

men left their work, or their beds, and made their way to Vittoriosa. The Vilhena Code required that every time that there was an urgent need for the galley and warship squadrons to leave harbour, the governor, after receiving written instructions from the venerable congregations of the squadrons, was to fire a gun signal as required by the ordinance dated 23 March 1722 issued by Grand Master Perellos and required by the tribunals of Malta.[101]

Life on the galley

The conduct of the Order throughout its stay in Malta was certainly not unblemished. Like all other occupying powers, it ruled with an iron hand and was primarily interested in quelling any unrest that might arise. The Maltese had to bear this yoke patiently but an even more pitiable fate awaited the slave population.

The knights had an equivocal relationship with their slaves. On one hand, they saw in the slave an image of God, on the other the slave was a valuable beast of burden that, properly looked after, could give a long useful service. Certainly a slave's life was harsh and rigorous. The very law of the grand master is evidence of how many slaves preferred poison to a life of hardship.[102] The Maltese, too, did not behave any better

Slaves at the oars by Sebille

towards the slave.[103] It cannot be denied, however, that a certain respect was shown to the slave as can be seen in the laws and decrees enacted by the Order.[104]

If civil life was uncompromising, life under military discipline on the galleys was still more strict. Even the knight himself had to submit to strict discipline but the penalties of disobedience were much harsher for the slave than for his master.[105]

Of all vessels, life on the galley was the hardest. It meant 500 or more people living together for three or more months on a vessel 50 metres long. One has to imagine the hardship, the cramped living conditions, and the stench. Life on the galley was not called 'a passage to hell' for nothing.[106] The slaves, more then 250 of them, were chained to their benches and could not even move to relieve themselves.[107] This naturally created an unbearable stench, especially when the slaves' excrement was not cleared for days because of fighting or more pressing work.[108] The odour seeped into the timber of the deck with the result that a stink would remain on the vessel all the time.

The knights obviously spent a more leisurely time at the poop which was reserved for them. There they could sleep, recreate themselves, and play cards when they were permitted to do so. The soldiers, too, spent whole days basking in the sun at the *rambata*, playing games, spinning yarns, polishing their weapons, and, if they could afford the money, drinking wine in the tavern below decks.[109] The sailors, on the other hand, had the normal duties of cleaning, general repairing, hoisting, and lowering sails and the thousand-and-one jobs that sailing such a vessel entailed.

On the galley, space was at a premium. Even the knight had to bed down on the floor on a blanket. Only the captain, the chaplain, and a few knights could sleep below deck. A few other knights could bed down in the cabin at the poop or on the stern *rambata* called the *spalliera*.

The Maltese soldiers and sailors fared worse. They had to find some place to lie down either on the *rambata* or along the side passage-ways. To further complicate things, 20 rams used to be tied to either side of the vessel close to the rowers' benches and the Maltese crew had to sleep in their vicinity.[110] Cows, rams, hens, and pigeons were carried on board. Some even took along their own hens letting them run loose under the slaves' benches. The Order, however, restricted the amount of chickens a captain could allow to run free on the galley.[111]

139

Two colour shoes issued to galley slaves

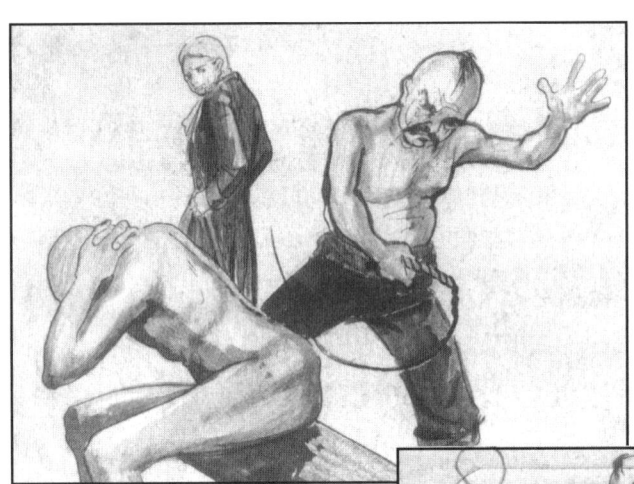

Flogging of slaves; courtesy Joe Mallia

Flogging of slaves: courtesy Joe Mallia

One could not even undress to sleep; indeed not even shoes could be taken off.[112] Because of the restricted space, nobody could take with him more than one canvas bag. The captain, who failed to see to this, was severely punished.[113] In this respect Vilhena's law was quite specific: 'Any cabin boy who fails to report baggage taken clandestinely on board will receive 100 lashes on his back or he will be condemned to row on the galleys for life.'[114] This order applied even to the captain. If found guilty of allowing merchandise to be loaded on board, even free of charge, he would lose command of the ship. The treasury would also confiscate two years' income from his commandery and he would forfeit four years seniority.[115]

The slave, however, fared worst of all. Tied with heavy chains, he passed his days on the rowing benches working, eating, and sleeping.[116] The slave was nonetheless protected from potential excessive ill treatment by the younger knights. The captain and the officers could not, for example, use the slaves for their own personal tasks on shore.[117] No knight could molest or beat a slave or order him about on the galley.[118] It should be remembered that a knight could take his valet with him on board, provided that the valet was more than 20 years old and he was to be treated decently.[119]

But the knights had their good aspects which must be mentioned for honesty's sake. The chapter general of 1603 issued an order number 58, that required the knights in the name of Holy Obedience not to insult or molest any member of the crew.[120] For religious brothers, an order issued in the name of Holy Obedience is the most binding and breaking it results in mortal sin.[121] This injunction shows the seriousness of the Order's intentions of curbing unnecessary violence on the part of the young bloods.

Excessive and unnecessary beatings did not do any honour to the captain and rather served to lower the morale of the crew.[122] The Order also supplied the slave with warm clothing and a pair of shoes.[123] In addition wine was distributed to the slaves whenever the *capitana* hoisted the signal.[124] Each slave received a small sum of money every month from the Order. A band also used to play on board. The slave could join this band and receive a small payment in remuneration.[125]

Punishment on the galley was very severe. The *baton* or goad was used regularly to keep the oarsmen on their toes. According to the Vilhena Code, any prisoner, slave, or *buonavoglia* who mutilated himself and

The punishment for cowards: courtesy Joe Mallia

could not row again was to be mercilessly hanged immediately. If, however, he recovered enough to be able to row again, he would be whipped without trial and his nose would be chopped off. This order was issued on 15 November 1674 and was strictly enforced. A slave was hanged the first time he tried to mutilate himself.[126] Dal Pozzo mentions an incident in early 1673 when about 100 slaves tried to escape from the island on a *pollacca* they had commandeered in the harbour. '*La Giustizia con una ricordevole punitione fece mozzare a ciascuno il naso, e l'orecchie, a terrore de gli altri*', after they were chased and captured.[127] If he maimed himself a second time but recovered, both his ears would be cut off. The third time he would be hanged and those who had in any way helped him to maim himself would be held responsible as well.[128] This shows the way that the knights considered their slaves as beasts of burden condemned to a life sentence on the oarsmen's bench.

There were other severe punishments for the rest of the crew as well. Anybody who showed cowardice in battle would pass a gauntlet of booing and catcalling along the entire *corsia* and would then be committed to the rowing benches for a number of years.[129] Anybody heard blaspheming, holding the Sacred Eucharist to ridicule, or caught duelling would be severely punished.[130] Blasphemy was also heavily punished on French galleys according to a law issued by Richelieu.[131] Blasphemers would be whipped or sentenced to a period of rowing.

Keel-hauling: courtesy Joe Mallia

The same penalties applied to anybody caught betting, provoking others to fight, or was found guilty of injuring someone else.[132] Harsh punishment was reserved for anybody who slept during a watch or who failed to keep his weapons in good condition.[133] Similarly anybody who carried daggers or small pistols was severely chastised.[134]

One of the worst punishments was the so-called 'plunge in the sea'. The culprit was tied by a rope round his waist and thrown violently from the spar or antenna of a vessel to the sea. One could be given the plunge for five times, depending on the offence. Sometimes the rope was only long enough just to reach the surface; this was called the dry plunge. In such cases the pain was much worse because the jolt was taken by the victim's waist.[135]

A period of rowing was, however, the most common punishment and this was obvious since the Order was always in need of people to man the oars.

No member of the crew could disembark in a Christian country without the galley captain's express permission.[136] Probably this was done to avoid the possibility of desertion for, naturally, only loyal and trusted men would be allowed to get on land. The knights, too, could be tempted to misbehave away from the watchful eyes of their captain. To avoid the risks of fighting and scandal, the Order did not want the crew to go ashore without legitimate reasons.[137] In Syracuse on 6

December 1658 a serious fray took place between the soldiers of the Order and those of the city.[138] This was certainly not an isolated case.

The knights had found out through experience that a good wholesome diet was essential on board.[139] Minestrone was the daily fare of the slaves,[140] although not of the other members of the crew. Although these had better food than the ordinary crew, there was no luxury or waste. The knights were meant to observe temperance as befitted the members of a religious Military Order.[141] The knights' food was frugal, of an honest but decent quality that did honour both to the members of the Order and to any guest.[142] When a galley left on the *corso*, it took on board about 220 *cantari* of shipbiscuit and 5,000 small loaves as well as four bulls or cows and other meat. It also loaded about 40 Sicilian rams, 150 hens, and 150 pigeons. Meat was eaten four times a week and every member of the crew was given a daily ration of four shipbiscuit or small loaves. The galley also carried quantities of wine, vinegar, oil, salted tuna, sardines, cheese, lard, salted beef, 5,000 eggs, dried fish, caviar, cocoa, rice, butter, peas, and flour.[143] Live animals could be carried on board galleys in order to supply fresh meat. Since consumption of salted meat resulted in scurvy and other illness, the Order took pain as much as possible to have a supply of fresh meat to minimize the incidence of disease on the galleys.[144]

Hierarchy on the galley

The knights, naturally, held all positions of command on the galley. Though the captain was the ultimate judge on board,[145] there were a number of ordinances issued by the reverend chapter of the Order and decrees published by the council meant for the keeping of discipline afloat. These restricted the powers of the captain.

The crew members of the galley were divided in a threefold hierarchy:
1) The knights who made up the upper class;
2) The middle class made up of those who were neither knights nor slaves;
3) The third class, the lowest of all, made up of the slaves, the *buonavoglie*, and the prisoners or convicts.

The first class was further subdivided as follows: first came the captain, then the second in command,[146] then the *re* and the *cercamar*. These

Hierarchy on the galley: courtesy Joe Mallia

latter two officers were not allowed to disembark for any reason whatsoever on enemy territory. The penalty for doing so was six months' service in one of the towers round the coasts of Malta.[147] They also lost all the service on that cruise and their share of that expedition.[148] Then there were the knights of fortune or voluntary knights followed by the other caravanists. For these latter, precedence was determined by the number of times they had been on a *corso*.

The *re* and the *cercamar* were the most important officers after the captain. The *re* was in charge of the knights and of the soldiers, while the *cercamar* was responsible for all weapons of war, guns, and munitions.[149]

In order to qualify for an appointment within the Order, the knight, after serving a five-month novitiate had to spend at least two years on the sea. The requirements that every knight had to undergo a five-month novitiate and be at least 18 years of age before he could go on a *corso* were not always respected and were later changed. In 1625 the minimum age was raised to 20[150] and in 1631 the *re* and *cercamare* had to be at least 25 of age.[151] During the last years of the Order in Malta, the minimum age was raised to 25.[152] Before leaving on a caravan, the knight had to be granted a written permit by his auberge.[153] A knight could not leave his galley during a *corso* or leave his auberge before completing his two years of compulsory service as a caravanist and without a permit from the grand master himself. However, he could always find somebody to substitute him for the remainder of his service at sea. The penalty for not observing this order was severe: *'sotto pena contrafacendo di esser castigato come dissubidiente'*.[154] This two-year period could be divided into four terms of six months each.[155] After five years in the Order and after having served his sea service, the knight was entitled to wait his turn for a commendary.

At one time the *corso* season lasted from 1 July to 31 December and from 1 January to 30 June.[156] Although shipping almost disappeared during the winter months, yet there was always the possibility of some fat prize being encountered. The Order felt that its ships sailing in winter reduced the number of young bloods roaming the streets in search of trouble.[157]

From 1528 onwards, the choice of the knights for the *corso* lay in the hands of a commission of two or three knights who were empowered to act as it deemed fit. The work of this commission generated a great deal of trouble and a lot of fighting.

It was later decided that this commission should be made up of representatives from every langue. The number of knights needed for the *corso* was first drawn up and then each langue had to supply its quota. The number of caravanists on each mission was determined by the type of attack planned.

The number of knights varied from time to time. In 1625 the *capitana* carried 35 knights while the other galleys carried 30 each. In 1733 the *capitana* had a complement of 14 knights, the other galleys had 12 knights each, and the remaining vessels had 13 knights each.[158] On 30 January 1739 the *capitana* carried 12 knights, the other galleys 10, and the remaining vessels carried six knights each.[159]

Very often the vessels of the Order carried four young knights each, while the general's galley carried five chosen from amongst the most courageous and the most keen to learn and to serve the Order. If more knights wanted to go on a caravan than were actually needed, the grand master himself selected them.[160]

While serving on the vessels of the Order or fighting the Muslim on land, the knight was known as a caravanist.[161] Some caravanists did their service on the great galleon, the small galleon, or the *petacchio*.[162] A caravan consisted of service on the warships of the Order or fighting on land. No distinction was made as to the rights and duties of the knight whatever the type of service performed.[163] The one with the greatest

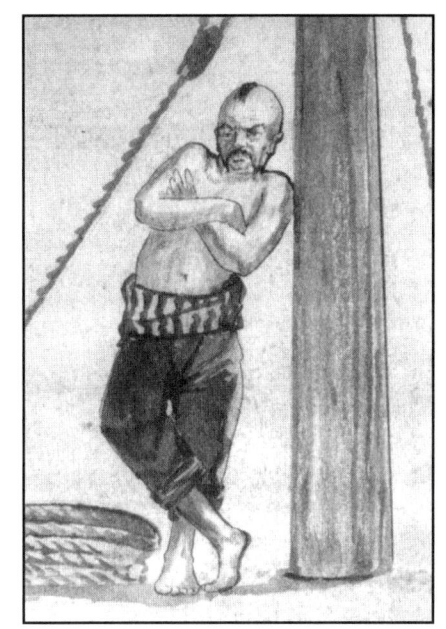

Chaplain of Obedience: NLM 627   *The* bonavoglia: *courtesy Joe Mallia*

number of caravans to his credit could be chosen as the *re* or the *cercamar*.[164] But both these positions were due by right to the so-called knights of fortune who had already done their service at sea of two years fighting the Muslim. This right was granted to a knight who volunteered to embark on the *corso* on 19 June 1664 and was confirmed on 12 July 1684. This right was kept for as long as the knight did not disembark from the galley.[165]

The second class of crew members included the doctor, the barber, the cooper, the caulker, the pilot, the carpenter, the slave driver or *argusin,* the cook, the clerk in charge of the distribution of food, the soldiers, and the sailors. The highest rank of a non-commissioned officer could aspire to was that of sergeant or that of chief bombardier. The 40 soldiers on board a galley included a trumpeter, four bombardiers, and 16 soldiers skilled in handling the arquebus.[166]

The chaplain came in a class of his own but he had the privileges as a knight and he took precedence over the *re* and the *cercamar*.[167] The chaplain was only in charge of spiritual matters but had to be present if a will was being drawn on board; otherwise the will had no effect.[168]

There were two types of chaplains. First there was the conventual chaplain[169] who formed part of the Order and, like his brother knights, had to go on the *corso* when his turn came.[170] He could, however, appoint another priest in his stead. In this case, the priest was called a chaplain of obedience.[171] A priest who substituted a conventual chaplain was remunerated for his services. During his period on board, the priest came under the jurisdiction of the Order and not of his bishop.[172]

In the selection of a chaplain, consideration was taken of his ability to look after the spiritual needs of the crew and of his knowledge of the liturgy. The first requirement was that he should be a good and holy priest.[173]

The lowest class on the galley was the *ciurma* and consisted of slaves captured by the knights, Maltese or foreign *buonavoglie* who sold themselves to the Order to row until they paid their civil debts, and the prisoners or convicts, those condemned to row on the galleys. The *buonavoglie* and the prisoners were considered on the same level as the slaves.[174]

One of Grand Master Manoel de Vilhena's laws said that 'each slave had to wear a plait of hair or *bezbuza* as thick as a *patacca* on penalty of 50 lashes on his back.' Another law said that 'no slave could wear similar clothes as Christians and he has to carry a six-ounce chainlink round his ankle, on penalty of 50 lashes to the slave and a fine of from two to ten ounces of money to his master.'[175] The same grand master also ordered that all *buonavoglie* should shave their heads on penalty of 50 lashes.[176] The *buonavoglie* could, however, keep a *moustache* as a privilege.[177]

Religious practice on the galleys

The Order of St John of Jerusalem was founded originally as a religious order and its members were therefore religious individuals. Indeed, a religious spirit can be seen in the Order itself and in its relationship with its subjects from its very foundation. A knight's whole existence was based on his faith in Christ, a faith he witnessed by devoting his life to the service of the Religion.[178] Both while sailing on the *corso* and in his everyday behaviour, the knight had to bear himself in a way that did honour to his Christian beliefs. In practice, however, his behaviour was often far different.[179]

The knights of Malta kept their title of Hospitallers even after they were expelled from Jerusalem and they took to fighting the Muslim at sea. The Hospitallers, true to their name, had the foremost medical service in Europe of their time which was available to everybody including Muslim slaves.[180]

It followed naturally that religion featured prominently in life on board. Every vessel carried a chaplain who formed part of the crew of all warships of the Order.[181] Frigates, tartanes prepared for the *corso*, the ship-of-the-line, the grand galleon, the small galleon, the *petacchio*, the chebecs together with the galleys all carried their chaplains.[182] A ship-of-the-line carried two priests to look after the spiritual needs of the crew.[183] Pope Sixtus V's brief said that a priest, approved by his bishop, who served on a galley, was able to absolve all those on board even in matters reserved to the pope.[184]

Jurien da la Gravière boasts that mass was said daily only on the French galleys. He says that this privilege existed on no other oar-propelled ship, not even the papal galleys.[185] However, it can be positively asserted that mass was said daily at sunrise on every galley of the Order during the *corso*.[186] The knights were also granted a decree by the pope, which was renewed every seven years, that allowed the chaplain to administer the *Viaticum* and the Last Rites on board the vessel.[187]

At sunrise the *capitana* raised the flag so that all the masses on the other galleys could start simultaneously. This flag consisted of a white field divided into four equal quarters by a red cross and with another small red cross in each quarter. It was known as the flag of the Holy Land.[188]

Only the carrack *Sant'Anna* had a chapel on board. The sacristy mentioned by the documents consisted of a box in which were kept the sacred vestments and other utensils used in liturgical services. There was another box which served as an altar.[189] The sacristy was kept in the same berth where the chaplain had his quarters with 12 other knights. This was the second room under the deck, next to the captain's.[190] One of these portable altars can still be seen in the Wignacourt Museum, Rabat.

Mass was probably said on the *spalliera* that is the *rambata* at the stern. In windy and rainy weather, mass was probably said underneath the canopy at the rear of the ship. When there was enough time for the crews to disembark, the service took place on the foreshore. On Sundays and principal feastdays when the galleys and the ships-of-the-line were in Malta, mass was said in a place where it could be followed from all the other seacraft.[191]

According to an inventory found in the Cathedral Museum Archives in Mdina, the chaplain had to carry with him a crucifix, a chalice, a paten, a pyx for the hosts, two cruets, a shallow plate to be used during

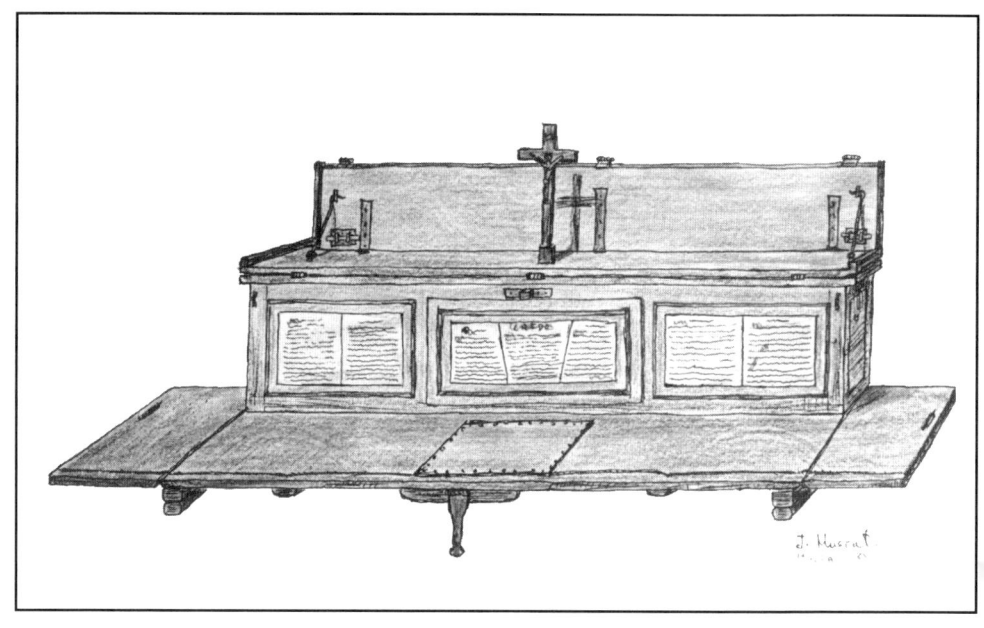

A galley's altar

The galley's altar prepared for Mass

Communion – four copes, one white, one red, one green, and one violet, a white stole and a small while altar cloth for the administration of the *Viaticum*, three altar cloths and three albs, two towels for the washing and drying of the hands before and after mass, two corporals for under the chalice, two chalice cloths to cover the chalice during Mass, 12 purificators to dry the chalice and the pyx, 12 handkerchiefs for the washing of the hands during Mass, three Credo cards, a missal, a bell, a box for the hosts, a collection box, a box with four lanterns, a crucifix to be used when administering to the moribunds, a violet stole and ritual, an iron for the preparation of the hosts, an *asperges* and a container for holy water, a wooden collapsible altar which closed up in the form of a box and which includes the holy marble, and a small wooden platform with its carpet. Probably such an inventory applied to all the galleys of the Order leaving for the *corso*, though this is actually the inventory of a *capitana*. The 'Inventario della Conventuale Chiesa di San Giovanni' found at the Cathedral Museum, Mdina lists all the sacred items that were included in the *casse delle galere* for the *capitana*, magisterial, *San Nicola*, and *Santa Caterina* galleys respectively.[192]

In addition to the celebration of mass, the chaplain had to conduct the morning prayers. He administered the necessary sacraments and conducted funerals. He was also in charge of teaching catechism to the children on the vessel.[193] These children were known as *proeri*. The ordinances of the Order refer to these *proeri* or *projeri* as being those boys who were recruited at a tender age and they grew up on a galley to become sailors. Others were assigned as apprentices to carpenters, caulkers, and oar-makers. Their number was not to exceed 48, with 11 assigned to the *capitana* and nine to the other galleys together with other supernumerary candidates. The venerable congregation of the galleys was free to add four other supernumerary for the *capitana* and two for the other galleys.[194]

The chaplain looked after the spiritual needs of the entire crew including the slaves.[195] He was meant to try his best to convert the slaves to Christianity. The chaplain even had books of morals intended for the Muslim slaves who wanted to become Christians. Amongst others can be mentioned the works by Emmanuele Sanz[196] Commendatore Cagliola, and Commendatore Manso.[197]

The chaplain had the duty of washing sick persons' hands before meal times.[198] In sickness, knight and slave, were considered equal and the same care was given to both. The chaplain had to look after and comfort all the sick without any discrimination whatsoever.[199]

There was a great difference between the conduct of the Christian and the Muslim in battle. Before Lepanto,[200] for example, the Christian chaplains and priests went round all the vessels confessing and absolving the combatants and encouraging them to be ready to shed their blood for God their Saviour. Before engaging battle, the Turks, however, took opium and fought in a drugged state, encouraged by the fearsome cries of their captains. As they moved towards the enemy, the Muslims used to utter bloodcurdling animal-like howls. Drug-taking before battle was common amongst the Muslims. Amongst the Saracens, the 'old man of the mountain' (*sceih el gebel*), was their leader and he had a group of assassins ready to do all that he ordered them to. These assassins used to be drugged by means of opium and other drugs and were thus kept under the control of their leader.[201] They trained their youths to become *feda vie* assassins or 'sicarians' as the Jews called them,[202] so that they were ready to do their leader's bidding. They used to be drugged so that they could experience 'heavenly' feelings in drug-induced dreams. The young men were promised the pleasures of heaven and were made to experience the forgetfulness of intoxication. However, before Lepanto the Christian chaplains went round warning the believers that heaven could not be won by those who opted for comfort.

Graffito of a galley at St Rocco church, Balzan showing the chaplain near the stern

Anybody who showed disrespect towards the Blessed Sacrament during the *Viaticum* was heavily punished. So that proper deference could be shown by the entire crew, the big bell at the stern was rung throughout the ceremony. The bell was the signal for all hindrance on the deck to be removed so that the chaplain could pass unobstructed. In front of the chaplain a man walked carrying a bell and flanked by two lantern-carriers. A knight accompanied the chaplain on either side to help him should the vessel pitch or roll unexpectedly.[203]

Before the galley left on the *corso*, the Blessed Sacrament was exposed for 40 hours and a special departure mass was said. The grand master and the Council used to order that '*si esponga per 40 ore il Venerabile* (the Blessed Sacrament) *acció si preghi Sua Divina Maesta per li prosperi successi delle arme marittime dell'Ordine*'. This is the kind of ordinance that was issued to order the devotion of the 40 hours. Many such ordinances can be seen in the Archives of the Order.[204] G.F. Abela wrote that the crews of galleys used to stop to hear mass at the church of St George in Birżebbuġa on their way out of the harbour.[205]

Before an encounter at sea the chaplain was expected to encourage the crew members of a galley to meet the Muslims with a full faith in Christ who forgives all sins and who will grant them victory over the enemy. During the short time that remained between the discovery and the assault, the chaplain would approach all the members of the crew and the knights themselves preparing them with a true contrition for their sins before imparting the sacramental absolution. The chaplain heard as many confessions as possible before the commencement of hostilities. With cross in hand, the chaplain would walk on the *corsia* from poop to bows encouraging all to do their duty while imparting the sacramental absolution. That was the time when the chaplain announced the plenary indulgence granted by papal breves *in ariculo mortis*.[206] All chaplains of galleys and third rates were authorized to confer the indulgence to all sailors and soldiers engaged on the warships of the Order of St John.[207] Then the chaplain joined the crew in the hailing out '*Viva Gesu, Viva Maria Vergine, Viva San Giovanni Battista!*' and after the last benediction he retired below deck to attend to the wounded who would be lowered to the sick bay to be cared by the doctor and the *barberotto*. The chaplain's services were deemed so important on board a galley that he was advised to take care and keep away from the *rambata* which was the bows' gun platform during saluting gunfire when accidents sometimes occurred which wounded or killed crew members.[208]

An interesting case of a last-minute conversion is found in the archives of the Order. During a battle, a fatally-wounded Turk started calling out for a priest to baptize him and invoking the names of God, Our Lady, and St Francis of Assisi to intercede for him. He passed away holding a holy picture of Our Lady saying that he was happy to die a Christian.[209] It was extremely difficult for the Muslim to change his beliefs because the Koran says that when one changes his religion is a worst guilt than when one is charged with murder.

The Church always looked after the spiritual needs of sailors. It was there to encourage them during the actual fighting and it did its best to ransom those who were enslaved. The *Monte della Redentione* was set up in 1607 for such work.[210] The Trinitarians and the Fathers of Mercy were also active and operated especially amongst the Christian slaves held in the bagnios of the Barbary Regencies.[211] It also comforted them at the moment of their death.[212]

On the galleys of the Order a dead knight used to be shrouded in his own blanket before being buried at sea. The corpse was always lowered from the starboard side and a gun salute was fired as the corpse slid into the water. Among sea-faring people it was considered dishonourable to lower the corpse from the port side which was reserved only for dead animals. For sailors to be punished on the port side of the vessel was considered far worse that the punishment itself.

When someone died near the coast, the corpse was always given a decent Christian burial on land. In this case it did not matter from which side the corpse was lowered. Those who died during the night were buried the following day after the evening prayers. Those who died during the day were buried the following day after the morning prayers.[213]

The Order distinguished between the knight and the other members of the crew even after death. However, it always supplied a winding sheet to anybody who lacked one.[214] The rules of the Order described how a knight should be shrouded. These rules also applied to those who died in the infirmary.[215]

The knights, the Maltese, and the galley

The Order partly enriched itself with the wealth of the Muslims even though it was far more interested in laying its hands on the enemy rather than on his wealth. The unbelievers were chased, captured, and committed to a lifetime on the rowing benches. Theirs were the arms and muscles that powered the galleys of the Order all over the Mediterranean in an endless search for yet more Muslim booty.

The Order, however, needed even more hands to man the oars and very often it turned its eyes on the Maltese, who, being fellow Christians, could not be treated like the unbelieving Muslims. Instead the Order found another solution by substituting terms of imprisonment by long periods of rowing on the galleys. The least crime was punished severely by years of rowing. Indeed, too often there was no proportion between the crime and its punishment.

A quick look at the codes of criminal law illustrates all this. An order issued by Grand Master de Valette in 1558 punished by four years of rowing on the galleys anybody who wore embroidered trousers.

Grand Master Verdalle's order of 1583 punished anybody guilty of sheltering a criminal with a life sentence of rowing on the galleys.

The pragmatic sanction of Grand Master Perellos of 1700 punished with five years' galley service anybody who wore clothes made out of *lamé* or that were brocaded or otherwise embroidered with gold or silver thread. The tailor himself received a similar sentence.[216]

A bonavoglia *by Joseph Muscat*

An even better witness is the codex of Grand Master Vilhena that was published in 1724. Amongst other laws it provided that:

Any *buonavoglia* or any member of a ship's crew who deserted and was recaptured was to be summarily sentenced to three years' rowing.[217]

Any *buonavoglia* who went out during the night was to be punished with five years' rowing without any payment.[218]

Any cabin-boy who does not inform about clandestine cargo carried on the ship ... could be condemned to a life sentence of rowing.[219]

Anybody who showed disrespect towards his father or mother had to spend ten years as a soldier on the galleys without any remuneration.[220]

Anybody who fired an arquebus or musket that was loaded with a ball or shot ... was punished with between three and five years' rowing on the galleys.[221]

Any prisoner, slave, or *buonavoglia* who injured himself in order not to be able to row was to be summarily whipped.[222]

Anybody who took out any weapon during a fight received a sentence of five years' rowing.

Anybody who kept a knife or a pointed instrument on his person or in his house ... could get up to five years of rowing.

Anybody who, on being arrested, showed resistance to the officers of the law could receive from three to five years of rowing on the galleys.[223]

Any man caught indecently dressed was given a five-year rowing sentence.

Any Jew or Turk who entered a house, even to buy or sell anything, became a slave and had to spend two years rowing on the galleys.[224]

Anybody who stole anything up to the value of 50 *scudi* was sentenced to rowing on the galleys for the rest of his life.[225]

Any innkeeper or shopkeeper who received anything in barter from a prisoner, a slave, or a *buonvoglia* stood to lose what he had received for a first offence ... The second time he was sentenced up to three years of rowing on the galleys.[226]

Anybody whose animals grazed on somebody else's land had to make up the damage and he was punished with up to three years of rowing, even if he did not let them in personally.[227]

Any Jew who failed to wear a conspicuous yellow headband or who wore a hat ... would either be whipped or be enslaved.[228]

Anybody who threw dirt against other people's doors received a ten-year rowing sentence.[229]

Anybody who practised a profession or a trade without a licence ... received three years of rowing. Any vagabond caught not gainfully occupied could receive up to four years of rowing.[230]

These were certainly cruel and excessive punishments symptomatic of the times and of the mentality of those who projected methods to recruit non-paid rowers on the galleys.

NOTES

1. G.A. Vassallo, *Storia di Malta Raccontata in Compendio* (Malta, 1854), 369: '*prede cosi vistose erano loro ignote* (when referring to corsairing prior to the arrival of the Order in Malta) *ne in conseguenza potevano rimanere indifferenti alla vista di tanta straordinaria provvidenza*'.
2. A.A. Caruana, *Frammento Critico della Storia Fenico-Cartaginese, Greco-Romana e Bizantina, Musulmana e Normanna-Aragonese delle Isole di Malta* (Malta, 1899), 474 quoting M. de Villebrun: '*In ogni tempo, i migliori marinari d'Europa, i quali forti, attivi e sobri riuniscono tutte le qualità del buon marinaro*'.
3. Bosio, ii, 295; G.F. Abela, *Della Descrittione di Malta* (Malta, 1647), 567.
4. Bosio, ii, 311.
5. Dal Pozzo, ii, 298 and E. Rossi, *Storia della Marina dell'Ordine di S. Giovanni, di Gerusalemme di Rodi e di Malta* (Rome-Milan, 1926), 12, note 1, 39, 490, for the contribution of the Order to these nations.
6. M.U. Ubaldini, *La Marina del Sovran Militare Ordine di San Giovanni di Gerusalemme di Rodi e di Malta* (Rome, 1970), 163; the author shows the attack by four galleys of the Order on two large Muslim galleons which took place on 22 April 1543.
7. AOM 1759, f. 390v.
8. Dal Pozzo, ii, 23.
9. Rossi, 110.
10. AOM 1839 f. 20.
11. Rossi, 111.
12. Lib. 223 s.v. *Scuola*; R. Cavaliero, *The Last of the Crusaders* (London, 1960), 15; Rossi, 110.
13. AOM 1764, f. 3.
14. Vassallo, 672; T. Zammit, *Malta – The Islands and their History* (Malta, 1971), 183.
15. Lib. 172, *passim*.
16. Lib. 568, *passim*; *L'Arte*, No.79, 22 February 1866.
17. Lib. 282, *passim*.
18. Lib. 223, s.v. *Idrografia*.
19. See Lib. 67, 223, 318, 317, 757, 254, 1101.
20. AOM 1839, f. 7.
21. Ibid., f. 31.
22. Dal Pozzo, ii, 65.
23. Ibid., 85.
24. Ibid., 251.
25. Vassallo, 369.

26 Ibid., 389.
27 AOM 1759, f. 384.
28 AOM 1839, f. 8.
29 AOM 1934A, f. 24.
30 AOM 1763, f. 6: '*Bombardieri pero, et altri Officiali quando presentemente non si trovino, doveranno per ora esser forastieri, finché col tempo la Natione maltese s'impratichisca come si spera.*' The same words are repeated in AOM 275, f. 21.
31 J. de la Gravière, *Les Dernier Jours de la Marine a Rame* (Paris, 1885), 115: '*Les galeres de Malte furent, pendant longtemps, la grande ecole de guerre de notre marine*'; see also C.E. Engel, *Histoire de l'Ordre de Malte* (Geneva, 1968), 228, 229: '*La reputatuion de la marine de l'Ordre etait immense, au point qu'elle devenait une sorte d'ecole navale internationale.*'
32 Dal Pozzo, i, 284.
33 Engel, 228, 243.
34 Dal Pozzo, ii, 327
35 Engel, 229: '*Les jeunes Russes laissent d'excellents souvenirs. Ils sont braves, disciplines, obligeants, tres consciencieux dans leur service.*'
36 Abela, 433, 442.
37 Vassallo, 244-6.
38 E. Schermerhorn, *Malta of the Knights* (Surrey, 1929), 32.
39 Bosio, iii, 840.
40 Dal Pozzo, ii, 384, 460
41 AOM 1767, f. 383 mentions Ascanio Attard; see Dal Pozzo, ii, 212, 328, 329 for the activities of various corsairs.
42 Dal Pozzo, ii, 460.
43 AFH, xiv, 1921, 490, 492, 494-6; Calahorra is quoted in ibid., *passim*.
44 L. DeCaro, *Storia dei Gran Maestri e Cavalieri di Malta* (Malta, 1853), 43: '*e tenere una perpetua crociata contro i nemici di Cristo*'. For more details, see J. Muscat, 'The Maltese Corso' in C. Villain-Gandossi, *Mediterranee, mer ouverte*, (Malta, 1997), 191-208.
45 Ibid., Prefazione. p. iv; *Regula Hospitalariorum et Militiae ordini Sancti Ionnis Baptistae Hierosolymitano* (Rome, 1556), f. 2.
46 Dal Pozzo, i, 100.
47 AOM 1766, ff. 53, 170.
48 Bosio, iii, 817; Dal Pozzo, i, 124; ii, 103
49 Dal Pozzo, ii, 348, 466; R.E., Cavaliero, 'The Decline of the Maltese Corso in the XVIIIth Century', *Melita Historica*, ii, No. 4 (1959), 224.
50 P. Earle, *Corsairs of Malta and Barbary* (London, 1970), 121.
51 P., Auphan, *Histoire de la Mediterranee* (Paris, 1962), 203.
52 Engel, 227-38.
53 One should keep in mind that Muslim corsairs, on their part, occasionally captured Maltese merchant ships especially during the winter season.
54 Rossi, 82.
55 Dal Pozzo, ii, 82 *et seq.*
56 Lib. 110, f. 16, no. 68.
57 Dal Pozzo, ii, 145: '*si risolve d'abbordarlo, ordinando ch'unitamente tre Galere da una parte u tre dall'altra l'investissero e tutte d'un colpo gli mettessero dentro l'artiglieria*'.
58 AOM 1771, f. 153.
59 Lib. 413, *passim*, see pictures; Lib. 110 f. 3, No.1.
60 MMM, MS 'Segni della Capitana', f. 2, Nos. 21-5; the attack on the enemy would be launched as necessary and at the appropriate time.
61 AOM 1771, f. 153.
62 Dal Pozzo, i, 20.
63 Lib. 112, f. 79.

64 Dal Pozzo, ii, 601; referring to the joint Order and Venetian attack on Modon in June 1686, the author says: *'La sera de' 28 il Battaglione Verde (cosí chiamavasi il nostro di Malta per i vestiti di livrea verde, che la Religione ad esempio de gli altri Principi haveva quest'anno cominciato a fare a suoi Soldati) ...'*.
65 AOM 1771, ff. 152 *et seq.*; Spinola's *capitana* came apart and sunk, see Vassallo, 689. Graviere, 125 says that this loss was deeply felt. Dal Pozzo, ii, 476 mentions the case when a Turkish vessel came apart after an intense bombardment but still the Christian crew wanted to board it to claim the prize.
66 Lib. 413, 193.
67 AOM 1823, f. 317.
68 Dal Pozzo, i, 295.
69 Lib. 413, f. 192.
70 Bono, 112.
71 Lib. 223, s.v. *Bottino*.
72 Lib. 413, f. 192; *Leggi e Costituzioni Prammaticali* (Malta, 1724), 98, XXX.
73 Dal Pozzo, i, 494; *Leggi*, 97, XXV; S. Bono, *I corsari barbareschi* (Turin, 1964), 113, says that in the Barbary States the pasha got 12% of the profits: *'Al pascia, cioe alle casse dello Stato, spettava il 12%'*.
74 *Leggi*, 97, XXV; Earle, 126, 127 gives exhaustive details. For the distribution of shares on Barbary ships, see Bono, 113.
75 Dal Pozzo, i, 167, 175, 327, 524; ii, 163, 167, 216.
76 DeCaro, prefazione, p. ii; for the dispute between the langues of Italy and Spain, see Dal Pozzo, i, 108.
77 Auphan, 155, 166, 167.
78 These are some of the prizes the Order captured but there were many others like:
   pink   AOM 1769, f. 93; AOM 276, f. 5;
   galleon   AOM 1769 f. 93;
   sultana   A. Guglielmotti, *Storia della marina Pontificia*, viii, 5;
   foist or *fusta* Bosio, iii, 149;
   maona   Dal Pozzo, i, 120;
   brigantine   Ibid.,166;
   galleot   Ibid., 540;
   petacchio Ibid., 578;
   galley   Ibid., ii, 205.
79 C. Brockelmann, *History of the Islamic Peoples* (London, 1952), 303, 304, explains in detail the administration of the Turkish fleet.
80 Auphan, 193.
81 Earle, 126-8.
82 Dal Pozzo, i, 243, 244.
83 Bono, 112; Auphan, 194: *'1% de la valeur allait aux wakoufs (biens religieux)'*.
84 Dal Pozzo, i, 238.
85 Vassallo, 433.
86 Lib. 223, s.v. *Campana, Nebbia, Segnali per la Nebbia, Segnali di giorno*; Lib. 413, f. 199; AOM 1839, ff. 32, 34; Guglielmotti, *Storia*, viii, 279; id., *Vocabolario marino e militare* (Milan, 1967), s.v. *Segnale*. In 1782 the English introduced a system whereby each flag stood for a letter of the alphabet.
87 See supplement in *Epoca*, No. 1068: *'Tavola di un antico codice dei segnali fra le navi'*.
88 At the Biblioteca Reale of Turin one can examine a manuscript 366/3 which is a copy of Lib. 110. Thanks to Furio Ciciliot who kindly provided a photocopy of the Turin MS.
89 For further information, see Lib. 110. Two other mss are to be found in the MMM; one is entitled MS 'Segni che fa la Capitana in tutti li occasioni su la Squadra delle Galere, della Sacra Religione Gerosolimitana, tanto di giorno, che la notte, tanto

alla vela che alla fonda'; the other MS is 'Segni che le Galere Sinsile farranno all Capitana, alla Vela ed alla fonda'.
90   Lib. 223, s.v. *Fanale*. The *capitana* of the galleys carried a large lanthorn for signals; see Lib. 110 f. 14, No. 57 and MMM, MS 'Segni che fa la Capitana', f. 6, No. 25: '*Il fanale di posta acceso serve per rispondere a tutti li segni.*'
91   Dal Pozzo, ii, 293.
92   Lib. 223, s.v. *Salutare colla voce*.
93   Ibid., s.v. *Salutare colla Bandiera* and *Salutare colle Vele*.
94   Ibid., s.v. *Salutare col Cannone*; sometimes only the powder chambers of periers were used for salutes.
95   AOM 269, f. 6.
96   Dal Pozzo, i, 647, 648.
97   AOM 1759, ff. 386-8.
98   Dal Pozzo, i, 493, 494.
99   AOM 270, f. 117v: '*Segnali per il giorno, e per la notte a chiamare la Gente d'arme della Campagna per portarsi nella Valletta immediatamente visto il segnale*'.
100 AOM 1761, f. 65. This order is dated 1709 but is in agreement with the order found in AOM 270 f. 117v; see also note 97 *supra*.
101 Leggi, 21, XXXVI.
102 Ibid., 74, X and 135, XVII.
103 Ibid., 111, X.
104 AOM 1761, f. 264; AOM 1759 f. 497; see also Lib. 413, f. 197
105 AOM 1759, f. 497.
106 *Histoire de la Marine* (Paris 1934), 151.
107 Lib. 413, f. 185.
108 Often the whole mess was simply cleared by a storm or downpour; see *Histoire de la Marine*, 151.
109 AOM 1759, f. 384.
110 Ibid., f. 541; Lib. 413, f. 148; Gravière, *Les Derniers*, 148.
111 AOM 1759 f. 451, order No. 7 of 11 March 1631.
112 Ibid., ff. 127, 458.
113 AOM 273 f. 143; AOM 1759 f. 497; AOM 1761, f. 265.
114 *Leggi*, 91, XII.
115 AOM 1761 f. 177.
116 Lib. 413, f. 178.
117 AOM 1759, f. 497.
118 AOM 1761, f. 264; AOM 1759, f. 407; Lib. 413, f. 197.
119 AOM 1761, f. 265.
120 AOM 1759, f. 497: '*Proibendo in virtu di Santa Obedienza a tutti i Religiosi* [to ill-treat any member of the crew]'.
121 *Regula*, 98.
122 Lib. 413, f. 197.
123 AOM 1761, f. 106; Lib. 413, f. 216; *Leggi*, 91, XV.
124 Lib. 110, f. 8, no. 30.
125 AOM 1759, f. 380.
126 AOM 125, f. 44; *Leggi*, 103, IX, mentions the article of law that deals with the slave who tried to main himself.
127 Dal Pozzo, ii, 408.
128 *Leggi*, 103, IX.
129 Lib. 413 f. 193.
130 Ibid., f. 187
131 Gravière, *Les Marins*, 195; see also Lib. 413, f. 189 and AOM 1761, f. 245
132 AOM 1761, f. 187.

133 Lib.. 413, f. 189.
134 Ibid. f. 191.
135 Lib. 223, s.v. *Dar la Cala;* according to Richelieu's laws, the guilty individual could be given three crashes, see Gravière, *Les Marins,* 44.
136 Lib. 413, f. 192.
137 Dal Pozzo, ii, 167, 631.
138 AOM 1769, f. 137: '*circa un incidente avvenuto il 6 dicembre 1658 in Siracusa tra alcuni sbirri di quella città e alcuni soldati delle galere dell'Ordine di Malta*'. See also Dal Pozzo, ii, 270.
139 Lib. 413, f. 180; Lib. 223, s.v. *Pietanza.*
140 AOM 1759 f. 519; AOM 1845, f. 233, mentions '*Minestre di Riso, Pasta, Fave, Fagioli, Ceci, Lente, Amandoli, Passoli, Taria*'.
141 AOM 1763, f. 10.
142 AOM 1761, f. 269.
143 Lib. 413, f. 186, describes the provisions taken for a *corso* mission in the Eastern Mediterranean.
144 AOM 1759 f. 451.
145 AOM 1761 f. 263.
146 Bosio, iii, 65; AOM 1934A, f. 3.
147 For more information about the coastal towers of Malta, see J. Muscat, 'Visitatio Turrium', *Melita Historica,* vii, No.2 (1981), 101-8.
148 AOM 1759, f. 162.
149 Bosio, iii, 65.
150 AOM 1759, f. 118.
151 Ibid., ff. 102, 103.
152 AOM 1934A, f. 3.
153 AOM 1761, f. 263.
154 AOM 1759, f. 115.
155 Lib. 223, s.v. *Caravano.*
156 AOM 1759, f. 115.
157 Dal Pozzo, I, 791.
158 AOM 269, f. 25v.
159 Ibid., f. 158.
160 AOM 1761, f. 263.
161 G.A. Ciantar, *Malta Illustrata* (Malta, 1772), 661.
162 AOM 274 f. 92v; AOM 1759 f. 117.
163 Lib. 223, s.v. *Caravano;* AOM 1579, f. 115
164 AOM 1759, f. 162; To be chosen as a *re* or a *cercamar* a knight had to be at least 25 years old and had to have taken part at least in two caravans. In 1631 the number of caravans was increased to three; see AOM 1759, f. 163.
165 Ibid., f. 164.
166 Lib. 413, 180.
167 AOM 1763 f. 11.
168 AOM 1761 f. 245.
169 Lib. 223, s.v. *Priori del Vascello.*
170 Ciantar, 661, note a.
171 AOM 269, f. 171v; AOM 1774 f. 96; AOM 1826, f. 222.
172 AOM 1926, f. 5v.
173 Lib. 223, s.v. *Priori del Vascello;* AOM 1761, f. 245.
174 See J. Muscat, 'Xogħol ta' lsir fuq Galera ta' l-Ordni', *Il-Pronostku Malti,* (Malta, 1996), 179-205.
175 *Leggi,* 112 XVII, The diameter of a *patacca* was $3^1/_2$ cm; information kindly provided by Joseph Sammut.

176 Ibid., 90, IV.
177 Gravière, *Les Derniers*, 29.
178 Dal Pozzo, ii, 405; DeCaro, 43; Lib. 110, f. 2.
179 DeCaro, Prefazione, p. ii. The knight carried the eight-pointed cross on his habit to signify a pure inner life; see *Regula*, f. 2.
180 L. de Boisgelin, *Ancient and Modern Malta* (London,1805), ii, 307.
181 AOM 1763, f. 11.
182 For the various nomenclatures, see AOM 1823, ff. 57, 158; AOM 1759, f. 117; AOM 1826, f. 630; Lib. 413, f. 182.
183 Lib. 223, s.v. *Priori del Vascello*.
184 Dal Pozzo, i, 311.
185 Gravière, *Les Derniers*, 52 cites Barras de la Penne.
186 Dal Pozzo, i, 311: '*E ch'i Capitani delle dette Galere in tempo di viaggio potessero far celebrare la Santa Messa due hore avanti il levar del sole*'. See also Pope Clement XI's brief of 22 March 1706 in AOM 1761, f. 245.
187 AOM 269, f. 195; see also J. Muscat, 'Maritime Exhibits' in J. Azzopardi, *St Paul's Grotto, Church and Museum at Rabat Malta* (Malta, 1990), 453-66.
188 MMM, MS 'Segni della Capitana', f. 2.
189 Lib. 223, s.v. *Sagrestia o cassa della messa*.
190 Lib. 413, f. 182; see also J. Muscat, 'An Altar from the Galleys of the Order of St John and The Celebration of Mass at Sea', *The Mariner's Mirror*, lxx, No.4 (1984), 389-95.
191 See Pope Sixtus V's brief in Dal Pozzo, i, 311 and AOM 1761, f. 245 which treats about the warships when in the harbour of Malta.
192 ACM, 'Inventario della Conventuale Chiesa di San Giovanni', ff. 119, 123, 127, 131.
193 AOM 1761, f. 245.
194 AOM 274, f. 210; AOM 1934A, f. 13.
195 Lib. 223 s.v. *Priori del Vascello;* see also AOM 1761, f. 248.
196 E. Sanz, *Breve trattato nel quale con ragioni dimostrative si convincono manifestamente i Turchi, senza che in guisa veruna possano negarlo, esser falsa la legge di Maometto, e vera solamente quella di Cristo* (Catania, 1691). Sanz was a Jesuit father in the college of Malta and consultant to the Holy Inquisition.
197 For Cagliola, see AOM 1926, 'Istruzione ai Cappellani' and for Manso, see AOM 1927, 'Istruzione ai Cappellani di Galera'.
198 AOM 1761, f. 284.
199 Boisgelin, 307; for more details see J. Muscat, 'Mass at Sea on Warships of the Order of St John' in J. Azzopardi (ed.), *Portable Altars in Malta* (Malta, 2000), 59-75.
200 Dal Pozzo, i, 21.
201 DeCaro, 105, 110.
202 T. Davidson, *Chamber's Twentieth Century Dictionary* (London, 1943), s.v. Assassin.
203 AOM 1761, f. 245.
204 AOM 270, f. 111v; AOM 1761, f. 245.
205 Ciantar, 99, 100.
206 Lib. 1222, ff. 42v, 60v; Lib. 273. f. 163; W. Schellinks, *Journey to the South* (Rome, 1983), plate 17, shows the chaplain standing on the *spalliera* of the Christian galley holding the clergy cross during an encounter at sea. A galley graffito at St Roque Church, Balzan shows the chaplain holding the clergy cross.
207 Lib. 1222, f. 61.
208 Lib. 211, f. 266.
209 AOM 1768, f. 80.
210 Dal Pozzo, i, 553, 554.
211 Bono, vii, *passim*.
212 AOM 1927, ff. 88v-92v: '*Dell'amministrazione del S. Viatico agli infermi sulle galere fuori*

di Malta' and ibid., 92v-7v: '*Dell'amministrazione dell'Estrema Unzione agli infermi sulle galere*'.
213　Lib. 223, s.v. *Morte*.
214　AOM 1761, f. 289.
215　*Regula,* 35v, 36v.
216　P.P. Castagna, *Malta bil-Gzejjer taghha* (Malta, 1869) Parti III, 21.
217　*Leggi*, 89, II.
218　Ibid., 90, VII.
219　Ibid., 91, XII.
220　Ibid., 101, I.
221　Ibid., 102, IV.
222　Ibid., 103, IX.
223　Ibid., 104, XIII.
224　Ibid., 105, I, III.
225　Ibid., 106, III.
226　Ibid., 107, XV.
227　Ibid., 108, XVIII.
228　Ibid., 113, XXIX.
229　Ibid., 135, XXIII.
230　Ibid., 136 XXVI, XXVIII.

Chapter V

THE FIGHTING TOOLS

The fast warships of the Order and the bravery and skills of their crews were of scarce value without the proper fighting tools.

The Order regularly spent large sums of money to obtain the necessary ammunitions and weapons such as guns, swords, muskets, and shot. Tons of steel, bronze, and iron had to be imported.

Artillery changed with the times. As time went on and especially towards the end of the eighteenth century, guns began to be more skilfully constructed and they became far more dangerous. New standardized types of guns also appeared.

It is best to describe the arms carried towards the beginning of the eighteenth century by the galley, the prime fighting vessel.

A galley carried five guns on the bows. The one placed in the middle under the *rambata* was known as the *coursier* and had two smaller ones placed at either side. The *coursier* fired 36- or 40-pound cannonballs. By 1750 a Maltese *capitana* carried a 36-pounder *coursier*, two 8-pounder sacres, and two 6-pounder minions under the *rambata* together with 18 swivel guns and 18 musquetoons.[1] The reserve *coursier* mentioned in the archives of the Order was not actually carried on a galley but, most probably, kept at the Birgu arsenal. There was absolutely no space for two coursiers under the *rambata* of a galley.[2] De la Gravière maintained that the Maltese galley carried two 48-pounder cannon, one of which lay in reserve in the *corsia*. It also carried four other 8-pounders and 14 swivel guns along the sides. According to the same author, a large 36- or 48-pounder coursier, two 8-pounders, two 6-pounders, and 12 swivel guns on the *apostis* were carried by the French galleys of the seventeenth and eighteenth centuries.[3] Apparently by the last decades of the eighteenth century the galleys of the Order were provided with 24-pounders for the *coursier* and 12-pounders for the lateral guns kept under the *rambata*.[4]

The figure mentioned in connection with a gun refers to the weight of the cannonball it could fire. Thus a 40-pounder gun fired a 40 lbs cannonball, while a 4-pounder fired a 4-lb-cannonball. The principal calibres of guns up to the eighteenth century were 36-, 24-, 18-, 8-, 6-, and 4-pounders.[5] In the fifteenth and sixteenth centuries there were cannon of different calibres primarily used on ships. Land guns were frequently much larger. The Turks, for example, carried gigantic land guns for their sieges.

Although it seems that the Maltese galley carried two coursiers, one in its proper place and one in reserve, only one was used at any one time. It was rather a difficult operation to change these guns around on the seas.[6]

On 15 November 1657 the council ordered that galleys should have two guns known as sacres on either side of the *coursier* in place of the *masfelti*. These sacres had already been in use for some time previously. Guidotti[7] gives a concise description of the armaments a galley used to carry. He gives fragmentary information but it seems the following armaments were carried: a large cannon not identified by name, two 20-pounders called *moiane* or moyanas,[8] two sacres, and four mounted heavy muskets. According to Bosio, in 1562, the galleys had a moyana which is positively identified in the description of Romegas's attack on an Algerian galleot.[9] After the victory at the Dardanelles in 1656, the Order's spoils included 73 bronze guns. Dal Pozzo says they were 76 in number, most of them 60- or 80-pounders and 24 swivel guns all made of bronze.[10] Seventeen of them were of the same type as those used by the Order and were retained. The others, on the advice of Fra R. Cotoner and Fra Fabrizio Ruffo, were to be melted down and recast as *masfelti* which were guns that weighed 8 *cantari* and fired 8 pound cannonballs. The two knights were of the opinion that these cannons were of a more useful size but only 12 were to be cast as an experiment. If they proved successful, they could utilize all the bronze, about 820 *cantari*, of the captured Turkish guns. This proposal of 15 October 1657 was approved by the grand master and the council and was later put into effect. Apparently these *masfelti* were not very popular because they were soon replaced once more by the sacres which were 8-pounder guns on the *capitana* and 6-pounders on the other galleys.[11]

THE FIGHTING TOOLS

A sacre *of a galley: Palace Armoury*

Model of a small swivel gun as found on the side of a galley

A musquetoon mounted on a fork

One such sacre at the entrance to the Palace Armoury in Valletta bears the legend M. MAG. LASCARIS AD USUM TRIREMIS SUAE FUND. ME. F.F. 1688 (*Magnus Magister Lascaris ad usum triremis suae fundavit me*) meaning 'I was cast by Grand Master Lascaris in 1688 to be used on his galley'.

Small swivel guns known as *petrieri* were placed along the side of the galley. Lib. 627 shows a representation of the grand galley of the Cotoner brothers. On one side, near the *rambate*, can be seen a cannon that is out of proportion with the rest of the ship. The periers were mounted on the *apostis* so as not to interfere with the oars.

Sometimes large heavy muskets known as musquetoons were fixed on the rambate. These muskets were too heavy to handle and so were mounted on a fork. An engraving by Jacques Callot to be found at the Cathedral Museum, Mdina shows such a large musket or arquebus mounted on a galley's rambate. Guidotti mentions '*quatro archibusi da posta*'.[12] On the papal galley *San Francesco* there were also '*sei archibusi da Posta*'.[13]

A proposal was also made for two small falcons to be fixed on the poop to defend that part of the galley.[14] The falconet was a small gun that fired small 1- or 2-pound cannonballs. In the fifteenth and sixteenth centuries, the different sizes of cannon were called after the names of reptiles or birds of prey. Since the art of fighting with guns was in its infancy, strange or frightening names of eagles and mythological monsters were used so that their very names could terrify the enemy.[15]

There were also hand-held arms such as muskets, pistols and swords.

The Vilhena Codex punished harshly anybody who took up arms during a quarrel, or kept pointed instruments either on his person or in his house.[16] Obviously this law applied even more strictly on the galley because of the danger that such weapons could fall in the hands of the slaves or could be used in a quarrel between seamen.

The guns

Guns in those days required far more skill to fire. It was important for the bombardier to be both precise and fast in his work. After every firing, the gun had to be drawn back from the gunport, the bore cleaned, the gunpowder loaded from the muzzle and the cannonball

THE FIGHTING TOOLS

inserted. Only then was the gun placed once more in its firing position and fired.[17]

When battle was engaged for a long period, the muzzle of the gun would become very hot. This would result in an expansion of the bore that reduced the strength of the powder charge. It could also bring about the explosion of the gun itself which would severely maim or kill anybody near it. The gunpowder could also ignite as it was being loaded, severely injuring the bystanders.

To reduce these dangers a hot gun used to be smeared with lard or tallow or if time did not allow it, simply wetted with vinegar. During the thickest of battle the gun used to be doused with water.[18]

Guns then needed many ancillary tools and a good bombardier had to be skilled in their use. The most important tools were:

1. Ropes with four blocks to pull the gun forward into its porthole. Two other blocks were used to pull the gun back after firing. All these blocks and tackles used to be hooked to the carriage which was sometimes painted red.[19] Red seems to have been a very popular colour with the Order. Even the decks of the ships occasionally were coloured red so that during battle the crew would not be demoralized by the sight of flowing blood running through the scuttles.

2. Two levers one straight edged and the other forked used for better directional aiming. The first one was used to move the carriage in position. The other crow-bar with one end that resembled a pig's foot, was used to raise or lower the gun's cascabel in position.

3. A worm and hook were used to clean inside the barrel after every round. The worm was a spring-like iron contraption which, like the hook, was fixed to the end of a wooden handle. These two tools were used to clean any cartridge debris left in the bore after each shot. Another soldier then washed the bore with a wet sponge.

4. The ladle and the ram; the former was used to insert a cartridge of gunpowder while the latter was used to press the cartrdige, the wad and then the shot into the barrel.

5. A lighted covered fire was carefully nursed. This container was meant to protect the fire from being put out by the wind and from igniting the gunpowder.

6. A powder flask filled with fine gunpowder. This was kept by

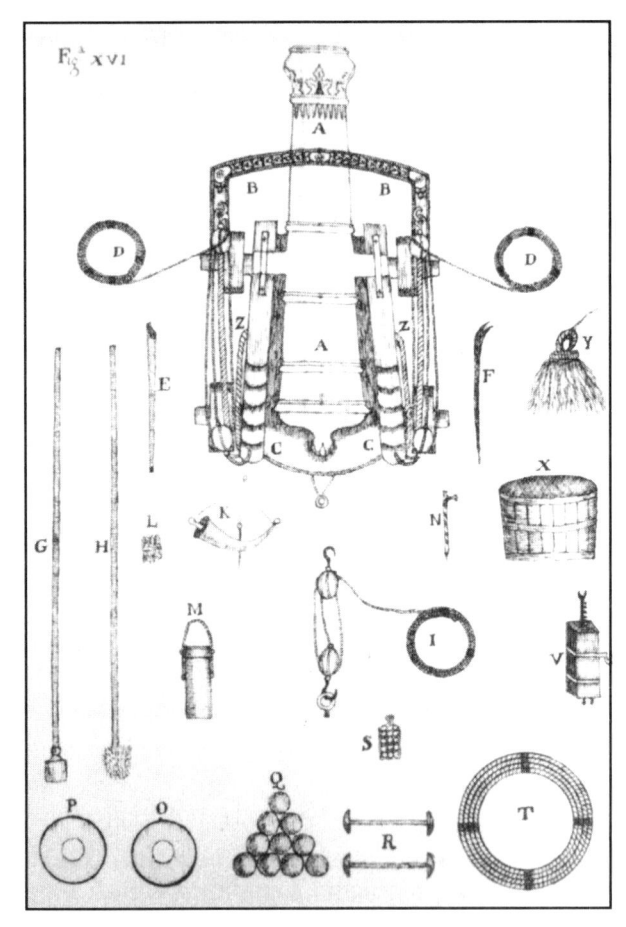

A naval gun and its accessories: NLM 172

An ivory powder flask: Palace Armoury

another soldier who had to fill the touch hole to assist the ignition. Before this a linstock used to be inserted through the touch hole to make sure that the cartridge was pierced so that the fuse could be embedded in the gunpowder. The touch hole was then primed and the cannon fired.[20]

The guns in Malta were made from imported metal. Sometimes the Order imported its raw materials from Salonica.[21] Like other powers, the Order must have bought some guns from Sweden which had a plentiful supply of iron ore.[22] However, the best and cheapest way to obtain guns was to seize them from the Turks. After the battle of the Dardanelles, for example, the Order's booty included 73 guns.[23] At another time a large ship was seized near Salonica which was carrying a cargo that included iron, lead, and tin, all materials that were used for the production of guns and shot.[24] The Order kept a particular watch for such ships which kept it supplied both with artillery and slaves.[25]

Guns were made either of bronze or of iron.[26] The iron gun was longer and slightly thicker than the bronze one.[27] It seems that only bronze guns were cast in Malta in the arsenal at Vittoriosa and the other just inside the main entrance to Valletta, Porta Reale.[28]

Since a gun could be cast with some flaw there were many tests intended to check the finished product.

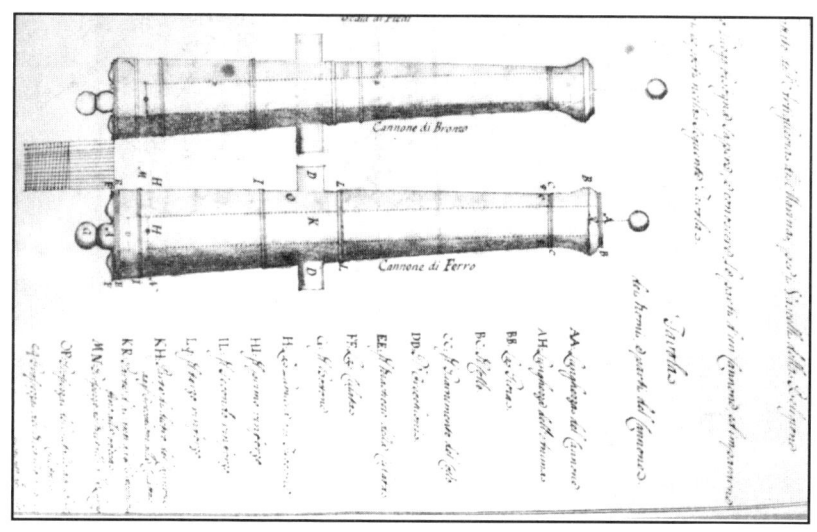

Comparison between a bronze (top) and an iron (bottom) naval gun

To see whether the barrel was cracked, the interior could be lit up by the sun's reflection by a mirror placed near the muzzle's mouth. A hooked iron rod was inserted to measure the depth of the cracks. If they were too deep, the gun would shatter after a short service. Flawed guns were melted down again.

Smoke and water were also used to inspect the gun from the inside. The touch hole and the muzzle were sealed and a little gunpowder in the barrel ignited. If there were the least crack in the gun, the smoke from the explosion would seep out. This experiment could also be performed with water instead of smoke.

Another test consisted of placing the gun in a trench and loading it with more gunpowder than it would normally ever be charged with. If the gun could withstand such an explosion, it would theoretically never shatter under normal use.[29]

After slaves, guns were the most useful and most sought-after prizes by the knights. Following a battle, after the number of slaves captured, prominence was given to the number of guns taken. This was so in the battle of the Dardanelles and in many other cases.[30]

The swivel gun

The perier or swivel gun looked like any other gun, except that its breech was half-open. A chamber was used instead of the cartridge of gunpowder. These chambers fitted exactly in the same place as the cartridge in the other type of cannon.

The perier had the advantage that one could prepare a number of charged chambers before battle was engaged. It was also quicker to clean and it could be turned round by one or two men.[31]

Periers were made either of bronze or of iron.[32] Such guns could not have been very large since they were mounted on a fork-like contraption where the trunnions fitted.[33] Some sources say that swivel guns could take up to 30 or 40 pounds of shot.[34] But such periers were certainly far too big to be mounted on the sides of a vessel. Since only a quarter of a *rotolo* of gunpowder was used for each chamber, the guns could not have been of a very large calibre. A swivel gun as mentioned by Darmanin Demajo could not take a 30- or a 40-pound shot as this required a 9- or 10-inch bore.

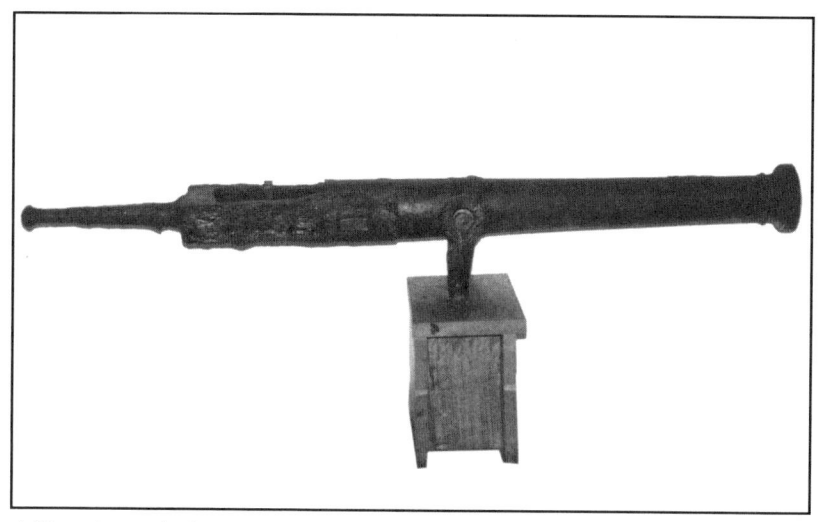

A Venetian swivel gun

The principal divisions till the sixteenth century were the culverin, a long and narrow cannon, the cannon used on land and sea, and the *petriera* which was somewhat short and had a wider bore than either of the others. The latter only fired stone cannonballs. This was not a swivel gun and it could fire projectiles of considerable size.

The Lascaris gun is called a demi-cannon by Darmanin Demajo and further down he gives its dimensions correctly as follows: length 7 feet and calibre 3.37 inches. Such dimensions were, however, those of a sacre and not a demi-cannon which was 11 feet long and had a 6-and-a-half inch calibre.[35] In his list the author inexplicably never mention the sacres and yet these guns were very often mentioned in the records of the Order. Later on, when the author gives the weight of cannon shot from 15 to 20 lbs, he refers to the half-swivel gun and says that 'The half swivel guns were abolished from the galleys and substituted by demi-cannon in virtue of a capitular decree dated 15 November 1657.' Here he is in disagreement with another decree[36] which says in the marginal notes, when referring to the artillery found on the galleys, that 'it was determined that the galleys should not be armed anymore with the *masfelti* which were introduced few years before but instead to carry four sacres as was established in November 1657. The *capitana* was to be armed with 8-pounder sacres while the other galleys to carry 6-pounder sacres. For saluting purposes the sacres of the *capitana* were to fire a five-pound charge while the other galleys were to use four pounds.' Therefore if the author is referring to the *masfelti* these had an 8 pound calibre[37] and they were replaced with 8- or 6-pounder sacres. Here it seems certain that the author is erroneously referring to the sacres as demi-cannons as he had done earlier in the case of the Lascaris gun.

Originally a perier, as the name itself indicates, used to fire shot made of stone. However, iron cannon balls were later substituted. Bits of iron, marble, stone, and other such projectiles were often used against human targets. Swivel guns were also put on the sides of vessels to deter boarding parties.[38]

Such periers were also found on caiques and on galleots and other small vessels.[39]

A good number of bronze chambers used for swivel guns can still be seen in the Malta Maritime Museum. These chambers were round and had a touch hole and a handle so that they could be quickly inserted and removed from the breech of the gun. They were narrower at one end to make insertion easier and so that they would not wobble when in position.[40] An iron or bronze wedge was passed from one side of the breech to the other fixing the chamber in place and preventing its sudden ejection after firing.[41]

Later on the swivel guns started being more used for saluting important personages.[42] They were still encountered, however, in the eighteenth century.[43] It could well be that its shape was much changed in the latter century.

In Malta, where no fifteenth- or sixteenth-century perier is to be found, only some chambers are left to remind us of this piece of artillery.

Gunpowder

The Order obtained its prepared gunpowder from Genoa and Leghorn, amongst other sources.[44] Very often, however, to reduce the possibility of some catastrophic explosion and for economic reasons, the knights imported only the raw materials which were then mixed together in Malta in special munitions factories as needed.[45] Grand Master Lascaris left a foundation for the acquisition of arms and munitions for the needs of the island. Amongst other things, it says: 'Moreover, the acquisition was to include refined saltpetre up to 5,000 *cantari* together with the necessary sulphur and charcoal in proportion to produce gunpowder.' However, this foundation was later availed of for the arming of a seventh galley.[46] The ingredients of gunpowder were saltpetre, sulphur, and charcoal, the proportions being varied for different intended uses. Occasionally the Muslims provided the gunpowder for the knights who seized it from captured vessels.[47]

Whenever the Maltese corsairs seized a vessel, the cannonballs, the gunpowder, and all other munitions became the sole property of whoever had armed it for the *corso*. None of the crew, not even the captain, received a share of the munitions.[48]

Gunpowder was first invented by the Chinese, from where the knowledge passed on to the Arabs.[49] From 1300 onwards the Arabs started using gunpowder; indeed, the first person to fire a gun was Ibn Khaldun.[50] The first recipe for gunpowder was written by the Greek Marc in 1300. While some ascribe the invention of gunpowder to Roger Bacon and Berthold Schwarts of Germany, Hitti unequivocally says that Bacon's recipe is apocryphal.[51]

A mill was necessary in the production of gunpowder.[52] It was one of those mills inside Fort St Angelo that exploded on the night of Tuesday 19 June 1565 during the Great Siege. Ten people died in the explosion which blew off the roofs of the mill and an adjoining store as two *cantari* of gunpowder exploded with a deafening roar. At first it was thought that the explosion was the result of sabotage but it had been continuously

A caique supplying a ship with powder, modern painting by Paul Busuttil

at work for a long time. A spark from the grinding stone had set off the disastrous blast.[53]

Close to the factory, there was the oven from which fine wood charcoal dust was obtained, the refinery and cauldrons for saltpetre, and the still for the saltpetre.[54] With all these fires about, it is small wonder that explosions were a fairly regular occurrence at munitions factories.

Saltpetre, sulphur, and wood charcoal used to be mixed in a ratio of 6:1:1 and the mixing operation could take 24, 30, and even 36 hours. So long as the mixture remained damp there was little danger of an explosion. The gunpowder was then laid out to dry. It was then reduced to powder and graded according to fineness.[55]

The Order apparently kept a monopoly of the manufacture of gunpowder. Anybody caught manufacturing gunpowder illegally was sentenced to three years on the galleys. Also anybody caught trying to export gunpowder clandestinely received a five-year rowing sentence. This applied to both buyer and seller and the gunpowder itself was confiscated.[56] Similarly, anybody caught with either gunpowder or even a fuse at his house or who sold the same either wholesale or retail received a five-year sentence on the galleys.[57]

Similar regulations applied to the galleys' crews. Ordinance 14 of 15 February 1684 forbade the selling of gunpowder on galleys, the penalty for which was five years of rowing.[58]

There were two keys to the room where the gunpowder was stored. One of these keys was held by the captain and the other by the chief bombardier. A very close watch was kept over the gunpowder and the lead shot. After every caravan the clerks had to account for every shot and every ounce of gunpowder.[59] Even during target practice an account was kept in the registers of the gunpowder stores of every shot fired.[60]

A particular store for gunpowder was situated in the place originally intended for the auberge of England. On 12 September 1634 this store exploded with a loss of 20 lives. Since the same store had also exploded six years previously, Grand Master De Paule decided that another store be built on the Marsamxett side of Valletta which was actually constructed years later.[61] A large building to serve as a munitions factory was eventually built at Floriana close to the hospice for old people. The building also included suitable accommodation for the knight in charge of the establishment. The inscription on the door said:

Aedificium Nitri
Summo consilio Em. Magni Magistri
F.D. Emmanuelis Pinto.
A Fundamentis Excitatum An. Dom. MDCC.LXII[62]

In 1662 the Order lost another great quantity of gunpowder when lightning struck a lookout post on the ravelin of the counterescarpment of Valletta. This finally decided the Order to distribute its gunpowder in a number of different sites[63] in order to minimize the danger of a vast explosion.

Another gunpowder store was sited on the Corradino side of the Grand Harbour at Ras Ħanżir. This was paid for by the Balì Fra Bartholomew Tommasi from Cortona to house the Order's munitions.[64] It is mentioned in the pragmatic order of 15 January 1795. This order shows how difficult the Order was finding it to cope with its expenses and was always trying to economize on everything.[65]

The mortar

The French invented the mortar. According to some historians, Chev. de Ressons was the first one to design a mortar for a ship[66] in 1680. Two years later Du Quesne built a successful prototype. At first the mortar was used to fire stones but a special bomb was later utilized.[67]

The mortar, which looked like a short tubby cannon, fired the largest projectiles. The knights had two types of mortars; the German mortar, which was comparatively long and narrow, and the French one, which was short and had a wide bore. A French mortar was cast with a length of four or three-and-three-quarters calibres while the German type used to be six times the calibre equivalent to the diameter of the bore.[68] In 1960 a small-four inch calibre iron French type of mortar was found in Marsamxett which can be seen in the Malta Maritime Museum.

The mortar bomb had two small handles or eyes from which two men could grip it by means of hooks. One mortar bomb can be seen in the Norman House, Mdina, while another one with a wooden cross on it was placed on top of the niche of St Paul at Saqqajja Square in Rabat. The one in Norman House clearly shows the two small handles. It was deliberately made out of the worst type of iron so that it could splinter into tiny bits on

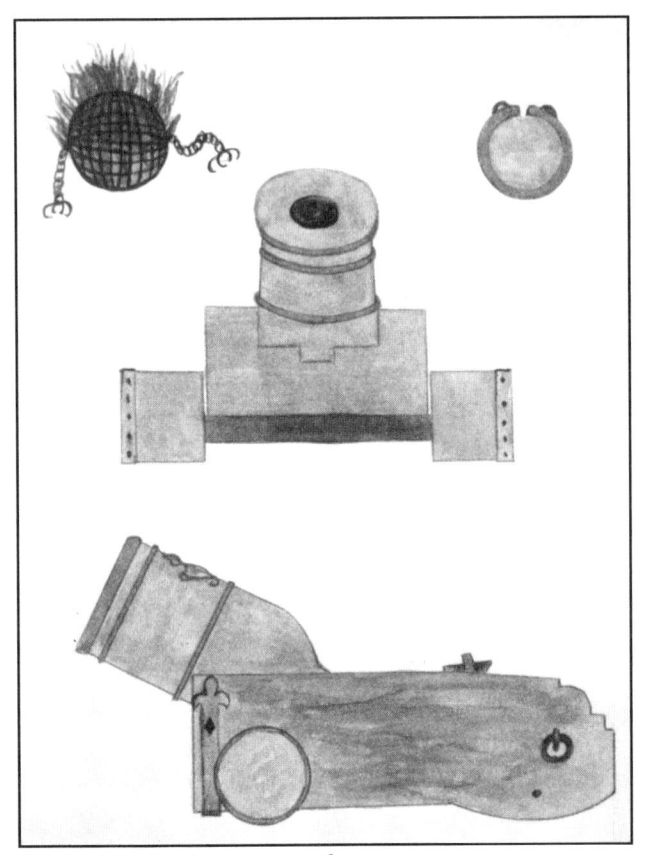

Mortar and bombs; seventeenth-century

A bomb shell

exploding.[69] It was a gunpowder-filled shell with the hole that had been used to insert the gunpowder being stopped by a wooden plug with a hole in it to serve as the fuse. The longer the fuse the longer the explosion was delayed; so a skilled bombardier had to judge exactly where it was wanted.[70] When the mortar was fired, the fuse ignited and so the bomb would be projected with its fuse alight. Although originally the fuse used to be lit before the mortar was fired, it was later found that the fuse lit automatically when the charge was ignited.[71] It was, of course, extremely hazardous work. Sometimes the bomb exploded within the mortar, killing the bombardiers themselves, while at other times it either exploded prematurely harmlessly in mid-air or even failed to go off at all. When the *palandra* or mortar ship, was used to attack coastal cities, the bomb stood a better chance of hitting its target. Care was taken to anchor the mortar ship in line with the target, out of reach of hostile fire.[72] In the nineteenth century the mortar bomb started being aimed better. The bomb retained its shape but the timing fuse became more efficient and the danger of premature explosions was greatly reduced. The mortar was permanently fixed at an angle of 45 degrees so aiming was simply the result of increasing or decreasing the charge.[73]

In the eighteenth century the mortar started being mounted on a carriage which allowed the muzzle to be raised and lowered. The mortar was, however, never lowered less than 12 degrees when used on land so that the bomb could bounce and reach a greater distance. At sea the mortar was always fired at the same 45 degrees elevation of the older mortars.[74]

Mortars could have different bores. The English and the French both had mortars with bores ranging from 10 to 13 inches, which obviously fired bombs with a similar diameter. The first mortar bombs had a 14-inch diameter and carried from 14 to 15 lbs of explosives. The bomb weighed 145 lbs, so to be projected over a distance of 1,900 *tese*, 38 or 39 lbs of charge were needed. In the eighteenth century it was possible to install 12-inch mortars on ships.[75] Most probably the mortar bomb exhibited in the Norman House did not belong to the knights at all for it has a diameter of only 10 inches. It could very well have belonged to the English who had brought two mortars from *Stromboli* to use against the French vessels anchored in the Grand Harbour.[76]

The mortar could also fire another type of bomb which was the carcass frame. The carcass was filled with rags socked in wax and oil which caught fire when the charge exploded.[77]

The cannonball

The cannonballs as used by the knights consisted of iron round-shot or hard stone or marble made to fit the bore of the cannon.

Occasionally the iron cannonball was heated till it became red hot and was then fired on its path of fire and destruction. It was a hazardous job to fire such red-hot cannonballs and, to prevent them from igniting the charge, a wooden plug and wet rags were inserted before the projectile.[78]

Another type of cannonball was known as the canister or grapeshot. This was a cartridge full of small shot which were meant to disperse on being fired, thus increasing its effectiveness.[79]

A cannon could also fire pairs of cannonballs. There were two types of pairs of cannonballs. The first-type balls were joined together by a chain and were thus known as 'chain shot'. In the other type each cannonball had a kind of hook meant to slip into the hook of the other. A pair of cannonballs was intended to tear the sails and the rigging of enemy ships as they spun on their deadly course. Every cannon had five of these handy to be fired[80] but it seems that, occasionally, there were ten to every gun.[81]

The cannon could also be loaded with old bits of iron, lengths of chain, nails, and other shrapnel. When this was fired, a frightening rain would sweep the decks of the enemy ship. Dal Pozzo recorded the deadly effect

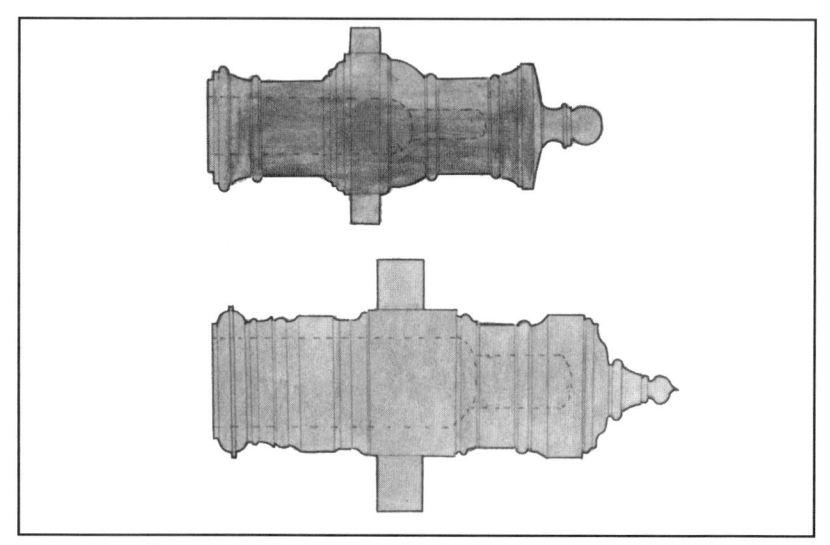

Comparison between a German (top) and a French type of mortar

of one similar great gun when it was correctly aimed and fired against a Turkish royal galley. The charge consisted of small lengths of chain, big nails and lead pellets, which '*vi fece una strage incomparabile, portando via la poppa*'.[82]

Hand bombs

The hand bombs of old were of two types: explosive or incendiary. The incendiary bomb, also known as the trumpet, looked like a large tin canister with two iron prongs meant to stick to the wooden sides of the vessel. It was fitted at one end of a metre-long wooden pole which was slung round before the hand bomb was released.[83]

The explosive hand bomb was equivalent to a hand-grenade. It was made out of worst quality iron so that it could shatter into tiny fragments on exploding.[84]

The throwing of these hand bombs demanded a fair degree of skill[85] and soldiers were specifically trained for such duties. Before a ship was boarded, skilled grenadiers placed on the galley's *rambata*, would sweep the hostile vessel's deck with a precise shower of hand bombs.[86]

The periers could be seen along the side of the galleys and big mounted muskets were placed on the *rambata*. The knights and the other soldiers

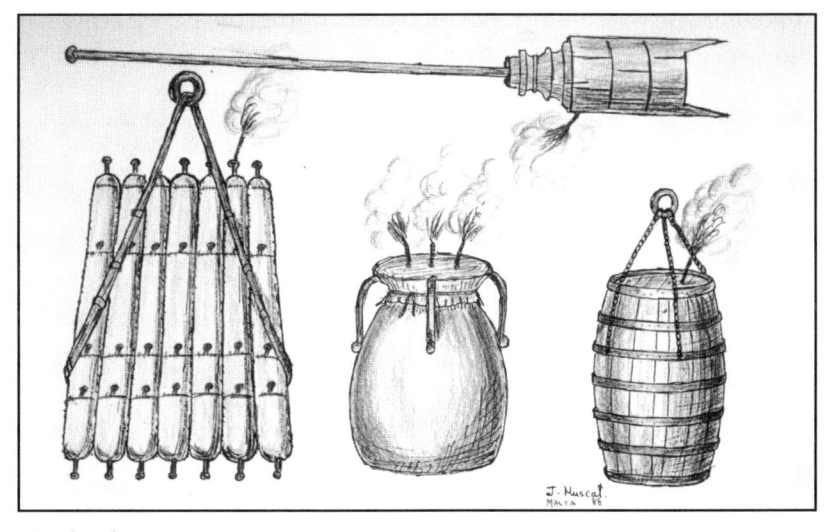

Fire bombs

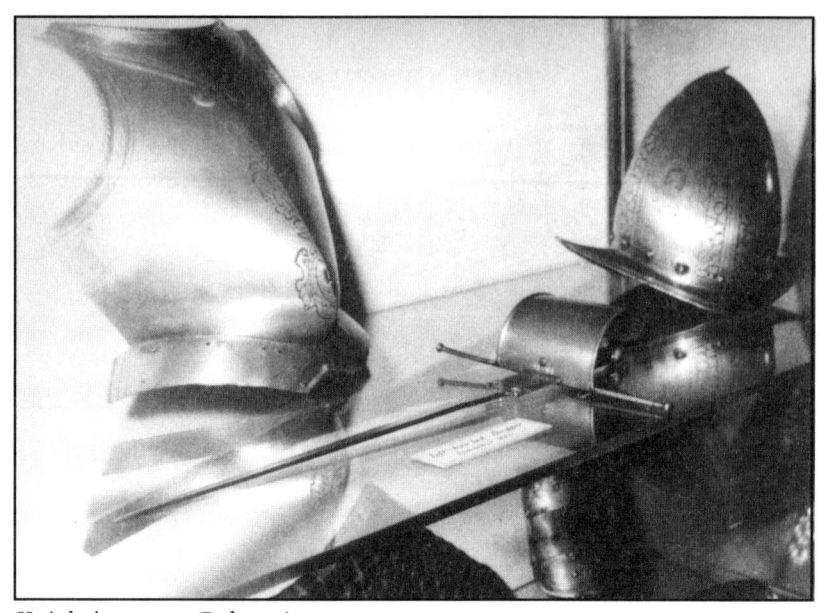

Knights' armour; Palace Armoury

could carry these muskets or arquebuses which fired solid iron or lead balls.

Each knight on a caravan took his own weapons.[87] He had to take with him on the galley a chain-mail hauberk which became obsolete by the first decades of the seventeenth century, a cuirass, a helmet or morion, and the red overall with a white cross known as *sopravesta* or surcoat. He also had to have two arquebuses or an arquebus and a crossbow with all its appurtenances, swords, and daggers.[88] Towards the beginning of the eighteenth century, a knight had to take two arquebuses on board which he could borrow from the palace armoury. The weapons were carefully examined on shore just before the departure to see whether they were carefully maintained.[89]

The fire barrel

A barrel could also be used as a deadly bomb. The barrel would be filled with gunpowder and hand bombs. Then, the fuse having been ignited, it would be swung from the vessel's spars or antennas with the intention of dropping it onto an enemy's vessel close by.[90]

Very often such a barrel exploded prematurely and so it was rarely made use of, especially since the deck of the attacking galley was always packed with soldiers and the *ciurma*. In addition it could not be used in choppy seas as this made the aiming of the swinging barrel almost impossible.

Swinging the fire barrel; drawing by Joe Mallia

The fire pot

The fire pot or *pigniatta* was the equivalent of the modern Molotov cocktail. A man could hurl it between 25 and 35 paces. The *pigniatta* or earthenware bottle, was made out of poorly-baked clay so that it could shatter more easily. It was filled with gunpowder, unrefined saltpetre, sulphur, oil, pitch, and other inflammable material.

The pot had a long neck and it was plugged with a thick piece of paper or a rag. It was then wrapped up with a musket's fuse which was ignited just before the bomb was thrown. The pot would then break and the fuse would ignite the explosive mixture spilled over a large area. Such a fire was not easy to extinguish.[91]

The fire shirt

The fire shirt or *camicia di fuoco* consisted of a number of compartments packed with gunpowder and sewn together. Each section had a particular fuse so that the shirt could explode simultaneously and cause large scale damage.[92]

As the knights and the Muslims were fighting it out on deck, some Maltese sailor on a caique would approach the enemy's vessel, nail the shirt to the far side, ignite it and make a hurried escape. The fire shirt the equivalent to a modern limpet mine, could also be used by night

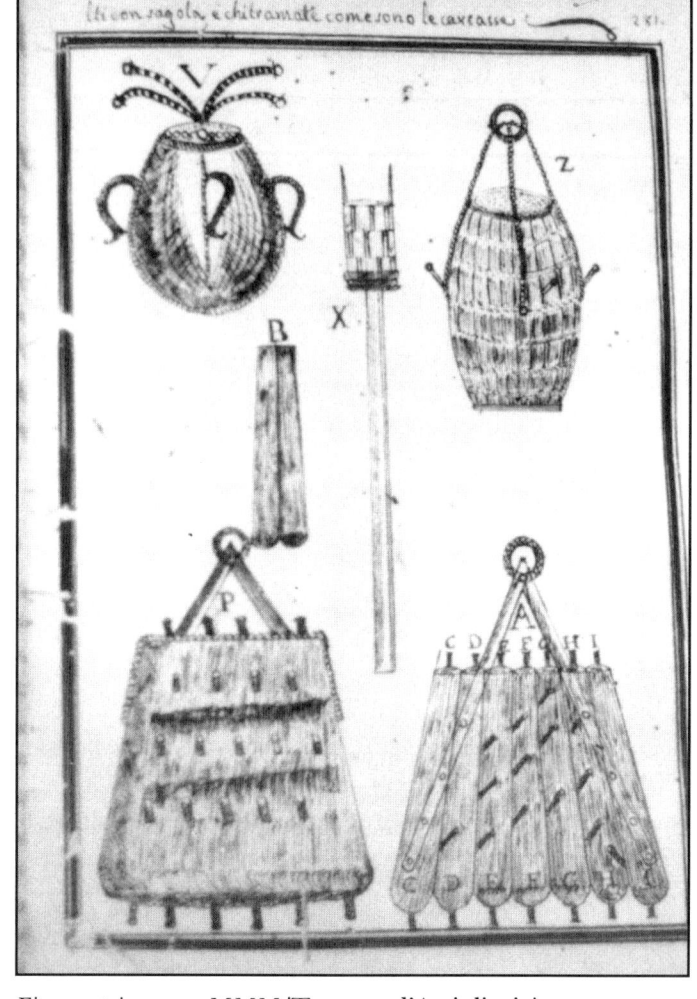

Fire contrivances; MMM 'Trattato d'Artiglieria'

when the enemy was sheltering within his walls. The fire shirt was also an excellent weapon for sabotage.[93]

It needed singular bravery to fix a fire shirt under an unceasing shower of cannonshot, musket fire and arrows. One had to get right along one's target and hammer a large nail to which the fire shirt was attached. The enemy naturally would try to douse the fire my means of bucketfulls of water but once ignited, the fire shirt was impossible to extinguish.[94] The sack was obviously nailed on the far side of the vessel from which the fighting was taking place and, as far, as possible, in a position sheltered from enemy fire. The fire shirt could also be used to burn down the gates of a fortress or a city.[95] However, to burn a city's gate, a petard was more frequently used.[96]

184

THE FIGHTING TOOLS

NOTES

1. F.H. Chapman, *Architectura Navalis Mercatoria 1768* (New York, 1967), see introduction under La Capitana; see also D. Macintyre and B.W. Bathe, *The Man-of-War* (London, 1968), 37.
2. AOM 1759, f. 388v.
3. J. de la Gravière, *Les Derniers Jours de la Marine a Rame* (Paris, 1885), 117, 194.
4. AOM 1934A, f. 15v.
5. 'Compendio', f. 58.
6. Dal Pozzo, ii, 489.
7. Lib. 413, f. 180.
8. For more information, see M. Lewis, *Armada Guns* (London, 1961), 30, 133.
9. Bosio, iii, 456.
10. Dal Pozzo, ii, 241.
11. AOM 1759, ff. 389, 390v.
12. Lib. 413, f. 180; see also AOM 1759, f. 386.
13. A. Guglielmotti, *Storia della marina Pontificia* (Rome, 1886-93), i, 185.
14. AOM 1759, f. 390v.
15. Guglielmotti, iii, 85.
16. *Leggi e Costituzioni Prammaticali* (Malta 1724), 103, XI.
17. Lib. 318, f. 176: *Esercizio del Cannone in cinque Tempi.*
18. Lib. 223, s.v. *Cannone Riscaldato.*
19. AOM 1877, f. 142.
20. 'Compendio', f. 12: *Cannone armato in atto di combattimento* and ibid., f. 42 lists tools for the firing exercise of a gun: *Baga, Pedisciat, Gancietto, Rifulatore, Anata, Garagoro,* and *Cocchiara.*
21. AOM 258, f. 230v.
22. Gravière, 162; see also AOM 271, f. 170v which mentions: *Cannoni alla Svedese, no.36 scudi 7200.*
23. While AOM 1759, f. 389 mentions that 73 guns were taken. Dal Pozzo, ii, 241 says that 76 were brought to Malta.
24. Ibid., i, 782, 783.
25. Ibid., ii, 55, 56.
26. 'Compendio', f. 15.
27. Lib. 318, f. 152.
28. A.P. Castagna, *Malta u il-Gzejjer Taghha*, 112; see also F. Denaro, 'Houses in Kings Way and Old Bakery Street, Valletta', *Melita Historica*, ii, No.4 (1959), 201.
29. 'Compendio', f. 42 *et seq.*; Lib. 223, s.v. *Cannone.*
30. AOM 1759, f. 389; Dal Pozzo, i, 587.
31. P. Earle, *Corsairs of Malta and Barbary* (London, 1970), 139.
32. Lib. 223, s.v. *Petriere.*
33. Ibid., s.v. *Maimonetti di Petrieri.*
34. G. Darmanin Demajo, 'Stray Leaves from the Navel History of the Order', *Daily Malta Chronicle*, 19 January 1927, 12, Swivel gun (*petriera*) under weight of cannon shot shows 30-40 lbs.
35. Macintyre and Bathe, 38.
36. AOM 1759, f. 390v.
37. Ibid., f. 389v.
38. One can see an eighteenth-century iron swivel gun at the MMM.
39. Lib. 223, s.v. *Maimonetti di Petrieri.*
40. Ibid., s.v. *Mascolo del Petriere.*
41. Ibid., s.v. *Chiavetta del Petriere.*
42. AOM 1759, f. 388; the marginal note reads: *Cannoni petrieri si portino dalle galere per*

il salutare.

43 Lib. 1222, f. 20: this is an eighteenth-century MS.
44 Dal Pozzo, i, 125; ii, 100.
45 Ibid., i, 477; ii, 142, 143.
46 Ibid., ii, 193.
47 Ibid., i, 587.
48 (Leggi), 99, XXXVII.
49 Guglielmotti, s.v. *Polvere*.
50 P. Auphan, *Histoire de la Méditerranée* (Paris, 1962), 103.
51 P.K. Hitti, *History of the Arabs* (London, 1970), 664.
52 Guglielmotti, s.v. *Polvere*, but see also s.v. *Mulino di Polvere*.
53 Bosio, iii, 566, 567. There are a few slight differences in F. Balbi, 82, 83 who says 112 lbs. of gunpowder were lost and that there were eight dead.
54 Guglielmotti, s.v. *Polvere*.
55 Lib. 318, ff. 187, 188.
56 *Leggi*, 136, XXXII.
57 Ibid., 136, 137 XXXII.
58 AOM 1845, f. 402.
59 Ibid., f. 386.
60 AOM 1845, f. 402.
61 Dal Pozzo, i, 828. This was actually built in 1665; see ibid., ii, 331 and AOM 261, f. 27.
62 G.A. Ciantar, *Malta Illustrata* (Malta, 1772), refers to '*Aedificium: Dirsi dovrebbe latinamente 'Officina Nitri ad Militores usus conficiendi'*.
63 Dal Pozzo, ii, 302
64 Ciantar, 80
65 Lib. 429, f. 38.
66 *Histoire de la Marine* (Paris, 1934), 160.
67 Lib. 223, s.v. *Mortaro*.
68 'Compendio', f. 104.
69 Lib. 223, s.v. *Bomba*.
70 Ibid., but see also 'Compendio', ff. 96, 99 which mentions the use of the fuse. Lib. 318, f. 180 describes briefly the timing of the bomb; the wooden plug for the fuse was made of pine, ash, or beech.
71 Lib. 223, s.v. *Bomba*.
72 'Compendio', f. 102.
73 Ibid., f. 101.
74 Ibid., f. 104. During their stay in Malta the French had similar mortars; see W. Hardman, *A History of Malta during the Period of the French and British Occupations 1798-1815* (London, 1909),160.
75 'Compendio', f. 101.
76 Hardman, 158, 206; Mcintyre and Bathe, 42.
77 Lib. 223 s.v. *Vasa a fuoco*.
78 Ibid., s.v. *Palle infocate*.
79 Ibid., s.v. *Mitraglie* and Lib. 318, f. 179. The Turks had something similar, see Bosio, iii, 219.
80 Lib. 1222, f. 20.
81 Lib. 318, f. 179.
82 Dal Pozzo, ii, 191.
83 'Compendio', ff. 95, 96; Dal Pozzo, ii, 397; Bosio, iii, 215.
84 'Compendio', f. 96; Bosio, iii, 771 gives detailed information. See also Francois de Malthe, *Traite de Feux* (Paris, 1640), 36. Dal Pozzo, i, 800, 827, describes the power of these hand bombs used by the Maltese soldiers against the Muslims.

85 Bosio, iii, 771.
86 Dal Pozzo, ii, 291.
87 AOM 1759, f. 118.
88 Bosio, iii, 457.
89 AOM 1761 f. 263: '*Fatta la rassegna delli armi delli caravanisti a finche tutte si trovino sufficienti e di servizio alle occasioni.*'
90 'Compendio', ff. 95, 96.
91 Bosio, iii, 561.
92 Lib. 318, f. 180; Lib. 223, s.v. *Camicie a fuoco;* see also 'Compendio', ff. 95, 96.
93 Dal Pozzo, ii, 35, 36 describes the attack on the harbour of Tripoli by means of fire-sacks.
94 Ibid., i, 635
95 Ibid., ii, 522: '*per attaccare una camicia di fuoco all Porta*'. This describes the attack on Santa Maura in 1684
96 Ibid., i, 648 and Francois de Malthe, 52 *et seq*. gives detailed information about the construction of the petard.

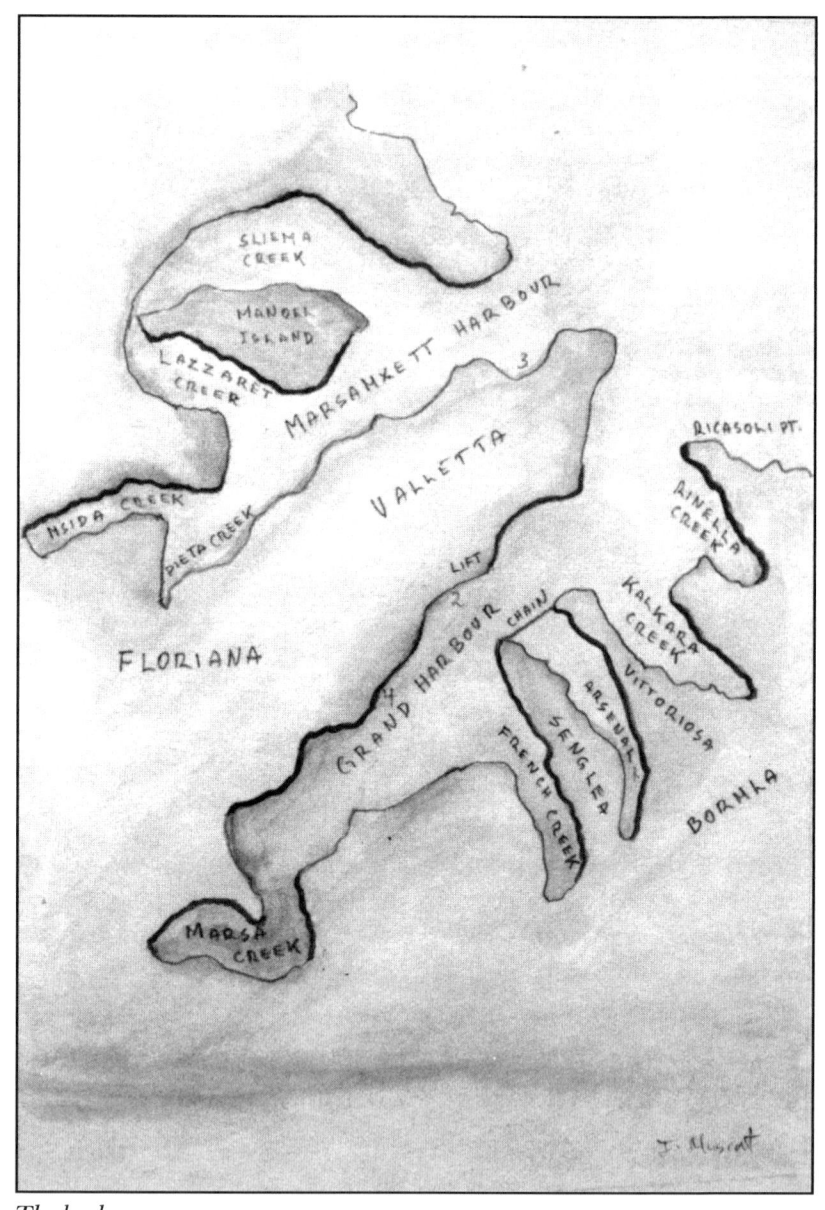

The harbour area

Chapter VI

BUILDING AND FITTING-OUT OF THE MALTESE GALLEY

Life in Malta always revolved around the harbour. The foreign occupier always sought to control the port and to have enough Maltese working there. The Order did not act any differently but, owing to the wealth it brought to the island, the Maltese as a whole saw a definite rise in their standard of living.

It was under the knights that the port flourished most. The Order of St John's and the island's whole existence depended on ships and, therefore, on the harbour.

Under the Order the Maltese shipyards became especially renowned for the construction of galleys.[1] Other vessels such as tartanes, *xprunari*, brigantines, chebecs, ships-of-the-line, and frigates[2] were also built locally but it seems that some large ships were sometimes built in foreign shipyards.[3] Large ships were sometimes built in Malta: the *Santa Caterina, La Santissima Vergine del Pilar e San Giuseppe*, and the *San Giovanni,* all large ships-of-the-line, were constructed locally at the ships' arsenal located behind Senglea.[4]

The shipyards

There were four galley shipyards in use in Malta during the Order's stay. The largest and the best-equipped shipyard or arsenal was the one at Vittoriosa which was built in 1597 and enlarged in 1696.[5] The first arsenal mentioned was that of 1538 but its whereabouts are not known. In the chapter general of 1538 it was stated that 'having considered that it is with great effort and expenses that timber, oars, sails, and other

The Birgu galley arsenal; drawing by Josian Bonello

munitions are bought for the construction and maintenance of the vessels of the Order, the sixteen reverend capitular members ordered and instructed that a suitable and convenient place be considered and chosen for the construction of an arsenal; and in the meantime [have also established] that the above-mentioned timber, oars, sails, and the rest of the munitions be placed and guarded securely in stores and also that an experienced commander of the arsenal be bound to give accurate and legal accounts according to our statutes'.[6] In 1554 a new *capitana*, the *Santa Maria della Vittoria*, was launched in Malta when Fra Stefano d'Arzac was the commander of the arsenal.[7] However, there was another galley, the *Santa Maria Madalena*, which was the first to be built in Malta. It was launched in 1545.[8] The creek between Vittoriosa and Senglea was well known as Galleys Port.

The three other shipyards were situated in Valletta. One was to be found near the lift in the area of the Customs House. That arsenal was built by the Prior di Venosa Fra Girolamo Salvago in 1652 who generously paid for all expenses incurred. It was built in a ditch of Valletta beneath the post of Italy known also as the Upper Barracca.[9] The arsenal had two arches as it is well-represented by one of the drawings by Schellinks.[10] Another one lay near Fort St Elmo on Marsamxett side. There is a hint about the existence of this arsenal in Dal Pozzo when he referred to the Post of Germany as extending from the head of the Forbici from the mouth of the arsenal up to St Elmo. That arsenal was abandoned also

The Santa Caterina *store, Bormla*

and taken to Birgu as that was the most convenient place for the building of galleys.[11] Rossi placed the location of this arsenal in an area on the Marsamxett side of Valletta comprising the space between St Andrew bastion and St Elmo. But near St Andrew bastion there was the *manderaggio* and not an arsenal. Most probably the arsenal was situated below the English curtain, exactly near the Jews Sally Port. It seems that this arsenal was a simple, provisional, wooden shed and not a strong masonry construction.[12] Some authors refer to a fourth shipyard which apparently was situated in the area known as the Old Calcara near Crucifix Hill. On 22 April 1667 the wooden roof of the Birgu galley arsenal was taken down and its timber was employed in the building of the Old Calcara arsenal.[13] This last shipyard could have been situated near where the Pinto Stores stand today.[14]

On the other side of the Grand Harbour, near No.1 Dock, there were the stores of the ships-of-the-line. One can still see their names on the doors of four of those stores to this day. These were more precisely known as *Cantiere delle Navi*.[15] The names that can still be seen are the *Nave S. Giovanni*, the *Nave S. Caterina*, the *Nave S. Giacomo*, and the *Nave S. Gioseppe M(aria)*.

The arsenal situated near the lift had the most unfortunate history of all. This was a real pity because this yard was much needed and was ideally suited for the building of galleys. Its stores were in the place where hired cars are parked nowadays.

This arsenal caught fire on 26 February 1685. It is said that the previous day a spark from the fire that was used to prepare the oakum for caulking had fallen unobserved on the sawdust and the other leftovers of wood. During the night this fire blazed unchecked and rapidly got out of control. On the other hand, Count Ciantar blames the fire on somebody who emptied the embers of a pipe onto the yard from the barracca high above it.[16]

Whatever its origin, the fire soon reached an almost-completed galley and the whole shipyard quickly became a raging inferno. All efforts to subdue the fire proved futile, especially since the bastions at the back of the yard served as a chimney and assisted the circulation of the air. In the end only ashes marked the place where the yard and the galley had been.

To make matters worse, since there was a gunpowder store in the vicinity of the yard, the residents quickly vacated the area. Fortunately the fire failed to reach the magazine, but the devastated shipyard was never rebuilt.[17]

Some people believe that the *manderaggio*, on the Marsamxett side of Valletta, was meant to become another shipyard. The *manderaggio* originally served as a quarry to provide the stone for the building of houses in Valletta. The idea was to keep cutting stone down to sea-level so that a sheltered galley-pen could be constructed. The stone, however, turned out to be too hard to be used for building purposes[18] and the galleys had to remain at Vittoriosa. After all the galleys were well protected at Vittoriosa, the *Porto delle Galere,* where there was even a chain boom across the creek to serve as a protection against some sudden attack.

Pilfering seems to have been quite common in the shipyards, especially in the largest one at Vittoriosa. When the galleys were in harbour, there used to be hundreds of sailors and soldiers roaming around the place. Annoyed by the regular pinching of shipbuilding material, the council of the Order issued a decree that all tools not actually in use were to be kept in the stores, which were only to be opened, even for airing, in the presence of a knight.[19] This need for a guard had been felt for a long time and in 1681 the grand master and the council were aware of this inconvenience.[20]

A group of French knights were specifically remunerated by the grand master to keep a watch over the shipyard.[21] A knight stood permanently on guard duty. He could not move away from Cospicua and was given enough provisions so that he would not have to leave his place of duty. He had the responsibility of welcoming and showing round the yard the admiral or any galley captain. He had to take note of the repairs suggested. If the guard left his post without permission, he would have to spend four days inside his auberge; for the second offence, he would be confined to his auberge for eight days. A further relapse was punished by fifteen days' work on the commander's ship-of-the-line.[22]

The Order enacted severe punishments to protect its property. These included whipping, rowing, exile, and death by hanging. The Vilhena Code was most severe about theft from the harbour and it said that anybody who steals wood that belonged to the Religion either from the *manderaggio* or the wood basin of Cospicua, the Marsa, or the foreshore would be hanged.[23]

The Order, at one time, forbade foreigners who came to arm a vessel for the *corso* and who intended to fly the Order's flag from employing Maltese sailors and soldiers.[24] Occasionally the Order did not find enough people to work at the arsenals and on board ships.

It is true that there was full employment in Malta under the Order but the wages paid were a mere pittance. The knights always took the lion's share of the Muslim booty.

The dry dock of the knights

The idea of a dry dock owes its origins to the knights. Grand Master Rohan started the construction of a dock during his magistracy but the work could not continue because of water seepage.[25] On 27 March 1765 there is information about the warship *San Giovanni* which could not be repaired in a local dock because there was not one on the island.[26]

The major problem in building a dock is the water that percolates into the site, particularly when there are no motorized pumps to drain it.

In 1681 Colonel Charles Grunemberg had come to Malta to visit the fortresses of the Order following a request Grand Master Gregorio Caraffa had made to the viceroy in Sicily. In Malta, Grunemberg devised a machine that could rapidly drain the water from a dry dock. It consisted of a wooden tube with one end placed on the bottom on one

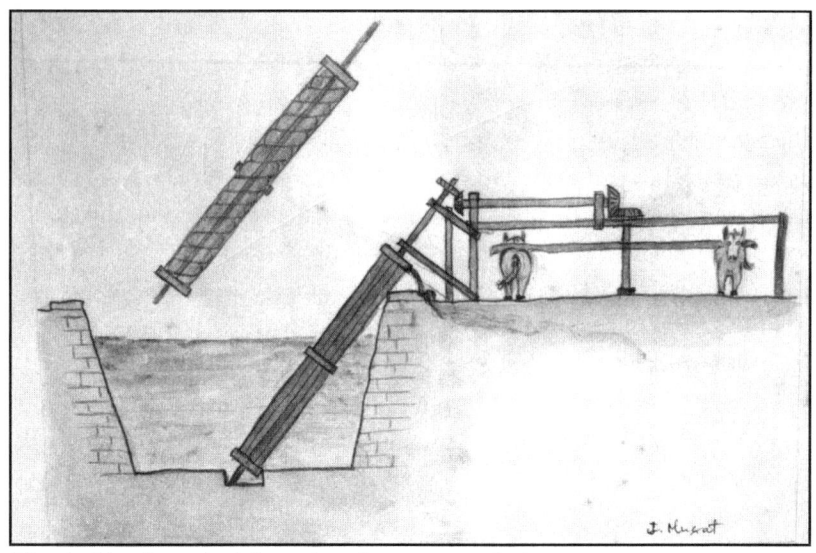

The Archimedes principle projected to empty a dock

side of the dock and the other end out of the dock site. In this tube a large Archimedian screw was used to pump the water out at a prodigious speed. Since the screw was very big and stiff to turn, the work was done by two mules at a time. As the mules slowly went round, a system of four gears turned the mechanism to reduce the difficulty of turning the screw full of water.[27]

A similar but smaller contraption was used to dredge the mud off the sea bottom.[28]

Careening and caulking

The hull of a vessel had to be cleaned regularly since wood tends to encourage the growth of barnacles and weeds more than metal, thus affecting the vessel's speed. A bonfire used to be lit under the vessel's hull to remove the old paint, dry the wood, and kill any woodworm.[29] Such work could best be done in a dock.[30] However, cleaning and caulking could also be done outside a dock.

Such work could also be done at sea. A special barge would moor a little distance away alongside the vessel. Ropes would then be tied from the vessel's mast to a capstan on the barge and, as the capstan was turned, the vessel would heel heavily to one side.[31] Two other barges, one

BUILDING AND FITTING-OUT OF THE MALTESE GALLEY

carrying the workmen and the other the fire for the pitch, then went near the side that had been lifted out of the water. The latter barge was known as the *pegoliera* or 'tar raft'.[32] Such work could also be done with a capstan fixed on the shore. At other times the vessel could also be grounded on a sandy beach.[33]

Since, when a vessel was made to lean to one side, water could enter through the gunports, before a careening operation these openings were sealed by means of wooden frames covered with waxed tarpaulin to make them waterproof. Such sealing was also carried out in stormy seas to prevent water from entering through the gunports.[34]

During the careening process, a fire was lit under the vessel's hull to melt the old pitch down and burn the old paint off. Necessary repairs were then carried out, worm-eaten planks replaced, and the seams sealed again with oakum and melted pitch. During the caulking operations, an officer knight supervised the work and he was expected to see that it was carefully done.[35]

Oakum consisted of old sails and ropes boiled together till they become one piece. This mash was then dried either naturally or in a furnace. During the caulking operation an officer knight supervised the work and had to see that it was carefully done.[36]

When the caulking operation was completed, the whole hull was covered with a mixture of pitch, sulphur, and resin.[37] While protecting the hull against rot, this mixture also increased the vessel's speed as this

Careening a galley; NLM 413

operation also cleaned and smoothened the hull below water-level.[38] The paint for the section above water level was made of red lead and linseed oil as primer, with a second coat of linseed oil, white lead, and colouring powder.[39] The whole caulking operation was not done regularly; instead the caulker quite often only sealed the seams, the heads of the nails, and the ends of wooden pins just with resin.[40]

Careening, on the other hand, was frequently carried out, especially when an operation of the *corso* was being prepared.[41]

Each vessel of the Order had its own caulker who was responsible to see that it did not make water during a voyage. He also repaired any damage caused by enemy gunfire in the sides of the vessel, especially below water level.[42] The vessels also carried all the necessary tools for caulking which had to be returned to their proper places on completion of the work.[43]

Quick repairs could be carried out by stopping the hole with a bale of oakum or covering it with a sheet of lead. If the caulker noticed that the vessel was making water, he was in duty bound to inform the captain without raising a panic amongst the other members of the crew. In such circumstances, a sail was thrown over the damaged side and securely fastened with ropes. Oakum was then inserted between the hull and the sail and the ropes drawn to tighten the sail.[44] The ship, temporarily repaired, made for the nearest landfall where more permanent work could be done.

The *Macina*

A painting exhibited in the Fine Arts Museum in Valletta shows a sort of large wooden crane jutting out on the sea from Sheer Bastion at Senglea. This crane was installed by the knights but it was also utilized by the English until they replaced it with an iron structure. The crane was dismantled and sold for scrap in 1927.

The knights' equipment consisted of two wooden beams jutting out over the sea from the top of the bastion that rose sheer from the water. It was used to lift masts off the vessels and to perform other heavy work. The masts, the guns, and all other heavy equipment were always removed whenever a vessel returned to harbour to reduce the unnecessary load and strain on the ship.[45] The crane's

BUILDING AND FITTING-OUT OF THE MALTESE GALLEY

The macina *or Sheer Bastion on Senglea side*

winch or capstan lay on the bastion. As it was turned, the ropes would tighten and the masts were slowly eased out of the ship and deposited onto the shore.[46]

While describing the Vittoriosa yard and its buildings, Count Ciantar describes the *macina* as being constructed out of wooden beams which could lift the masts off ships by means of its blocks and ropes.[47] The wooden beams themselves were regularly replaced.[48] Whenever the third rates would be out of harbour, the person in charge of the *macina* was expected to paint this contraption with pitch and to strengthen and repair it as necessary.[49]

The gun pontoon

While the *macina* was mostly used for the removal and the installation of masts, guns were more frequently loaded and unloaded by means of a special barge. This barge or pontoon had a relatively low freeboard and it used to moor alongside the vessel that was to be armed. The guns were lifted with a winch by means of a rope tied to the barge's mast. In this way guns could be loaded and unloaded without interfering with other work on the ship.[50]

The gun pontoon; MMM 'Compendio'

This barge was also used to transport guns to and from Gozo or where necessary. On such missions the galleys accompanied the barge to tow and protect it.[51]

Large ships had their own means to load and unload their guns which consisted of a thick rope, like the one used for anchors, tied to the main and fore tops of the mainmast and the foremast. These burten pendants were provided with iron eyes at their ends and were suspended a little below the tops of these masts. They used to tie a large block that could be used for loading and unloading heavy objects from the deck or the hold.[52]

The weaving of sails

Malta had established a reputation for weaving a long time before the arrival of the knights. This explains why Maltese sails were much sought after,[53] although this work continued to flourish under the knights. The Order mainly used its own slaves to weave its sails.

Sails were woven at Vittoriosa near the arsenal. When the Order built a new bakery in 1545, the top floor was divided between an office for treasury officials and quarters for the sailmakers.

Bosio almost seems to imply that the weaving of sails was introduced to the island by the Order, possibly meaning that such work increased with the heavy demand of the galleys and other vessels. At one time Pietro della Calibia, a converted Muslim, instructed the slaves in weaving.[54]

Sailmaking was primarily entrusted to female slaves. Young and strong slaves committed to the rowers' benches on galleys but older ones, or ones who were weak or crippled, were made to weave sails. The following are two sample entries from a list of 78 slaves taken at sea from a Turkish galleot near Sapienza:

- 20 Caramemet, son of Bubarca from Tripoli, aged 20, a Negro having a great wound and seven small ones on his right arm;
- 21 Musa Caradinghis, who does not know his father's name, aged 31 *circa*, with various crescent-shaped cuts on his left arm.[55]

A selection for the various tasks for the slaves was carried out on their return to Malta.

The weaving of sails was considered as important as the forging of weapons. The slaves detailed for weaving sails were to perform no other duties, according to an order of the Council. Moreover, their overseer had to submit monthly reports of the work done. Any sick slave had to be reported to the council by the overseer who had to give his name, surname, any distinguishing marks, and the number of days missed from work. The overseer could not change the work routine of the slaves without permission.[56]

A Muslim slave by Joseph Muscat

The dredging carrack

No remains of the Order's galleys have ever been found in the Grand Harbour which the knights used to keep spotlessly clean. They forbade the dumping of the ballast into the sea in the fear that this could ultimately render the creek between Vittoriosa and Senglea too shallow for the galleys.

The knights had a special barge to dredge the bottom called 'carrack'. This vessel had a large wheel turned by slaves, which rotated a chain to which a number of buckets were attached. The rotating wheel sent those buckets to the bottom of the harbour to scoop up the sediment from the sea floor.[57] Another barge was moored alongside the carrack to take away the dredged material.

In normal circumstances 29 slaves worked on the carrack, together with a guard and a clerk.[58] In emergencies more workers were detailed to help in the operation. A bill paid by the congregation of the galleys on 27 September 1738 for the dredging of Cospicua creek illustrates the lack of available slaves. Indeed, in addition to paying for the barge which transported the mud to Marsa, the Order had to pay for the services of a watchman, two divers, and seven young men who lifted the dredged material. The mud and sediment were carried in canvas or gauze containers.[59] Between 1 May 1745 and 30 April 1746, 784 gauze-wire containers were returned to the shipyard's stores.[60]

A dredger in front of the galley arsenal

It often happened that ships lightened themselves while in harbour by dumping the ballast. Severe laws prohibited the dumping of the ballast in harbour. A third offence brought about the confiscation of the vessel.[61] The ballast stones were transported to Marsa on barges.[62] Though the entry in the document is here referring to the dredged mud, even stones were dumped in the same place. A captain had to obtain his ballast stones from specific localities.[63] Since the ballast was normally placed in very restricted quarters on ships, it was usually loaded and unloaded by young children.[64]

The recovery of anchors

It was fairly common for a vessel to lose an anchor either because of violent seas or because it stuck so firmly to the sea floor that they had no other alternative other than to cut the cable and let it go.

The recovery of lost anchors was carried out by two caiques working together. A rope weighted down with two cannonballs stretched from one caique to the other was lowered to the sea bottom so that it could entangle with abandoned anchors. The two caiques traversed a wide stretch of sea at any one time.[65]

When an anchor was found, a man in a bronze diving bell was lowered to the bottom. The diver then hooked the anchor and gave the signal to

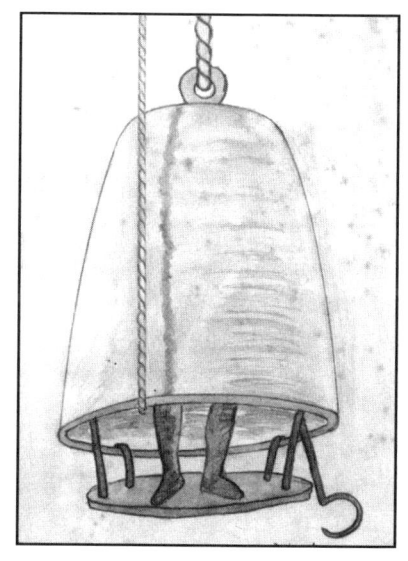

A diving bell

the attending vessel,[66] which hauled it aboard. Captains of ships were reminded that when they lost an anchor in the harbour they had to recover it and also not to leave any rubbish behind.[67]

The chain boom

During the siege of 1565, a creek of the Grand Harbour was protected by means of a chain boom. This was nothing unique to Malta, because an etching by Erhard Reuwich shows a chain protecting the port of Rhodes.[68]

Until 1546 the Grand Harbour was never protected by a boom defence. In 1533, when there were rumours of an imminent Turkish assault, the knights closed the harbour's entrance by lining all their ships side by side. They also moored the great galleon in front of them and a large Venetian vessel at their back for a better protection.[69]

In 1546, during the magistracy of Juan D'Omedes, the first *gran catena* or great chain was brought from Venice to protect the creek between Vittoriosa and Senglea.[70] Such a chain boom was cheaper and easier to handle than closing the main harbour opening with vessels.[71] A chain was also quite safe since galleys moored alongside each other could easily be burnt by hostile incendiary devices.

The chain boom mentioned in the Great Siege was not the one bought by D'Omedes. In 1563 it had been replaced because it had become greatly weakened by rust. Grand Master de Valette therefore ordered the forging of a stronger and longer chain which stretched from St Angelo point to Senglea point. According to Bosio, it was 300 paces long and that it was the longest and thickest chain of its time.[72]

At the Senglea end, the chain was fastened to one of the large anchors which belonged to the grand carrack and which had been firmly embedded in the solid rock and at the St Angelo end, a large winch could stretch the chain when and as needed. This meant that ships could only enter and leave from the side closer to Fort St Angelo.

In place, the chain stood about a metre above sea level. During the siege of 1565, a wooden ladder-like structure and well-caulked barrels were tied beneath it to stop even the smallest boat from getting through.[73]

The chain was only put in place when there were rumours of a Turkish assault. The chain was still operational in 1643, 1644, and 1645 and

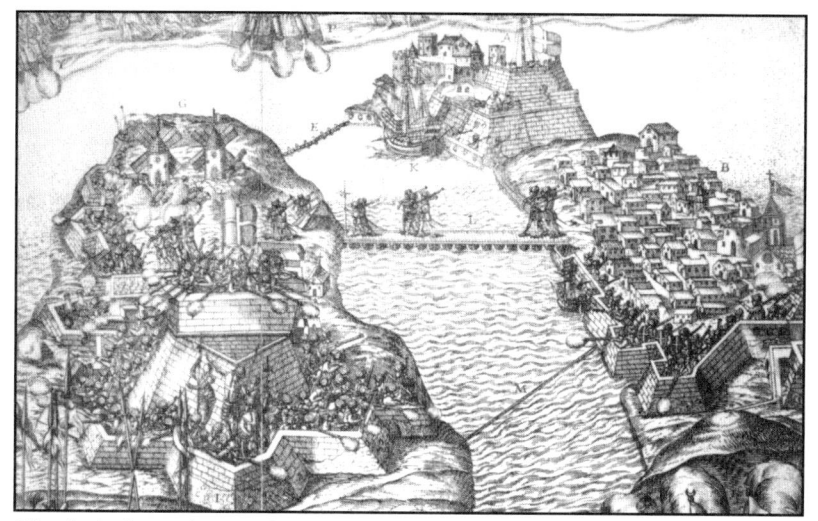

The chain boom during the 1565 Siege; Perez d'Aleccio

every time it is mentioned with the same remark: 'The chain was stretched at the usual place for a greater security of the Harbour.'[74] In 1687 Grunemberg remarked on the chain which used to close Galleys Port, suggesting the building of a low battery at Senglea point which would be more useful than the chain.[75]

Conclusion

The well known chroniclers of the Order of St John like Bosio and Dal Pozzo wrote invaluable information about the knights and their ships but when reading them one will not be able to visualize the portraits of such ships. Yet it is retained that when writing about the ships of the Order the contributions by these two chroniclers is invaluable.

Recent publications by Rossi, Ubaldini, Dauber, Wismayer and Scarabelli were a good step forward for the study of the history of the navy of the Order and together with the scholarly unpublished works by Quintano, Fava, Chetcuti, Caruana Curran and especially Grima established reliable ground work for the study of the organisation of the fleet of the Order.

The great number of drawings of portraits of the ships of the Order included in this study provides an inkling of the days of sailing when the Grand Harbour used to present a fascinating scene of grandeur, colour and busy life of the multishaped ships and boats maintaind by those gentlemen who were the elite of the best European families. Perhaps the work misses the odd vessel of foreign origin and probably not popular amongst the local masters but the iconography presents the great majority of ships and small crafts that once enhanced the charm of the natural beauty of the Grand Harbour.

The study of the period in Maltese history which includes the sojourn of the knights on the Island shows how many local people were employed with the Order especially on the ships. Many others worked at the arsenals and the local workforce developed various skills which subsequently were transmitted as a legacy especially for the people of the Cottonera area. At present one can hear the last boatbuilders round the harbour area repeating words and frases reminiscent of the galley and shipbuilding technology as practised by the knights.

A present-day knight of the Order of St John

Amongst other benefits the local sailors and soldiers gained valuable experience on the ships of the Order as regards discipline, standard of living as they were assigned a regular salary and shares from the prizes taken at sea and above everything else they travelled frequently in the Mediterranean hence gaining a valuable experience as regards the mercantile activities at sea.

The knights brought with them in Malta new hopes and valid scope for the Christain religion. Indeed, Catholicism in Malta flourished as in no other period of the Island's history. The ships of the Order proved to be a reassurance against Muslim intrusion on the Island. However, the local people had to accept and live up with a new phenomenon which was the slavery problem. Muslim slaves men, women and children in their thousands roamed especially round the Harbour area with all the inherent problems for the local people. Such a situation affected the social scenario of the Maltese life and consequently brought with it great social, religious and economic upheavals. Yet when the ships of the Order, for various reasons, were not able to continue with their capturing of slaves at sea there were various repercussions affecting even the local population.

The Order of St John, which since the eleventh century registered unprecedented successes on land and sea, found in Malta the best conditions for the organisation of the fleet. The ships of the Religion meant so much for all Christians and Muslim captains retreated, when possible, whenever the ensign of the Order appeared on the horizon. Indeed, it is hoped that the great work done by the Order will continue in a modified way today especially through the variegated works of charity so long as the members of the Order maintain the original zeal for their institution.

The navy of the Order was a small one, similar to others of her time established in the Mediterranean but it enjoyed a great reputation based on results attained in active service at sea against Muslim shipping. All the crowned heads of Europe were somehow or other connected with the ships of the Order and it was a great honour to travel on one of its galleys.

When delving into the many, yet unsounded, documents deposited in the National archives at Valletta and Rabat together with those found at the Notorial office and at the Mdina Cathedral Museum, one is liable to come across numerous references for the study of the navy of the

A galley of the Order badly damaged but victorious, trailing the enemy's colours behind the stern

Order. The story of the ships of the Order is the same one for the many Maltese who worked, fought and died for a living and for survival during a period when Malta changed fast from a *quasi* insignificant island to a well established centre of attraction in the centre of the Mediterranean.

NOTES

1. E. Rossi, *Storia della Marina dell'Ordine di S. Giovanni di Gerusalemme di Rodi e di Malta* (Rome-Milan, 1926), 103, 105 gives indications of the possible first arsenal for 1538. Bosio, iii, 353 mentions another arsenal for 1554. Dal Pozzo, ii, 12 refers to one built round 1636 and AOM 1877, f. 171 speaks of one in 1782. See also G. Darmanin Demajo 'Stray leaves from the Naval History of the Order', *Daily Malta Chronicle,* 2 February 1927.
2. Rossi, 105; Stray leaves from the Naval History of the Order, *Daily Malta Chronicle* 29 January 1927.
3. AOM 1759, f. 364; Lib. 413, f. 168; Bosio, iii, 22; Dal Pozzo, i, 458 all mention vessels that were constructed outside Malta.
4. Rossi, 83, 93.
5. Ibid., 103; J.F. Darmanin, 'The Building of the Order at H.M. Victualling Yard', Malta *Melita Historica,* 1957, 67, see under Darsena.
6. AOM 286 f. 89; Rossi, 103.
7. Bosio, iii, 353.
8. G.A. Vassallo, *Storia di Malta Raccontata in Compendio* (Malta, 1854) 386, note 1.

9   Rossi, 105.
10 W. Schellinks, *Journey to the South 1664-1665* (Rome, 1983) plates 51, 51A.
11 Dal Pozzo, I, 67.
12 Rossi, 106.
13 AOM 647, f. 90.
14 Castagna, i, 129.
15 AOM 636, ff. 219 *et seq.*
16 G. A. Ciantar, *Malta Illustrata* (Malta, ????), 18.
17 Dal Pozzo, ii, 548
18 Ibid., i, 67: '... *non si fece* (the *manderaggio*), *o sia per la difficolta di tagliar la pietra, trovata durissima in quel sito, o sia per evitare la mal aria ch'averebbe cagionato l'ingresso del mare; o perche in fine cosi convenisse alla Fortificatione, e quel sito si chiamò Manderaggio'*.
19 AOM 1934A, f. 21.
20 Dal Pozzo, ii, 484.
21 AOM 1826, f. 97.
22 AOM 1764, f. 17.
23 *Leggi*, 107, X.
24 Ibid., 93, XXVII, XXIX.
25 Lib. 223, s.v. *Forma o Bacino*; for information about the dry-dock, see K. Ellul Galea, *L-Istorja tat-Tarzna* (Malta, 1973), 34.
26 AOM 272, f. 18v.
27 Dal Pozzo, ii, 483.
28 A. Guglielmotti, *Vocabolario marino e militare* (Milano, 1967), s.v. *Cavafango*.
29 Ibid., s.v. *Spalmare, Spalmo, Brusca*.
30 Lib. 223, s.v. *Spalmatura*.
31 An old painting in the Franciscan Minors convent in Valletta demonstrates the process; see also Lib. 223, s.v. *Puntone*.
32 Lib. 223, s.v. *Pegoriera;* AOM 1899, f. 75; AOM 1899 bis, f. 149; Guglielmotti s.v. *Pegoliera* and *Chiatte*.
33 Lib. 223, s.v. *Dare alla Banda*.
34 Ibid., s.v. *Contro Portello*.
35 Ibid., s.vv. *Scaldare il Vascello* and *Spalmatura;* Guglielmotti s.v. *Calafato*. Occasionally even the deck and the masts were scoured; see Lib. 223, s.v. *Raschiare un Vascello*.
36 Ibid., s.v. *Stoppa*; AOM 1934A, f. 23; AOM 1761, f. 225.
37 Lib. 223, s.v. *Rasa*; AOM 1899, ff. 1, 100.
38 Lib. 223, s.v. *Rasa per la Spalmatura*.
39 AOM 1923, f. 65; AOM 1877, f. 115.
40 Lib. 223, s.v. *Spalmatura Secca*.
41 AOM 269, ff. 24, 27.
42 Lib. 223 s.v. *Calafato*; Guglielmotti, s.v. *Calafato*.
43 AOM 1767, f. 144.
44 Lib. 172, Figure XII.
45 Lib. 223, s.v. *Macchina per Alborare*; AOM 1899 bis, f. 45; Guglielmotti, s.v. *Mancina*.
46 AOM 1899, f. 81: '*Per fare due aspe dell'argano della Machina ...*'; see also Guglielmotti, s.v. *Mancina*.
47 Ciantar, 83.
48 AOM 1899, ff. 44, 69, 83, 86; apparently a new *macina* was built in 1745-46 because it is always referred to as the *nuova Machina*.
49 Lib. 273, f. 114.
50 Lib. 223, s.v. *Puntone*; 'Compendio', ff. 13, 14 gives detailed information as to how cannon were loaded on and unloaded from ships.
51 AOM 269, f. 12.
52 Lib. 223, s.v. *Surponte*.

53 Ibid., s.v. *Tela per far le Vele*.
54 Bosio, iii, 242.
55 AOM 1770, f. 305.
56 AOM 1759, f. 461.
57 Lib. 223, s.v. *Puntone*; AOM 1823, f. 130; Van de Velde, *Drawings* (Cambridge, 1958) 329 includes a 1672 drawing of the dredger.
58 AOM 1823, f. 127.
59 AOM 271, f. 170v.
60 AOM 1899, f. 80.
61 Vilhena, 79, XXX.
62 AOM 1823, f. 130: '*Barcia per trasportare le ciatte alla Marsa*'.
63 Vilhena, 137, XLI.
64 There are many references to *Figlioli che lavorarono in levar la saborra*; see, for example, AOM 1823, f. 134 and AOM 1839, f. 298.
65 Lib. 223, s.v. *Pescare l'Ancora*.
66 Ibid., s.v. *Campana*.
67 *Leggi*, 79, XXX.
68 Chatterton, DETAILS, Plate 2.
69 Bosio, iii, 223.
70 Ibid., 245.
71 Lib. 223, s.v. *Darsena* and *Catena del Porto*.
72 Bosio, iii, 518.
73 Bosio, iii, 510, 518.
74 AOM 261, f. 177v; Dal Pozzo, ii, 72, 80, 103; AOM 258, f. 44, '*si levi la catena dal porto*' and ibid., f. 82 '*che non si metta la catena del porto*'.
75 Dal Pozzo, ii, 633.

GLOSSARY

Admiral – The commander in chief of the Order's navy. The title was used for a period of time during the Order's stay in Rhodes. In Malta the title referred to the head of the auberge of Italy who managed the affairs of the navy but not necessarily embarked on the warships.

Altar – The warships of the Order carried a wooden, collapsible altar for the celebration of Holy Mass when possible. The only known surviving altar is exhibited at the Wignacourt Museum, Rabat.

Altar box or *sagrestia* – A chest carried by a chaplain on board a ship of the Order. It contained all the requisites for Mass and for the administration of the Sacraments.

Antenna – The long and narrow spar to which the lateen sail was tied. It was always made of two parts securely lashed together. The top part, to which an extension for a larger sail could be added was called the *penna* (feminine). The lower part was called the *carro* (masculine).

Apostis – A thick piece of hard wood projecting over the sides of the galley, forming the rectangle of the *talar*. The oars rested on the *apostis* and worked against the thole pins held in it. The *apostis* enabled the oars to touch the water at the same time and at the same distance.

Argusin – The slave driver in charge of the *ciurma* or rowing force on the Order's galleys.

Armateur – The person who invested his money in arming a vessel for the *corso* or for a mercantile activity.

Arquebus – The long and heavy, smooth-bore gun used by the ordinary soldiers. It was fired by means of a lighted match.

Artillery – A group of cannon on a galley or on a ship-of-the-line.

Auberge – A building that housed all the young knights of the same langue together.

Balestriera – A narrow gangway or *courroir* between the rowers' benches and the *apostis* on either side of the galley. Before the introduction of firearms, men with crossbows or *balestre* stood on it during the fighting.

Ballast –Extra weight made up of stone, cannonballs, or lead, stowed away along the hold of a vessel to counteract the force of the wind and to steady the ship on its course.

Banks of oars – see **bench**.

Barbary Coast – The states of the North African coast from Egypt to Morocco.

Barber or *barberotto* – The skilled man who could shave and trim the crew members' beards and hair. He also assisted the ship's doctor in elementary surgical work.

Barrel – Flat-ended cylindrical wooden vessel of hooped staves that could be opened at one end and was used to store salted meat, ship biscuit, and other solid victuals.

Barrel fire – A barrel filled with powder and other combustible material, suspended from a yard of a warship, and swung a few times ready to be dropped on an enemy ship.

Barrel for water – A small type of barrel that could be carried by one man and used to store fresh, drinking water. Those in use on galleys were not round but of elliptical form and were stored near the benches of the rowers.

Baton – The pointed ended stick held by the *argusin* and the *comito* to impose their commands when necessary.

Battery – The cannons on one side of each deck of a ship-of-the-line.

Battallotto – A special type of spur used on the lateen-type of merchant ships like the *tartana* and the *pinco*.

Bench – The place where the oarsmen sat on galleys. The size of a galley was indicated by the number of benches it carried. Benches could be moved about in emergencies.

Bezbuża – The forelock which the members of the *ciurma* were obliged to keep as a sign of their servile condition.

Biscuit – The principal food on ships. It was flat bread which was baked twice for longer keeping. It was considered a provision of war and was prepared in the Order's bakeries. The knights had large stores for provisions and munitions in Messina, Syracuse, and Augusta in Sicily.

Boat – A small type of vessel still common in Malta. It accompanied the galley for running urgent errands. It could even be rigged with a sail and small canopy at the stern, if needed.

Bombarda – see *palandra*.

Bombardier – A skilled man who had to load and fire the cannon. He also had to prepare other weapons such as hand-bombs, fire-sacks, and so on.

Bonadventure – The fourth and smallest mast on a ship. The carrack and the sixteenth-century galleon both had one. The bonadventure later became obsolete on big vessels.

Bonnet – An extra sail rigged up at the lower side of square sails in a good wind, to increase the speed of a vessel.

Bow chaser – A gun, normally a culverin, placed on the bows of a ship.

Breech – The end part of a breech loader gun which is open to take a chamber or *mascolo* which fits the barrel ready for firing.

Brigantine – Square-rigged cargo ship that first appeared at the end of the eighteenth century. It had two masts and a bowsprit. The second mast was rigged with a spanker sail and it was rigged also to take a jib or two. There was another smaller type of brigantine, a freighter with 12 oars and one lateen sail. It had no deck or cabin at the stern although eighteenth-century ones carried a type of stern cabin or awning. It only carried two small cannons

GLOSSARY

and six periers. It was frequently used for the *corso* by Maltese private owners.

Bonavoglia – A freeborn person who commuted a debt into an agreed period of rowing service on the Order's galleys. He was treated just like a slave but could keep a *moustache* as a special privilege.

Caique – One of the galley's tenders. It had a pointed prow and a tramson at the poop and could be propelled either by means of oars or by sails. It was used to attack hostile shipping, drop the galley's anchor, and to fetch water and kindling wood for the mother ship.

Calibre – The fixed measure in pound weight of the round shot that fitted into the relative barrel of a gun.

Camicia di fuoco or **fire shirt** – A fire contraption made up of various components filled with gunpowder and other highly inflammable materials, which was normally attached to an enemy ship and set on fire.

Canne, canna or ***qasba*** – A unit of measurement of length equivalent to 2.096 metres.

Caramousal – A square-rigged Turkish vessel with a very high stern commonly used to carry cargo in Eastern waters.

Caravan – The period of service a young knight had to fight the Muslim either on sea or on land.

Caravanist – A young knight during the period of his caravan.

Carosse – On a galley, the stern cabin or *carosse* was a beautifully adorned and finely furnished covered area reserved for the captain and important guests. On ships without a deck only a canopy could be erected.

Carrack – The largest type of square-rigged sailing ship the Order ever had. It had six decks and a very high freeboard. It was a very heavily-armed vessel and could stand up well to rough seas. There was also a dredging vessel bearing the same name in Maltese. It was a somewhat ungainly vessel with buckets or square boxes fitted on an endless rotating chain to dredge the sea-bottom.

Cask – A flat-ended cylindrical wooden vessel of hooped staves. It had one small opening that could be stopped with a small cork. A cask could also be used to store wine, oil, vinegar, and other liquids.

Cercamar – The young caravanist on board a galley responsible for the cannon, munitions, and all fighting material. He came just after the *re* in seniority.

Chain shot – A solid spherical shot cut in two but joined together with a chain and fitting the relative calibre of a gun. It was meant to be fired against sails and rigging of the enemy. There were various types of chain shot which are indicated in manuscripts of the Order as *angoletti*.

Chamber or ***mascolo*** – The firing charge of the perier. It could be dismantled and loaded beforehand. It fitted in the open breech and was kept in place by a metal key until fired.

Chaplain – The conventual chaplain was a priest, a member of the Order of St John who had to look after the spiritual needs of the knights both in Malta and in the Order's other commanderies all over Europe. A chaplain of obedience was a priest or friar chosen by a conventual chaplain to perform the latter's duties in his stead against payment of a salary.

Chapter General – The high dignitaries of the Order meeting under the presidency of the grand master to draw up administrative rules and to legislate for the entire state.

Chebec – A three-masted lateen rigged ship. It could be propelled by means of oars and could be heavily armed for corsairing. It had a wide beam and could stand up well to winter conditions. It was introduced into the Mediterranean around 1630 but it reached its apex in the eighteenth century with the Algerian corsairs.

Chiourme or ***ciurma*** – The slaves, convicts, and *buonavoglie* who provided the manpower to row the galleys. The same word was sometimes used to mean the entire crew of a vessel.

Clerk – The person on a ship responsible for keeping a written record of events aboard. He also had to keep an inventory of captured prizes.

Comito – The non-commissioned officer of a galley who, like a boatswain, was in charge of the daily running of the vessel.

Commandery – The property of the Order spread all over Europe and administered by a knight, hence called a knight commander.

Congregation of the Galleys – A committee of four senior knights under the presidency of the general of the galleys. This committee was first set up in 1596 and was responsible for all that had to do with the galleys. The congregation of the ships-of-the-line consisted of a senior knight and four other knights and was responsible for all the needs of the squadron of the ships-of-the-line.

Convict – A prisoner condemned to a period of rowing on the galleys.

Corsair – Anybody who armed a vessel to prey on Muslim shipping. The Order had specific laws relating to the prizes, the flag, the munitions, the ransoming of prisoners, and the *ciurma*. Even Muslim corsairs had their own rules.

Corsia – A narrow gangway or passageway between the rowers' benches in the middle of a galley, leading from the *rambata* to the *spalliera*.

Coursier – The 36 to 40 lb. cannon on the galley. It was placed under the *rambata* facing forward on the same line as the *corsia*.

Corso – In Malta, the *corso* meant the official or private war against the Muslims licensed by the grand master. Corsairing was a continuous and profitable venture carried out only against Muslim shipping. The Muslims carried out corsairing activities of their own against all Christian shipping.

Corvette – A type of small square-rigged warships introduced by the French. It had one deck and carried only a few guns. It could be propelled both by sails and by oars.

Culverin – A type of cannon with a very long barrel occasionally used on ships.

Demi-cannon – Small version of a cannon that could fire a 30 lb. cannonball. The barrel had a bore of $6 \frac{1}{4}$ ins and was from 20 to 22 times the length of the calibre.

Demi-galley – A smaller two-masted version of the galley with about 14 to 20 oars, each pulled by a single oarsman. The Order adopted the demi-galley by the second half of the eighteenth century.

Dghajsa – A typical Maltese boat used mostly in the harbour to carry passengers, also known as *dghajsa tal-pass*. The *dghajsa tal-latini* was a large type of *luzzu* that used oars and lateen sails. Until the beginning of the Second World

GLOSSARY

War, it was still regularly used to carry freight between Malta and Gozo.

Dolphin – A dolphin-shaped handle found only on bronze cannons. The handles were two in number and were not always shaped like dolphins.

Dragant – The transversal strong timber resting on the stern stem and which supported the *carosse*.

Falconet or **falcon** – Small cannon, very elongated for its width. It had a 50 calibre length and could fire a ball of 1 $\frac{1}{4}$ or 2 lbs.

Falki – see **washboards**.

Felucca – A type of small vessel that later increased in size. It used to accompany the galleys of the Order but could also operate on its own. The felucca, an extremely light vessel, had pointed bows and stern and was propelled by means of lateen sails and oars that worked on the gunwale.

Figurehead – Ornamental carving, usually breast or full-length figure over the ship's cutwater. On galleys there was no figurehead but they carried the statue of their saint's name on the *carosse* at the stern while the name was put on the *dragant*.

Fireship – This was a ship packed with gunpowder and other incendiary material. It was towed near an enemy ship and set on fire.

Firepot – An earthenware pot filled up with grenades and gunpowder which was hurled over an enemy ship after igniting the fuse.

Flag – The flag on a vessel had a practical rather than an ornamental purpose. It showed nationality and communicated signals. Ships were decked with flags on festive occasions.

Foist or *fusta* – A small corsairing vessel, more common amongst the Muslims. It had one lateen sail, a big jib, and 20 oars. It stood very low in water and carried two or three guns.

Foot – A unit of measurement equivalent to 12 inches.

Foot rest or **stretcher** – A long thick strip of wood fixed to the underpart of the oarsmen's bench so that the rowers could stand on it when pulling at the oars.

Fork – A small two-pointed fork-like iron contraption on a caique on which the antenna rested when not in use. A perier's fork consisted of a thick two-pronged support on which the barrel rested. The fork fitted in the gunwale and could then rotate for directional aiming.

Forty hours' devotion – Forty hours of continuous prayer in front of the Blessed Sacrament, exposed in St John's Conventual Church in Valletta, for victory over the Muslims.

Foundation – An amount of money or property left by a knight to maintain a galley or some other institution by its funds.

Freeboard – That part of the hull between the water level and the gunwale.

Fregatina – A small tender in the service of galleys and other warships. It was similar to a double-ended, small, open boat.

Frigate – A square-rigged vessel smaller than a third rate, that first appeared in the Mediterranean and in Europe in the eighteenth century. The French were renowned for the construction of frigates. Another type was the lateen-rigged frigate, a two-masted open freighter. It also had a few oars, a low freeboard, and a jib. It was common all along the Mediterranean seaboard.

Galione – A nomenclature which referred to a great galley or *capitana*, and was in use by the end of the seventeenth century.

Galeass – A large Venetian galley with lateen sails and oars. It resembled a floating castle and was well armed with guns in the bows.

Galleon – A square-rigged vessel, smaller but faster than the carrack. It was armed with a few large cannon and could sail long distances. Until the seventeenth century, 'galleon' was the generic name for a square-rigged vessel.

Galley – A low, lateen-rigged, multi-oared, extremely fast and manoeuvrable fighting ship. It only carried guns on the bows and it attacked its victims head-on. An armed galley not only carried the artillery required but had a full complement of the *ciurma*, skilled men, and knights.

Galley, *capitana* –The black-painted galley of the general of the galley squadron; it was the senior galley.

Galley, common – The ordinary or common galley in the squadron normally equipped with 26 oars on each side.

Galley, great – A large galley, often with three masts, so called because of its relatively large size.

Galley *padrona* – The second-in-command in a galley squadron.

Galley, royal – The leading galley in a royal squadron.

Galleot – A small extremely fast vessel similar to a galley. It had no *rambata*. It carried only one gun and was a favourite corsairing vessel with the Maltese.

Gavon – Any small compartment of no importance on a galley or other sailing ship. A galley had one in the bows and another under the *carosse* at the stern.

General – The commander in chief of the Order's galley squadron. He was in charge of the squadron while at sea. For a long time this appointment was held only by knights of Italian nationality.

Germa – An eastern cargo carrier, very common among the Turks and sometimes used for corsairing. It had a square sail on the mainmast and a lateen sail on the mizzenmast. The jibboom could also be rigged with a great jib if needed.

Gondola, magisterial – The ceremonial vessel of the grand master used for short trips. It was propelled by means of lateen sails and oars.

Gozo boat or *tal-latini* – The traditional Maltese boat similar to a great *luzzu* which was equipped with lateen sails, hence its nomenclature *tal-latini*. It plied regularly between Malta and Gozo.

Grenade – A round hollow iron shell filled up with gunpowder, made up of the worst material, so that on explosion it would break up in numerous pieces of shrapnel.

Grippo – A large Greek and Roman vessel that carried spices and medicinal herbs from India and Ethiopia. In time it came to mean a hospital ship. It could even be armed for corsairing.

Hatch – One of the six openings on the deck of a galley through which passed all provisions and spare parts for the galley below deck.

Hydrography – The art of navigation, commanding ships, and the preparation of marine charts.

In articulo mortis – Literally 'in the article of death' meaning at the point of death.

Inch – A unit of measure; the twelfth part of a foot.

Infidels – Christians referred to Muslims as Infidels and vice versa.

GLOSSARY

Jib – A large triangular sail rigged in the front section of a ship.

Knot – A nautical measure of speed (one sea mile per hour) and formerly measured by a logline divided by knots at equal distances of 1/120 of a geographical mile (every 14.7 yards). The number of knots travelled in half-a-minute corresponded to the number of sea miles travelled per hour. One sea mile equals one and one-sixth statute miles. Time was kept by an hour glass.

Lanthorn – The great lantern rigged on the stern of a ship.

Lateen rig – Ship using oars and triangular sails on antennas.

Levant – The eastern Mediterranean waters from Sicily to Palestine.

Londra – A Turkish cargo carrier, much used in the Black Sea. The same size as a demi-galley, it was sometimes armed for corsairing.

Luzzu – A typical Maltese open boat, with pointed ends used mostly for fishing.

Maona – A Turkish vessel. In the thirteenth century, it resembled a galley with a lateen rig and was used mostly to carry cargo. In the fifteenth and sixteenth centuries, the same word came to mean a square-rigged three-masted vessel. It used to be well armed and was normally deployed in the vanguard of the galley squadron.

Manderaggio – A shelter pen on a sea front for galleys or boats.

Marabout – A type of Muslim hermit especially common in North Africa.

Marana – Venetian vessel, mostly used in the Adriatic to carry firewood and building material.

Marciliana – Round-bellied Venetian sailing ship, mostly used in the Adriatic. It had a very high prow and vertically cut poop. Sometimes it carried four instead of three masts.

Mascolo – see **chamber**.

Masfelt – A type of cannon of the same size as a saker or sacre.

Mogarbina – The largest Muslim sailing ship of the sixteenth century. It resembled a heavily-armed galleon and frequently the Muslim squadrons. It was then known as the *sultana*.

Moiana or *mojana* (minion) – A cannon similar to a saker or sacre but of a slightly smaller calibre and less power.

Moor – An Arab from the Maghreb.

Mortar – Squat piece of ordnance for firing bombs at high angles. A mortar always kept the same inclination and approximate aiming was achieved by increasing or decreasing the amount of gunpowder used as a charge.

Musket – A gun, smaller and lighter than an arquebus, much preferred by the knights.

Muslim – A follower of the Islam.

Musquetoon – A great musket which fitted on an iron fork as it was too heavy to fire it from the shoulders.

Oakum – Loose fibres obtained by picking old ropes and pieces of cloth and boiled for a long time, then woven into lengths of various thickness and used to fill spaces between seams while caulking.

Oar – The wooden instrument by which one rows a boat or a vessel. The blade was the flat part that enters the water. The shaft was the round part which extends from the sea to the tholepin. The loom was the rest of the oar from the tholepin inwards. The loom of a galley was provided with grips for the benefit of the rowers.

Oculi – A high relief or painting of a human eye placed on either side of the bows of Maltese traditional boats to ward off the evil eye.

Orca – A square-rigged cargo carrier much used by the Venetians, the Turks, the Dutch, and the Swedes. It was flat-bottomed but had well rounded sides. It had three masts and a very long jibboom. It stood up well to wintry conditions.

Ordinances – Authoritative decrees issued by the chapter general either to strengthen or to repeal existing laws.

Pace – A unit of measure equivalent to one pace; about five feet.

Padrone – Local master of a vessel.

Palandra – A ship that carried one or two mortars; it was also known as bomb ketch.

Palma – Length of the hand used as a unit of measure. It was equivalent to $9\,{}^2/_3$ ins. A palm is today equivalent to $10\,{}^5/_{16}$ ins.

Patacca – A coin equivalent to one fourth of a brass *tari* and was *c.* $3\,{}^1/_2$ cm in diameter.

Pavesades – A sort of protective planks of wood that could be fitted to a galley's rail before battle. When entering or going out of harbour, the pavesades were made of cloth and bore the colours of the Order.

Pedana – The wooden board beneath the rowers' feet on a galley which was placed on but leaving a space from the deck and was provided on one side with a foot rest.

Pegoliera – see **tar raft**.

Pendant – Long triangular flag used for signals or for decoration.

Perier – A type of small cannon with the barrel half-open at the breech, from where it was loaded with a chamber. It was mounted on a rotating fork and in a way that the barrel could be raised and lowered for aiming.

Petacchio or *patache* – A type of ship, similar to a small galleon, that first appeared in the Mediterranean in the sixteenth century. It could stand up well to winter conditions and was used to carry cargo or for corsairing. It carried from eight to ten guns.

Petard – A specially prepared type of mortar formerly used to blow in gates of besieged cities. It could make a great explosion with a loud report.

Petriera – A piece of ordnance similar to a short cannon with a large calibre that fired a stone cannonball. It was often made out of bronze with a large bore but narrowing at the breach.

Pignatta – see **firepot.**

Pilot, royal – The one employed on a *capitana* of a monarchy like that of Spain or France. See also **steersman**.

Pink – Square-rigged ship with a high stern used both for fighting and for carrying cargo.

Pollacca – A type of ship with a lateen-rigged foremast and square-rigged mainmast and mizzenmast. It was principally a cargo-carrier but it was sometimes prepared for corsairing. It could stand up well to rough winter conditions.

Pollacca chebec – A type of chebec with square sails on mainmast and mizzenmast. This type of rigging increased the vessel's speed.

Port – The left side of a ship looking from stern to bows.

GLOSSARY

Portulan – A manual that provided charts of the sea bottom indicating depth and safe anchorages. It also indicated sources of fresh water on the shores.

Privateering – Naval activities whereby a private vessel could attack and capture an enemy ship and to take it as a prize. This activity was practised between belligerent countries especially in the Mediterranean and during the first decades of the nineteenth century.

Prize – The corsair's booty including cargoes, the crew, and the captured ship itself.

Proeri – Young boys, aged eight to twelve, joining the Order's ships to learn a sea-going trade.

Qantar – A Maltese unit of weight equivalent to 100 *rotoli* and one *rotolo* is equivalent to 30 ounces.

Rails – Long, thin but strong pieces of wood that fitted on top of the *apostis* like a banister. To them were tied the flagpoles on festive occasions or when the vessel was entering harbour.

Rambate or *rambata* – The forecastle of a galley, the section where the guns and the boarding party were to be found.

Ratal – Maltese unit of weight equivalent to 30 ounces.

Re – The senior caravanist in charge of the other knights and soldiers on a galley.

Renegade – Apostate, especially anybody who forsook Christianity for Islam. Such men were mostly of Italian, French and North European nationalities. Maltese renegades were extremely few in number.

Resin – Adhesive, highly inflammable substance, hardening on exposure to air, formed by secretion naturally exuded from trees such as pines and firs. It obtained its colour by being processed twice over the fire.

Saetta – A Muslim corsairing vessel. Extremely light and fast, it was very narrow and had a very low freeboard. It could tear across like lightning, hence its name, Italian *saetta* meaning 'lightning'. It had three lateen sails and long supple oars for increased speed.

Sagrestia – see **altar box**.

Saker or **sacre** – A type of long, narrow cannon with a $3\,{}^1/_2$ inch calibre resembling a demi-culverin. Its barrel was 32 calibres long and it fired mostly in Malta 6 or 8 lb. cannonballs.

Salettina – A fighting ship that carried 16 guns. Originally from Salè in Morocco.

Salma – The weight of a corpse. A unit of weight equivalent to about one-sixth of a ton or three *cantari*. The Maltese *salma* was slightly heavier than other *salme*.

Scaloccio **rowing** – A *scaloccio* was a method of rowing with more than one man pulling at the same oar. Subsequently, after the middle of the sixteenth century, the oars were lengthened and pulled by between three and seven oarsmen each. The oars were all laid out in one row and pivoted on thole pins on the *apostis*.

Saracen – A name which refers to Muslims, especially those of Syria and Palestine. Medieval writers used to attribute the name to all Arabs in general and to the Arab-Berber races of North Africa.

Scudo – A coin equivalent to eight or nine cents.

Sensile – The method of rowing on galleys with one rower to each oar which prevailed till the middle of the sixteenth century when three rowers sat on the same bench each pulling a separate oar.

Skiff – Generic nomenclature referring to a small, double-ended boat.

Slave – Any Muslim captured by the Order became its absolute property. Healthy males were sent to row on the galleys; the others were consigned to weaving and other duties.

Spalliera – The platform across the whole width of the back section of the galley extending from the *carosse* or cabin to the last row of benches. This was also known as the stern *rambata*.

Speronara – A small Maltese vessel, the size of a large *luzzu*, and without any decks. It was rigged with one lateen sail and a *pollakkun* which was a kind of a jib and had from six to eight oars. It was popular amongst private Maltese owners to carry freight and passengers to and from Sicily and other Mediterranean sea ports.

Spur or ***sperone*** – A triangular wooden extension at the bows of a sailing ship. On galleys it was used mainly as a boarding plank when attacking the enemy.

Square rig – That on ships using four-cornered sails extended on yards and spars. Except for the corvette, vessels so rigged did not use oars.

Standard – The distinctive flag of the Order. It consisted of a white cross on a red background.

Starboard – Right hand side of a ship looking from stern to bows.

Steersman – The man in charge of guiding the ship. He had to know every bit of the coast and how to read the weather. He was responsible for steering the ship under the direction of the pilot and the overall command of the captain.

Stem – Curved upright timber at fore end of vessels to which ship's sides are joined. In some boats such as the *dgħajsa* or *ferilla* the stem extended considerably above the level of the gunwale.

Sultana – The leading vessel or flagship, in a Muslim squadron.

Swivel gun – A small gun which fitted on an iron fork and was aimed normally against boarders.

Tabernacle – The chest for the navigational instruments located in a prominent place on the *spalliera* from where the captain could watch proceedings, and especially direct the fighting.

Talar – The rectangular framework that binds the upper structure of the rowing section. It included the *balestriera* and the rowers' benches that slanted slightly towards the stern; it also served to strengthen the *apostis*.

Tambouret – The flat triangular surface in front of the *rambate* of a galley, on which the anchors were handled from, animals were slaughtered for food and the cannons under the *rambata* were cleaned and loaded. This provided also toilet facilities for the crew but not for the *ciurma*. On a square-rigged vessel the *tambouret* signified the platform on which stood the helm or wheel.

Tar raft or ***pegoliera*** – A raft or pontoon which transported hot tar to a ship undergoing a caulking operation.

Tari – Twelfth part of a *scudo*.

Tarkija – A sprit sail as employed on small local merchant ships like the *xprunara*

GLOSSARY

or the felucca.

Tartana or **tartane** – A lateen-rigged cargo carrier often rigged with square sails by Maltese sailors in good weather conditions. The deck of a seventeenth-century *tartana* extended beyond the stern. The eighteenth-century *tartana* was equipped with a stern cabin, too. Sometimes it was used for corsairing and it sailed to every far corner of the Mediterranean.

Tavern – A compartment of the galley below deck near the foot of the mainmast where wine was stored and sold to ordinary crew members who could afford it.

Tese – A unit of length equivalent to the height of a man, approximately six feet.

Ton – A unit of weight equivalent to 20 *cantari*.

Treo or **jury sail** – A small, square sail which was rigged up instead of the normal lateen sail in an emergency.

Tromba or **trumpet** – A gunpowder filled canister with two sharp prongs, meant to be hurled at and to stick to a ship's side.

Tromboncini – Small guns or large muskets with a wide bore, mounted on the gunwale of a ship.

Thwart – see **oar**.

Università – The local government which consisted of a number of jurats who were the representatives of the Maltese. It was still important in the first decades of the nineteenth century and it managed certain obligations in favour of the people.

Versa – A width of sailcloth woven by a loom. Sometimes the sails of galleys were made of alternating red-and-white widths.

Votive picture – a picture offered to a church in fulfilment of a vow. Such maritime pictures always depict the ship involved and always carry the initials V.F.G.A. (*Voto Fecit Gratiam Accepit*) – 'I made a vow and I received grace.'

Washboards or *Falki* – Rectangular, removable pieces of wood that fitted on the gunwales of certain traditional Maltese boats such as the *luzzu*, the *kajjikk*, and so on.

Xprunara – see *speronara*.

Zenzile – see *sensile*.

BIBLIOGRAPHY

Primary Sources

Exhaustive use has been made of the Archives of the Order in Malta (AOM) with special reference to the manuscripts of section XII which deal with the Navy of the Order. Other references are made to other MSS of the above-mentioned archives.

At the National Library of Malta (NLM), there are also many other manuscripts dealing with the Navy of the Order, some of them being of the utmost importance for the scholar of sea lore in Malta.

The Malta Maritime Museum in Vittoriosa has a few manuscripts dealing with galleys, artillery and signals.

The Cathedral Museum, Mdina has a unique inventory of sacred objects carried by the galleys of the Order.

Secondary Sources

Abela, G.F., *Della Descrittione di Malta Isola nel Mare Siciliano con le sue antichita ed altre notitie* (Malta, 1647).
Album De Colbert (Nice, 1988).
Aliotti, G.T., *Il Gran Maestro Tommasi e l'Ordine di Malta a Cortona* (Cortona, 1995).
Anderson, R.C., *Oared Fighting Ships* (London, 1976).
Archibald, E.H.H., *The Wooden Fighting Ship* (London, 1968).
Arenson, S., *The Encircled Sea* (London, 1990).
Aubin, N., *Dictionaire de Marine* (Amsterdam, 1702).
Auphan, P., *Histoire de la Mediterranee* (Paris, 1962).
Azopardi, Barone, *Giornale della Presa di Malta e Gozo dalla Republica Francese e della susseguente Rivoluzione della Campagna* (Malta, 1836).
Azzopardi, J. (ed.), *The Order's Early Legacy in Malta* (Malta, 1989).
 – *St Paul's Grotto, Church and Museum at Rabat Malta* (Malta, 1990).
Balbi di Correggio, F., *The Siege Of Malta*. Translated from the Spanish by Major Henry Alexander Balbi (Copenhagen, 1961).

Bamford, P.W., *Fighting Ships and Prisons* (Minneapolis, 1973).
Barras de la Penne, *Lettre Critique* (Marseilles, 1726).
Bathe, B.W., *Ship Models* (London, 1966).
Bedford, W.K.R., *The Regulations of the Old Hospital of the Knights of St John at Valletta* (London, 1882).
Beeching, J., *The Galleys at Lepanto* (London, 1982).
Bellec, F., *Quand voguaient les galeres* (Madrid, 1990).
Bergna, P.C., *Tripoli dal 1510 al 1850* (Tripoli, 1925).
 – *La Missione Francescana in Libia* (Tripoli, 1924).
Blackburn, G., *The Illustrated Encyclopaedia of Ships, Boats, Vessels, and other Water-Borne Craft* (London, 1978).
Blouet, B., *The Story of Malta* (London, 1967).
Boisgelin, L., *Ancient and Modern Malta* (London, 1805).
Boismele, A., *Histoire generale de la Marine* (Paris, 1764).
Bono, S., *I Corsari Barbareschi* (Turin, 1964).
 – *Corsari nel Mediterraneo* (Milan, 1993).
Borch, Le Comte de, *Lettres sur la Sicile et sur L'Isle de Malthe* (Turin 1782).
Bosio, G., *Historia della Sacra Religione et Illustrissima Militia di S. Giovanni Gierosolimitano* (Venice, 1695).
Bowen, F.C., *From Carrack to Clipper* (London, 1948).
Boudriot, J., *Le Vaisseau de 74 Cannons* (Grenoble, 1974).
 – *L'Artillerie de Mer* (Paris, 1992).
Boyer, P., *La Vie Quotidienne a Alger* (Monaco, 1963).
Braudel, F., *The Mediterranean and the Mediterranean World in the Age of Philip II*. Translated by S. Reynolds (London, 1973).
Brockelmann, C., *History of the Islamic Peoples* (London 1952).
Brockman, E., *Last Bastion* (London, 1961).
Brydone, P., *A Tour through Sicily and Malta* (London, 1774).
Bugeja, L., M. Buhagiar, and S. Fiorini (eds.), *Birgu – A Maltese Maritime City* (Malta, 1993)
Buhagiar, M. and J. Muscat, 'The Gran Carracca' in J. Azzopardi (ed), *The Order's Early Legacy in Malta* (Malta, 1989).
Cabal, J., *Piracy and Pirates* (London, 1957).
Campodonico, P., *La Marineria Genovese dal Medioevo all'Unita d'Italia* (Milan, 1989).
Canale, C., *Della Milizia Marittima* (Venice, 1929).
Caruana, A.A., *Frammento Critico della Storia Fenico-Cartaginese, Greco-Romano e Bisantina, Musulmana e Normanno-Aragonese delle Isole di Malta* (Malta, 1899).
Cassar, J. and Muscat, J., 'The Gozo Prisons Graffiti', *Melita Historica*, xi, No.3 (1994), 241-73.
Cassar P., *Medical History of Malta* (London, 1964).
Castagna, P.P., *Malta bil-Gzejjer taghha* (Malta, 1869).
Cavaliero, R., 'The Decline of the Maltese Corso in the 18th century', *Melita Historica*, ii, No.4 – (1959), 224-38.
 – *The Last of the Crusaders* (London, 1960).
Chapin, L.F., *Venetian Ships and Shipbuilders of the Renaissance,* (Baltimore, 1934).
Chapman, F.H., *Architectura Navalis Mercatoria* (New York, 1967).
Chatterton, E.K., *Old Ship Prints* (London, 1967).

BIBLIOGRAPHY

Chetcuti, P., 'Direct Employment of the Maltese with the Order of St John: 1775-1798', unpublished BA dissertation presented to the Royal University of Malta, 1968.
Ciantar, G.A., *Malta Illustrata* (Malta, 1772).
Concina, E., *Navis – L'umanesimo sul mare: 1470-1740* (Turin, 1990).
Constructrion des Vaisseau Du Roy (Havre de Grace, 1723).
Contarini, G.P., *Historia delle cose successe dal Principio della Guerra mossa da Selim Ottomano a Venetiani* (Venice, 1645).
Coronelli, V., *Ships and other sort of craft used by the various nations of the world – Venice 1690* (London, 1970).
Courcy Ireland, J., 'The Corsairs of North Africa', *The Mariner's Mirror*, lxii, (1976), 271-83.
Cowburn, P., *The Warship in History* (London, 1966).
Crescentio, B., *Nautica Mediterranea* (Rome, 1607).
Culver, H.B. and Grant, G., *The Book of Old Ships* (New York, 1924).
Currey, E.H., *Sea-wolves of the Mediterranean* (London, 1913).
 – *The Man-of-War* (London, 1914).
Cuschieri, A., *Chiesa e Stato in Malta* (Salamanca, 1971).
Cuschieri, A. and J. Muscat, 'Maritime Votive Paintings in Maltese Churches', *Melita Historica*, x, No.2 (1990).
Dal Pozzo, B., *Historia della Sacra Religione di Malta.* Parte Prima, (Verona, 1703).
 – *Historia della S. Religione Militare di S. Giovanni Gerosolimitano detta di Malta.* Parte Seconda (Venice, 1715).
Dan, P., *Histoire de Barbarie et de ses Corsaires* (Paris,1636).
Darmanin, J.F., The Building of the Order at H.M. Victualling Yard, 'Malta', *Melita Historica*, ii, No.2, 1957
Darmanin Demajo, G., 'The Grand Harbour of Malta and its surroundings in 1530', *Daily Malta Chronicle*, 26 January 1927.
 – 'Stray Leaves from the Naval History of the Order', *Daily Malta Chronicle*, 29-31 January 1927.
 – 'L'Albergia d'Italia', *Archivio Storico di Malta*, i, No.1 (1930).
 – 'The Old Crucifix in the Victualling Yard', *Daily Malta Chronicle*, 28 February 1935.
Dauber, R.L., *Die Marine des Johanniter – Malteser-Ritter Ordens* (Austria, 1989).
Dearden, S., *A Nest of Corsairs* (London, 1976).
De Caro, L., *Storia dei Gran Maestri e Cavalieri di Malta* (Malta, 1853).
Del Diritto Municipale di Malta (Malta, 1784).
Denaro, V.F., 'Houses in Kingsway and Old Bakery Street, Valletta', *Melita Historica*, ii, No.4 (1959).
Desroches, *Dictionnaire des Termes Propres de Marine* (Paris, 1688).
Dimensions des Canons de Fer pour la Marine, approuvees par le Roi, Le 26 Nopvembre 1786.
Dudszus, A. and Henriot, E., *Dictionary of Ship Types* (London, 1986).
Duhamel du Monceau, *Elemens de l'Architecture Navale* (Paris, 1752).
 – *Moyens de Conserver la Sante aux Equipages* (Paris, 1759).
Dumas, A., *The Speronara* (Boston, 1902).
Earle, P., *Corsairs of Malta and Barbary* (London, 1970).
Edits Declarations Reglemens et Ordonnances du Roy sur le fait de la Marine (Paris,

1675).
Ellul Galea, K., *L-Istorja tat-Tarzna* (Malta, 1973).
Encyclopedie Methodique Marine (Paris, 1787).
Engel, C.E., *Knights of Malta* (London, 1963).
- *Histoire de L'Ordre de Malte* (Geneva, 1968).
Falconer, W., *An Universal Dictionary of the Marine* (London 1970).
Fava, P., 'Malta and Venice: The War of Candia 1645-1669', unpublished MA dissertation presented to the University of Malta, 1976
Fennis, J., *La Stolonomie 1547-1550 et son vocabulaire Maritime Marseillais* (Amsterdam, 1978).
- *Un Manuel de Construction des Galeres 1691* (Amsterdam 1983).
- *Tresor du Langage des galeres* (Tubingen, 1995).
Fincati, L., *Le Triremi* (Rome, 1881).
Fincham, J., *A History of Naval Architecture* (London, 1851).
Fournier, G., *Hydrographie contenant La Theorie et la Pratique de toutes les parties de la navigation* (Paris, 1667).
Francois de Malthe, *Traite de Feux* (Paris, 1640).
Frost, H., *Under the Mediterranean* (London, 1963).
Furttenbach, J., *Construction des Navieres en usage sur Mer et le Long des Cotes*, (Paris,1939).
- *Architectura Navalis* (Hamburg 1968).
Gardener, R., *The Age of the Galley* (London, 1995).
Gatti, L., *L'Arsenale e le Galee* (Genoa, 1990).
Gentilini, E., *Pratica di Artiglieria* (Venice, 1641).
Gli Statuti della Sacra Religione Gerosolimitana (Borgo Novo, 1719).
Gorgolione, S.G., *Portulano del Mediterraneo* (Naples, 1705).
Gosse, P., *The History of Piracy* (London, 1954).
Graviere, J., *Les Marins du XV et du XVI Siecle* (Paris, 1879).
- *Les Derniers Jours de la Marine a Rame* (Paris, 1885).
- *Les Chevaliers de Malthe et la Marine de Philippe II* (Paris, 1887).
- *Les Corsaires Barbaresques* (Paris, 1887).
- *La Guerre de Chypre et la bataille de Lepanto* (Paris, 1888).
Grima, J.F., 'The Galley Squadron of the Order of St John: Its Organisation between 1596-1645', unpublished MA thesis presented to the Royal University of Malta, 1975.
- 'The Maintenance of the Order's Galley-Squadron (*c*.1600-1650)', *Melita Historica*, vii, No.2 (1977), 145-56.
- 'Galley Replacements in the Order's Squadron (*c*.1600-1650), *Melita Historica*, viii, No.1 (1980), 48-60.
- 'The Organisation of the Order of St John's Fleet in the 18th century', unpublished Ph.D. dissertation presented to the University of Malta, 1999.
Guglielmotti, A., *Storia della marina Pontificia* (Rome, 1886-93).
- *Vocabolario marino e militare* (Milan, 1967).
Guilmartin, J.F., *Gunpowder and Galleys*, (Cambridge, 1974).
Hansen, H.J., *Art and the Seafarer* (London, 1968).
Hardman, W., *A History of Malta during the period of the French and British Occupations 1798-1815* (London, 1909).
Hennique, P.A., *Les Caboteurs et Pecheurs de la Cote de Tunisie* (Nice, 1989).

Histoire de la Marine (Paris, 1934).
Hitti, P.K., *History of the Arabs* (London, 1870).
Hogg, I., *Naval Gun* (Dorset, 1978).
Hogg, O.F.G., *Clubs to Cannon* (London, 1968).
Hoste, P., *L'Art des Armees Navales* (Lyon, 1727).
Howard, F., *Sailing Ships of War 1400-1860* (London,1979).
Hughes, B.P., *Firepower* (London, 1974).
Humbert, J., *La Galere du XVIIeme Siecle* (Grenoble, 1986).
Istruzione per i Cavalieri officiali delle Navi (Malta, 1778).
Istruzioni sopra gli obblighi piu principali de Cavalieri di Malta, (Malta, 1758).
Jal, A., *Archeologie Navale* (Paris 1840).
– *Glossaire des Termes nautiques* (Paris, 1848).
– *Nouveau Glossaire Nautiques* (Netherlands, 1970).
Jobe, J., *The Great Age of Sail* (Cambridge, 1977).
Jullien, P., *Journal de la Prise d'Alger 1830* (Paris, 1960).
Kermainguy, A., *L'Esclave des Galeres ou Malte sous les Chevaliers* (Paris, 1841).
King, C., 'The Naval Collection of Malta', *The Mariner's Mirror*, xvii (1931), 187.
Laferla, A.V., *The Story of Man in Malta* (Malta, 1939).
Landstrom, B., *The Ship* (London, 1961).
Lane-Poole, S., *The Barbary Corsairs* (London, 1890).
Leggi e Costituzioni Prammaticali (Malta, 1724).
Lehmann, L.T., *Galleys in the Netherlands* (Amsterdam, 1984).
Lewis, M., *Armada Guns* (London, 1961).
Lobley, D., *Ships Through the Ages* (London, 1972).
Ludwig, E., *The Mediterranean –Saga of a Sea* (New York, 1942).
Luke, H., *Malta – An Account and an Appreciation* (London, 1960).
Macintyre D., and B.W. Bathe, *The Man-of-War* (London, 1968).
Mallia-Milanes, V., *Venice and Hospitaller Malta 1530-1798 – Aspects of a Relationship,* Malta 1992
– *Hospitaller Malta 1530-1798 – Studies on Early Modern Malta and the Order of St John of Jerusalem* (ed.) (Malta, 1993).
Manfroni, C., *Storia della Marina Italiana*, Leghorn, 1899).
Marteilhe, J., *Memoires d'un Galerien du Roi-Soleil* (Paris, 1982).
Marzari, M., *Navi di Legno* (Grado, 1998).
Medrano, S.F., *El Pratico Artillero* (Brussels, 1680).
Michaud, A., *Storia delle Crociate* (Milan, 1878).
Miege, M., *Histoire de Malte* (Paris, 1841).
Mordal, J., *Twenty-Five Centuries of Sea Warfare* (London, 1965).
Munro, C., *Sailing Ships* (London, 1973).
Muscat, J., 'Visitatio Turrium', *Melita Historica*, vii, No. 2 (1981), 101-8.
– 'An Altar from the Galleys of the Order of St John and The Celebration of Mass at Sea', *The Mariner's Mirror*, lxx, No. 4 (1984), 389-95.
– 'The Dghajsa – In Memoriam', *The Mariner's Mirror*, lxxvii, No.4 (1991), 389-405.
– 'Maltese Ship Graffiti' in C. Villain-Gandossi (ed.), *Medieval Ships and the Birth of Technological Societies* (Malta, 1991), ii, 323-78.
– 'Le Xprunara – Un Batiment traditionel maltaise', *Neptunia*, No. 185 (1992), 22-32.

– 'Maltese Ship and Boatbuilding 18th and 19th centuries' in K.A. Damianidis (ed.), *The Evolution of Wooden Shipbuilding in the Eastern Mediterranean during the 18th and 19th centuries* (Athens, 1993), 69-89.

– 'The Arsenal: 1530-1798' in L. Bugeja *et al.* (eds.), *Birgu –A Maltese Maritime City* (Malta, 1993), i, 256-325.

– 'The Building of a Maltese Galley' in *Proceedings of Seminar: The Navy of the Knights of St John* (Malta, 1995), 2-16.

– 'The Warships of the Navy of the Order of St John in S. Fiorini (ed.), *Proceedings of History Week 1994* (Malta, 1996), 77-113.

– 'Xoghol ta' Lsir fuq Galera ta' l-Ordni', *Il-Pronostku Malti* (Malta, 1996), 179-205.

– 'The Maltese Corso' in C. Villain-Gandossi, *Mediterranee, mer ouverte* (Malta, 1997), 191-208.

– 'The Xprunara' in K. Sciberras (ed), *Proceedings of History Week 1993* (Malta, 1997), 123-49.

– 'Traditional Maltese Naval Architecture' in *Living Shipbuilding Tradition of Eastern Mediterranean Countries* (Greece 1997), 71-94.

– 'In Memoriam de Dghajsa' in *Maritem Erfgoed Vlaanderen* (Antwerp, 1997), 8-17.

– 'The Dghajsa and The Luzzu', *Treasures of Malta*, iii, No.3, 37-41.

– 'Arsenali maltesi: dal Sei all'Ottocento' in M. Marzari(ed), *Navi di Legno*(Trieste, 1998), 193-203.

– 'Graffiti on the Exterior Walls of St Paul's Shipwreck Church, Wied il-Qliegha Mosta', *Melita Historica*, xii, No.2 (1992), 179-194

– 'St Paul's Shipwreck Church Mosta Graffiti', in S.M. Haslam and J. Borg (eds), *The River Valleys of the Maltese Islands* (Malta, 1998), 161-3.

– 'Maritime ex-voto Paintings', *Treasures of Malta*, iv, No. 3 (1998), 13-8.

– 'French Influence on Maltese Ship and Boatbuilding', *Proceedings of Seminar: Aspects of Maritime Relations with France Through the Years* (Malta, 1998), 1-4.

– *The Maltese Galley* (Malta, 1998).

– 'Ship Graffiti – A Comparative Study', *Journal of Mediterranean Studies*, ix, No.1 (1999), 74-105.

– *The Dghajsa and other Traditional Maltese Boats* (Malta, 1999).

– *The Maltese* Vaxxell (Malta, 1999).

– 'Influences Affecting Maltese Ships and Boats' in K.A., Damianidis (ed.), *Shipbuilding and Ships in the Eastern Mediterranean during the 18th and 19th centuries* (Chios, 1999), 233-52.

– Mass at Sea on Warships of the Order of St John in J. Azzopardi (ed) *Portable Altars in Malta* (Malta, 2000), 59-75.

– *The Carrack of the Order* (Malta, 2000).

– *Il-Flotta ta' l-Ordni ta' San Gwann* (Malta, 2000).

– *The Xprunara* (Malta, 2000).

– 'The *Xprunara*' in G. Allotta (ed) *Girgenti La Magnifique e La Speronara* (Agrigento, 2000), 49-68.

– 'The Maltese Brigantine' in C. Vassallo (ed), *Consolati di Mare and Chambers of Commerce* (Malta, 2000), 199-214.

– The Dghajsa of Malta in B. Cadoret (ed), *Maritime Life and Traditions*,

March 2001, No.10, 54-71.
- 'Maltese 18th-century Merchant Ships' in A. Fehri (ed), *L'Homme et la Mer* (Sfax, 2001), 105-30.
Nance, R.M., *Sailing Ships Models* (London, 1949).
Ordonnance du Roi (Paris, 1787).
Padfield, P., *Guns at Sea* (London, 1973).
Pantera, P., *L'Armata Navale del Capitan Pantero Pantera* (Rome, 1614).
Pierredon, M., *L'Ordre Souverain et Militaire des Hospitaliers de Saint Jean de Jerusalem (Malte)* (Paris, 1924).
Plaisse, A., *Le Rouge de Malte* (Rennes, 1991).
Pope, D., *Guns* (London, 1965).
Porter, W., *Malta and its Knights* (London, 1871).
Prins, A.H.J., *In Peril on the Sea* (Malta, 1989).
Pritchard, J., *Louis XV's Navy 1748-1762* (Canada, 1987).
Pryor, J.H., *Geography, Technology and War: Studies in the maritime history of the Mediterranean 649-1571* (Cambridge, 1992).
Quintano, A., 'The Establishment and Organisation of the Order of St John's Sailing Ship-of-the-line Squadron 1701-1741', unpublished MA dissertation presented to the University of Malta 1995
Regula Hospitalariorum Militiae ordinin Sancti Ioannis Baptistae Hierosolymitani (Rome, 1556).
Rossi, E., *Storia della Marina dell'Ordine di S. Giovanni di Gerusalemme di Rodi e di Malta* (Rome-Milan, 1926).
Rubin De Cervin, *La Flotta di Venezia* (Milan, 1985).
Ryan, F.W., *The House of the Temple* (London, 1930).
Sanz, E., *Breve trattato nel quale con ragione dimostrative si convincono manifestamente i Turchi, senza che in guisa veruna possano negarlo, esser falsa la legge di Maometto, e vera solamente quella di Cristo* (Catania, 1691).
Saverien, A., *Dizionario Istorico, Teorico, e Pratico di Marina* (Venice, 1769).
Scarabelli, G., *La Caravana Marina di Fra Francesco Antonio Mansi 1728-1729* (Lucca, 1986).
Schellinks, W., *Journey to the South 1664-1665* (Rome, 1983).
Schermerhorn, E.W., *Malta of the Knights* (Surrey, 1929).
Scicluna, H.P., *The Order of St John of Jerusalem and Places of Interest in Malta and Gozo* (Malta, 1969).
Segnali Istruzioni, Manovre, e Tattica per La Marina di Guerra (Naples, 1822).
Sonnini, C.S., *Travels in Upper and Lower Egypt* (London, 1800).
Steel, D., *Elements of Mastmaking, Sailmaking and Rigging* (New York, 1932).
- *The Elements and Practice of Naval Architecture* (London, 1977).
Stevens, C.F., *The Nautical Pocket Dictionary* (Malta, 1854).
Suetonius, *The Twelve Caesars*. Translated by Robert Graves (London, **Year??**).
Tarassuk, L. and C. Blair, *Arms and Weapons* (New York, 1982).
Tartaglia, N., *Quesiti et Inventioni Diverse* (Venice 1553).
Taurisano, P.J., *Antologia del mare* (Florence, 1913).
Tenenti, A., *Piracy and the Decline of Venice 1580-1615* (London, 1967).
Teonge, H., *The Diary of Henry Teonge* (London, 1825).
Testa, C., *The Life and Times of Grand Master Pinto 1741-1773* (Malta, 1989).
Townsend, G.F., *The Sea-Kings of the Mediterranean* (London, 1891).

Traite de l'Administration Des Bois de l'Ordre de Malte (Paris, 1757).
Ubaldini, M.U., *La Marina del Sovran Militare Ordine di San Giovanni di Gerusalemme di Rodi e di Malta* (Rome, 1970).
Valiero, A., *Historia della Guerra di Candia* (Venice, 1679).
Van De Velde, *Drawings* (Cambridge, 1958).
Vassallo, G.A., *Storia di Malta Raccontata in Compendio* (Malta 1854).
Vella, A., *Storja ta' Malta* (Malta, 1979).
Vertot, R.A., *Histoire des Chevaliers Hospitaliers de S. Jean de Jerusalem, appellez depuis Chevaliers de Rhodes, et aujourd' hui Chevaliers de Malthe* (Paris, 1726).
Vingiano, G., *Storia della Nave* (Rome, 1954).
Viviani, L., *Storia di Malta* (Turin, 1933).
Vivielle, J., *Navires et Marines de la Rame a l'Helice* (Paris, 1930).
Willaumez, R., *Dictionnaire de Marine* (Paris, 1820).
Wilson, T., *Flags at Sea* (London, 1986).
Wilsen, N., *L'Art de Batir les Vaisseaux* (Amsterdam, 1719).
– *Architectura Navalis et Regimen Nauticum* (Amsterdam, 1690).
Witt, M.M., *A Bibliography of the Works written and published by David Steel and his successors* (London, 1991).
Zammit, T., *Malta – The Islands and their History* (Malta, 1971).
Zarb, J., *Zabbar Sanctuary and the Knights of St John* (Malta, 1969).
Zysberg, A., *Les Galeriens* (Paris, 1987).

Periodicals
Daily Malta Chronicle
Epoca
L'Arte
Malta Government Gazette
Mariner's Mirror
Melita Historica
Neptunia

Votive Paintings
In Malta, one can still find visual references by the hundreds in the votive paintings, most of them still *in situ*. These are the principal churches where they can be found:-
Mellieħa Sanctuary has a good collection although most of them refer to the nineteenth century;
Qrendi, Tal-Ħniena church has a few good examples which represent the ships of the Order;
Birkirkara, Tal-Ħerba Sanctuary has a good quantity and some of them are of artistic value also and show the galleys of the Order;
Żabbar Sanctuary Museum is the first attempt at classification and authentication. The genuine votive pictures in this Museum are of great importance and a few refer to the ships of the Order.

All over the Maltese islands there are rural churches which possess the odd votive picture but they are still very interesting.

INDEX

Abela, G.F., 153
Aboukir, 50
Acton, General, 5
Alexandria, 26
Algerians, 106, 107
Algiers, 10, 34, 50, 57, 69, 101, 107, 118, 126
Altar, 149, 151
Amalfi, 77
Amsterdam, 22
Anchor, 45, 201
Angevins, ix
Apostis, 165, 168
Apprentices, 115, 151
Aquila, 42
Arabs, ix, 175
Aragonese, ix
Archimedes, 194
Archimedian screw, 194
Argentine routes, 97
Argusin, 147
Armenian, 128
Arquebus, 182
Arsenal, 23, 41, 49, 165, 171, 190, 191, 192, 198
Arsenal, Civil, 89
Arsenal, Commander of the, 190
Artillery, 171
Asia, 125
Assassins, 152
Atlantic Ocean, 15, 21, 66
Attard, Ascanio, 51, 123
Auberge, 145
Auphan, Paul, 9, 133
Azzupardo, Giuseppe, 34
Bab Assan, 34
Bacon, Roger, 175
Bagnios, 154

Baia, 3
Bakery, 198
Baldacchino, Antonio, 118
Ballast, 37, 38, 200, 201
Band, 141
Barbary Coast, 10, 26, 70, 107, 109, 113, 129, 132, 133
Barbary Regencies, 154
Barberini, Cardinal, 124, 125
Barberotto, 153
Barca Maltese, 91
Barche di guardia, 92
Barrel, 172
Battalotto, 100, 103
Baumes, 23
Baumes, see Colans, Baldassere 24
Bebazon, 34
Bell, 153
Benedictines, 77
Benghen, 129
Betting, 143
Beżbuża, 148
Bible, 62
Bichi, Prior, 118
Bidoux, Fra Preanni de, 87
Bidoux, Pregeant, de, 120
Birgu galley arsenal, 190
Birgu, 3, 165, 191
Birżebbuġa, 153
Birżebbuġa, Church of St George, 153
Biscain pilot, 24
Bishops, Maltese, x
Bizerta, 42, 50. 79, 93
Black Sea, 93, 97, 125
Blaspheming, 142
Blessed Sacrament, 153
Boat, 90
Bocage, Emanuel, Balì, 96

Boisboudron, Commander, 27
Bomb shells, 178
Bomb-ketch, 71
Bomb-vessels, 73
Bombard, 72
Bombarda, 71
Bombardier, 168, 176, 179
Bombs, 178
Bomensor, Abu Tamin, Caliph, 77
Bonello, Josian, 190
Bonnet, 80
Bormla, 191
Bosio, Giacomo, 16, 19, 34, 62, 78, 166, 198, 202, 203
Branca Leone, 58
Braudel, F., 39
Brazil, 15
Breughel, 12
Brigantine, 4, 7, 14, 19, 51, 64, 74, 78, 89, 94, 95, 96, 99, 189
Brigantine, Ceremonial, 63, 65
Britain, 5
British blockade, 93
British forces, 50
British period, 97
Bronze chambers, 174
Bubarca, 199
Bucentaur, 65
Bulls, 144
Buonavoglia, 46, 56, 141, 144, 147, 148, 155, 156
Burial at sea, 154
Busuttil, Paul, 175
Byzace, 73
Byzantines, ix

Cabin boy, 141, 156
Cabin, 35, 139
Cagliola, Commendatore, 151
Caicco in fagotto, 61
Caique, viii, 19, 24, 55, 59-61, 73, 92, 93, 174, 175, 183, 201
Caique, Assault, 60
Calabria, 58, 103
Calahorra, 124
Calves, 41
Camicia di fuoco, 183
Candia, 3, 8, 73, 77, 78, 130, 134
Canea, 76
Canister, 180
Cannonball, 180, 201
Cannoni Finti, 87
Canoncini, 57
Canopy, 33
Cantiere delle Navi, 191
Cantu, 125

Copanion way, 36
Capitana, 21, 28, 30, 31, 32, 34, 35, 41, 42, 46, 53-5, 57, 64, 129, 130, 135, 136, 137, 141, 146, 149, 151, 166, 173, 190
Capobuono, 91
Capstan, 45
Captain's berth, 36
Captain, 144
Caracoggia, 27, 28, 101
Caradinghis, Musa, 199
Carafa, Gregorio, 126, 193
Caramemet, 199
Caramousal, 21, 51, 132
Caramousal, Muslim, 52
Caravan, 145, 176, 182
Caravanists, 145, 146
Carcass, 179
Cardena, Knight, 123
Careening, 194, 196
Carrack, 2, 6, 7, 13, 14, 15, 16, 17, 21, 21, 24, 25, 26, 67, 73, 79, 200
Carthage, 27, 29, 73
Carthaginians, ix, 26
Cartridge, 169
Caruana Curran, P., 203
Caruana, A.A., 113
Caruana, Bishop, x
Casha, Bartolomeo, 118
Cassar, Paul, 77
Castelvi, Knight, 114
Catarinetta, 44
Cathedral Museum Archives, 149, 151, 205
Catherine II, 121, 122
Catholicism, 205
Caulker, 196
Caulking, 194
Cavaliero, R.E., 158
Cephalonia, 9
Cercamar, 144, 145, 147, 161
Cerche, Victor, Fra, 58
Ceremonial barges, 63-5
Chain boom, 202
Chain shot, 180
Chamber, 172
Chapel, 149
Chaplain, 33, 36, 147, 147, 148, 149, 151, 152, 153
Chaplain, Conventual, 147
Chapter General, 36, 32
Charcoal, 175
Charles V, Emperor, 3, 6, 7
Chatterton, E. Keble, 79
Chebec, 14, 57, 103, 106-10, 133, 149, 189

INDEX

Chebec, Algerian, 107, 109
Chebec, French, 109
Chebec, Small, 108
Christian fleets, 136
Chetcuti, P., 203
Chickens, 39, 41, 39
Chinese, 175
Churchill, Winston, Prime Minister, 5
Ciantar, G.A., Gount, 192, 197
Ciurma, 148, 182
Civitavecchia, 3, 45, 50, 54
Cleremont, Fra Francesco de, 19
Coal, 39
Codex Vilhena, 98, 156
Colans, Fra Baldassare de, 23, 24
Colubovich, Girolamo, 125
Combreux, Knight, 70
Comiti, 33
Commander-in-chief, 57
Commanderies, 44, 47
Compendio d'Artigliera, 59, 60, 75, 198
Concessione Immacolata e le Ani, 103
Congregation of the galleys, 47, 129, 151
Consolato di mare, 89
Constantinople, 26, 124, 125
Conversion, 154, 199
Convicts, 46, 144
Convoys, 14
Cook, 31, 39
Copper, 18
Corfu, 58, 90, 91
Cornaro of Venice, Cardinal, 124
Corneto, 3
Coron, 4, 113
Corona, 42
Corradino, 177
Corsair felucca, 58
    galleot, 52
    galleys, 124, 125
    ships, 121
    warships, 125
Corsairing activities, xi, 113
Corsairing crew, 103
Corsairing, 22, 51, 89, 109
Corsairs, 2, 14, 26, 42, 51, 53, 66, 96
Corsairs, Algerian 107
Corsairs, Barbary, 9, 14, 15, 27, 34, 66, 68, 70, 90, 93, 101, 123, 131, 132, 133, 134
Corsairs, Christian, 125
Corsairs, Maltese, 68, 93, 113, 114, 124, 175
Corsairs, Muslim, 89, 100, 101, 121
Corsairs, North African, 15, 106
Corsia, 33, 48, 63, 93, 142
Corso, 8, 39, 53, 70, 77, 99, 101, 109, 114, 121, 123, 125, 126, 131, 133, 144, 145, 146, 147, 148, 149, 153, 175, 193, 196
Corso, decline of, 11
Corso, Maltese, 121
Cortona, 177
Corvette, 14, 49, 69-71
Cospicua, 63, 193, 200 (see also Bormla)
Cossacks, 93, 125
Costruzione delle Radici Quadra, 117
Cotoner brothers, 35, 54
Cotoner, Nicholas, Grand Master, 126
Cotoner, Rafael, Grand Master, 126, 166
Cotton articles, 94
Cottonera, 204
Coulonga, Knight, 123
Couroirs, 38, 56
Coursier, 38, 48, 165, 166
Cowardice in battle, 142
Cows, 139, 144
Crete, see Candia
Crew members, 147
Crime, 155
Criminal law, 155
Crossbow, 182
Crow-bar, 169
Crucifix Hill, 191
Cuirass, 182
Culverin, 173
Customs House, 190
Cyprus, 9, 21
Czechoslovakia, 5

D'Aleccio, Matteo, Perez, 203
D'Anville, Luigi, 93
D'Arzac, Stefano, Fra, 190
D'Asia, Langravio, Prince 29
D'Avola, Paolo, 118
Daggers, 143
Dal Pozzo, Bartolomeo, 27, 50, 68, 93, 98, 115, 120, 121, 142, 166, 180, 190, 203
Daniel, Captain, 123
Dardanelles, 120, 166, 171
Dardanelles, Battle of the, 172
Darmanin Demajo, G., 172173
Dauber, R.L., 203
Delia, Grazio, 130
Della Calibia, Pietro, 199
Demi-cannon, 19, 173
Demi-galley, 30, 41, 44, 45-50, 56
Denmark, 107
Digut, Commander, 22
Dingli, viii
Discipline, 144
Diving bell, 201

231

Dizionario della Marina, 117
Djerba, 23, 78
Dock, 194
Doctor, 153
Don Carlos, 39
Drago Grande, 15
Dragut, 44
Drydock, 193
Du Quesne, Knight, 177
Duelling, 142
Dutch, 9, 10, 66, 73, 96, 101, 103

Earle, P., 104, 109
East, 114
Eastern Mediterranean, 106
Eastern trade routes, 15, 77
Ecumenicsm, 8
Egypt, 47, 50, 93, 125
Egyptian campaigns, 99
Egyptian sultan, 16
Engel, C. E., 91, 120, 126
England, 9, 19, 39, 65, 77, 94, 107
England, Auberge of, 176
English corvettes, 70
    curtain, 191
    ships, 91
English, ix, x, 5, 8, 18, 24, 66, 67, 73, 74, 78, 96, 101, 179, 196
Escrainville, Knight d', 123
Esgarambe, 58
Eucharist, 142
European nations, 115
European navies, 69
European, 5, 8, 20, 65, 107, 126, 204
Ex-voto, 98
Explosive hand bomb, 181

Falconet, 168
Falcons, 168
Falka morta, 85
Falka viva, 85
Falki, 59
Farrugia, Michele Angelo, 117
Fathers of Mercy, 154
Fava, P., 203
Favignana, 91
Feda vie, 152
Fehri, A., 110
Felucca, 53, 55, 56-8, 73, 91, 98
Fighting ships, 14-5
Fighting tools, 165
Fire barrel, 182
Fire bombs, 73, 181
Fire contrivances, 184
Fire shirt, 183, 184
Fireship, 15, 60, 73-6

Firewood, 39
Fitting-out, 189
Flanders, 23
Floriana, 176
Fluyt, 103
Food, 36, 37
Food, Knights', 144
Foot rest, 32
Forbici, 190
Forfeit, 30
France, 4, 5, 9, 20, 35, 47, 48, 65, 94, 96, 107, 114, 115, 118, 120, 120, 121, 126
France, king of, 109
Franciscan Fathers, 41
Franciscan friars, 8, 123, 124
Franciscan Minors convent, 134
Franciscans, 124
Fregata del passo, 98
Fregata, 97
Fregatina, 61-2
French crown, 121
nationality, 126
naval officers, 120
navy, 71
Revolution, 47
ships, 73
French, ix, x, 5, 8, 26, 39, 47, 50, 56, 66, 67, 78, 91, 93, 94, 99, 106, 107, 109, 110, 117, 120, 177, 179
Frigate, 14, 67-9, 73, 96
Frigate, Small, 71
Frigates, 149, 189
Fugazza, Captain, 123

Gabes, Bay of, 92
Galea Naudi, Francis, 65
Galione, 53, 54, 55
Galleas, 73, 74
Galleon, 2, 7, 12, 13, 14, 20-4, 26, 27, 29, 67, 68, 146
Galleon, Muslim, 23, 128
Galleon, Small, 25, 146, 149
Galleon, Turkish, 118, 129Galleons, 19
Galleot, 7, 24, 30, 50-3, 125
Galleot, Algerian, 166
Galleot, Turkish, 19, 199
Galleots, viii, 74, 93, 174
Galleots, Muslim, 50
Galley Hierarchy, 144, 145
Galley soldier, 133
Galley squadron, 42, 78, 128
Galley tenders, 56
Galley's altar, 150
Galley's caique, 60
Galley's *rambata*, 181

INDEX

Galley, 2, 6, 8, 12, 14, 25, 26-45, 46, 48, 50, 55, 56, 58, 59, 61, 63, 74, 77, 90, 91, 93, 93, 96, 97, 98, 100, 101, 103, 114, 115, 118, 123, 129, 130, 134, 136, 138, 139, 144, 147, 148, 153, 165, 176, 191, 200
Galley, Experimental, 46, 48, 54
Galley, French, 32, 36, 39, 45, 142, 149, 165
Galley, Magisterial, 42, 134
Galley, Maltese, 9, 10, 28, 35, 40, 41, 47, 120, 121, 131, 133, 165, 166, 189
Galley, Turkish, 134
Galley-pen, 192
Galleys of antiquity, 32
Galleys of the Order, 154, 155, 166
Galleys Port, 190, 203
Galleys, viii, 4, 6, 7, 9, 23, 42
Galleys, Bizertan, 41
Galleys, construction of, 2, 189
Gallipoli, 5
Garcia, Damiano, 137
Gattineau, Knight, 16
General's galley, 146
General of the galleys, 64
Genoa, 7, 50, 70, 174
Genseric, 73
George VI, king, 5
Gerald (Founder of the Order), 77
Gerenti, Knight de, 26
Germa, 132
German mortar, 177
German, 117
Germany, 47, 175
Gibraltar, Straits of, 94
Goletta, 19, 25, 29, 73, 106
Gondola, 64, 65
Gondola, Magisterial, 63, 64
Gondola, Wignacourt, 85
Gouttes, Fra Filippo de, 79
Gozo, vii, 57, 63, 70, 90, 90, 98, 198
Graffito, 152
Gran Carracca, 16
Gran Catena, 202
Gran Nave, 16
Grand carrack, 202
Grand galleon, 55, 149, 168, 202
Grand Harbour, xi, 6, 98, 109, 177, 179, 191, 200, 202, 203, 204
Grand Master's palace, 17, 34
Grand Master, 63, 131, 146
Grand Vizier, 120
Grapeshot, 180
Grasse, Knight de, 120
Gravière, J., 32, 35, 45
Great caique, 61

Great Siege, 4, 24, 175
Greece, 4
Greek Islands, 58
Greek Orthodox Church, 8, 124
    citizens, 126
    patriarch, 124
Greek shipping, 8, 124
Greek vessels, 125
Greek, 58, 59, 76, 106, 124, 125, 132
Greenwich, 45
Grima, 203
Grippi, 87
Grippo, 76, 77
Grog, British, 36
Grunemberg, Charles, Colonel, 193, 203
Guerre de course, 89
Guglielmotti, A., 25, 26, 29, 30, 47, 48, 50, 54, 56, 57, 68, 71, 100, 104, 109, 134
Guidotti, 21, 22, 25, 26, 30, 30, 37, 41, 51, 98, 134, 166
Guidotti, Opizio, 1, 20, 34, 132
Guillaume Tell, 86, 110
Gun pontoon, 197, 198
Gunpowder, 174, 176, 177
Gunpowder, recipe for 175
Guns, 168, 169, 171, 198

Ġgantija, vii

Hadrian VI, Pope, 4
Half galley, 30, 130
Half-swivel gun, 173
Hamilton, William, Sir, 5
Hand bombs, 181
Hand-grenade, 181
Hand-to-hand fighting, 130
Hanging, 142
Harbour area, 205
Harbour, 189, 201
Harraka, 15
Hatches, 33
Hauberk, Chain-mail, 182
Helmet, 182
Henry Count of Malta, 113
Henry VIII, 19
Hens, 40, 41, 139, 144
Herberstein, Carlo Leopoldo d', 43
Hitti, P.K., 175
Hocquicourt, Knight d', 120
Holland, 94
Holy Land, 4, 77, 124, 149
Holy League, 120
Holy Obedience, 141
Holy Places, 8, 77, 123, 124, 125
Holy See, 124

233

Holy Shrines, 8
Hompesch, Ferdinand von, 67
Hoquincourt, Knight, 123
Hospital ship, 76-8
Hospitallers, 2, 4, 77, 123, 148
Hypogeum, vii

Ħal Saflieni, vii
Ħaġar Qim, vii

Ibernia, Prior of, 58
Ibn Khaldun, 175
Ibraim, sultan, 129
Ice, 39
Ice-boxes, 39
Il Trionfo in Mare, 117
Imbroll, Carlo, 117
Imnajdra, vii
In articulo mortis, 153
Incendiary bomb, 181
India, 18, 76
Indiscret, 109
International school, 120
Inventario della Conventuale Chiesa di San Giovanni, 151
Inventory, 149
Iron gun, 171
Italian vessels, 134
Italy, 44, 47, 70, 94, 190
Ivory powder flask, 170

James I, 78
Jerusalem, 77, 124, 148
Jesuit's College, 115
Jews Sally Port, 191
Jews, 126, 128, 152, 156
John of Austria, Don, 120
June 1919, x, 7

Kitchen, 38
Knights of fortune, 145, 147
Knights of St John, ix, x, 2, 3, 4, 7, 16, 18, 19, 24, 29, 36, 39, 39, 42, 47, 49, 51, 53, 54, 59, 63, 93, 113, 115, 117, 121, 125, 126, 139, 142, 143, 144, 146, 148, 148, 153, 174, 180, 182, 192, 198, 204, 205
Koran, 154

L'Aquila, 50
L'Immacolata Concezione, 106
L'Isle Adam, Philippe Villiers, 3, 4, 6
La Cassiere, Jean de, 64
La Gravière, Jurien de, 30, 33, 36, 37, 38, 149, 165
La Richoidie, Gabriel de, 91

La Santissima Vergine del Pilar, 68, 189
La Sengle, Claude de, 44
Ladle, 169
Lampedusa, 53
Landgrave of Hesse, 34
Landstrom, B., 54, 104
Lapparelli, Knight, 70
Lascara, 43
Lascaris gun, 173, 174
Lascaris, Jean Paul, 42, 126, 174
Last Rites, 149
Lateen-rigging, 13, 14, 45, 93, 97, 98
Latini, tal-, 59, 90
Latino, Giorgio, 58
Leghorn, 27, 90, 92, 96, 174
Lepanto, 5, 7, 8, 10, 33, 78, 130, 152
Levant, 19, 26, 38, 51, 58, 169
Libro della Marina, 81
Licata, 14
Life-expectancy, 65
Light frigate, 69
Limpet mine, 183
Lisbon, 92, 94, 99
Liturgical services, 149
Loaves, 144
London Archaeological Institute, l, 8
Londra, 92, 93
Luftwaffe, 5
Luzzu, 59, 90

Macina, 196, 197
Madonna della Concezione, 51
Madonna della Grazia, 43
Maldonato, Antonio, Fra, Comman 15
Mallia, Joe, 32, 38, 140, 142, 143, 145, 147
Maltese, 94
    armateurs, 114
    battalion, 130
    bombardiers, 115
    brigantines, 96, 97
    capitana, 165
    life, 205
    nation, 119
    pink, 102
    seamen, 117
    small warship, 69
Maltese, ix, viii, x, xi, 2, 5, 6, 7, 8, 10, 15, 18, 23, 24, 33, 43, 46, 47, 50, 51, 53, 59, 68, 69, 89, 94, 99, 106, 113, 121, 123, 126, 129, 131, 138, 148, 189, 204, 206
Mancuso, Enrico, 123
Manderaggio, 191, 192, 193
Mannarino, Gaetano, Don, x
Manoel de Vilhena, Antonio, 64, 70,

INDEX

148, 156
Manso, Commendatore, 151
Maona, 133
Marabouts, 134
Marani, 87
Marc, 175
Marciliani, 87
Maritime Museum, Malta, 1, 35, 41, 45, 46, 47, 49, 65, 66, 67, 113, 119, 134, 174, 177
Maroccans, 110
Marsa, 6, 193, 200, 201
Marsamxett, 176, 177, 190, 191, 192
Marseilles, 9, 105
Mascoli, 137
Masfelti, 166, 173, 174
Mass, 149, 150, 151
Mastrillo, Giovanni Battista, 125
Mattresses, 36
Maurin, Giuseppe, 48, 67, 68
Mazzarelli, 93
Mdina, 137, 177, 204
Men-of-war, 8
Merchant ships, 14
Messina, 3, 16, 63, 77, 78, 79, 94
Metal, Imported, 171
Micciolo, Pawlu, 123
Michele di Malta, 114
Middle class, 144
Milan, 47
Minestrone, 144
Mint, Order's, 17
Modon, 4, 17, 78, 113
Mogarbina, 16
Mogarbina, Muslim, 16
Moiane, 166
Molotov cocktail, 183
Monroy, Gonsalvo, ix
Montagna, Pasquale, 119
Montalto, Vincenzo, Fra, 91
Monte della Redentione, 154
Moor's head, 64
Moorish vessels, 23
Moorish, 8, 51
Moors, 8, 16, 17, 24
Morat Aga, 23
Morion, 182
Moro, Giacomo, 45
Mortar ship, 72, 75, 179
Mortar, 71, 72, 177, 178, 179
Mortar, French, 177
Mortars, 73, 86
Mosques, 134
Moustache, 148
Mufti, Muslim, 127
Mula, Martinu, 123

Muscat, Joseph, 40, 46, 72, 80
Museum of Fine Arts, 34, 196
Musicians' gallery, 17
Muskets, 168
Muslim booty, 155, 193
  chiefs, 124
  merchant shipping, 9
  minister, 127
  slaves, 21
  threat, 115
Muslims, xi, 5, 24, 25, 26, 27, 27, 35, 45, 49, 51, 53, 59, 64, 78, 93, 99, 101, 103, 109, 114, 123, 124, 126, 126, 129, 132, 146, 147, 148, 152, 153, 154, 155, 175
Musquetoons, 165, 167, 168

Naples, 2, 7, 9, 39, 44, 92
Napoleon, x, 5, 47, 50, 66, 74, 93
Narducci, pilot, 118
National Archives, 205
National Library of Malta, 35
Nautical school, 119
Naval battle, 128
Naval gun, 170
Naval student, Maltese, 119
Nave S. Caterina, 191
Nave S. Giacomo, 191
Nave S. Gioseppe M(aria), 191
Nave S. Giovanni, 191
Navigation, 115
Nazareth, 123
Nazi Panzers, 5
Neapolitan galley, 45
Negro, 199
Nero, Emperor, 39
Netherlands, 65, 96, 107
Neuchese, Captain, 129
Nice, 3, 9, 17
No. 1 Dock, 191
Norman House, Mdina, 45, 177, 179
Normans, ix
North Africa, 39, 73, 78, 91, 123
North European, 103
Notorial Knights, 205
Novitiate, 145
Nursery, 120

Oakum, 195
Oar-maker, 31
Oars, 30, 31, 109
Oarsmen, 30, 31, 32, 44, 50, 33
Old Calcara, 191
Old galley, 78
Omedes, Juan d', 19, 134, 202
Opium, 152

235

Orca, Venetian, 26
Order of St John, viii, xi, xii, 2, 3, 4, 5, 6, 7, 8, 10, 14, 15, 16, 17, 20, 21, 22, 23, 24, 26, 27, 29, 34, 35, 39, 41, 42, 44, 45, 46, 47, 48, 49, 50, 51, 53, 54, 56, 57, 58, 64, 65, 66, 67, 70, 74, 76, 77, 78, 89, 91, 92, 94, 96, 99, 101, 103, 104, 106, 107, 113, 114, 115, 117, 118, 119, 120, 123, 124, 125, 129, 130, 131, 132, 134, 137, 141, 143, 144, 145, 146, 148, 149, 153, 155, 165, 171, 173, 174, 176, 177, 189, 193, 198, 203, 205, 206
Ottoman empire, xi, 4, 9, 10, 125, 126
    fleet, 133
    forces, 7
    shipping, 9
    sultan, 9
Oven, 39

Pace, Giuseppe, 117
Pace, Silvestro, 117
Padrona, 31, 42, 129, 136
Pagnini, Giovanni, 117
Paid rowers, 46
Palace Armoury, 168, 170
Palandra, 71-3, 179
Palermo, 70
Palestine, 8
Papal fleet, 48
Papal galleys, 56, 149
Papal squadron, 47, 78
Papal States, 49
Paschal II, Pope, 77
Patacca, 148, 161
Patras, 4, 113
Patriarch of the Maronites, 122
Paule, Antoine de, 176
Pavesate, 33
Pedana, 32
Pegoliera, 195
Peloponnese, 8, 73
Pepiniere, 120
Perellos, Ramon, 65, 67, 129, 138, 155
Perier, 172, 174, 181
Pescara, marquis of, 8
Petacchio, 14, 24-6, 129, 133, 146, 149
Petriera, 173
Philibert, Prince, 136
Philip II, 7
Phoenician, ix, vii, 26
Piccola Barriera, 34
Pigeons, 139, 144
Pigniatta, 183
Pilots, 116, 118, 119
Pilots, Maltese, 117, 118

Pink, 14, 77, 93, 101-3, 133
Pinto de Fonseca, Emanuel, 35, 54, 96, 115, 121, 134
Pinto stores, 191
Polaccone, 104
Polacre, 104
Poland, 5
Pole-type masts, 104
Pollacca, 104-6, 109, 133, 142
Pollacca, French, 104
Pollacca, Maltese, 105
Pollacca-chebec, 108, 109
Porta Reale, 171
Porter, Whitworth, 5
Porto delle Galere, 192
Portolano del Mediterraneo, 117
Portolano, 117
Portugal, 20, 65, 94
Portuguese, x, 15
Portulan, 118, 119
Post of Germany, 190
Poussielgue, Antoine, 47
Powder flask, 169
Powder magazine, 36, 37
Prehistory, vii
Priests, Muslim, 123
Prince Frederick's boat, 65
Printing press, 117
Prisoner, 156
Private Maltese shipowners, 103
Proeri, 151
Proverb, 119
Puis, Raymond de, 77
Punic Wars, ix
Punishment, 141, 142, 143, 154, 157

Quinqueremes, Roman, 32
Quintano, A., 203

Rabat, 149, 177, 204
Rabat, Ta' Ġiesu Friary, 4
Ragusa, 15
Rais, Soliman, 25
Ram, 169
Rambata, 33, 36, 45, 53, 78, 139, 149, 153, 165, 166, 168, 181
Rams, 41, 139, 144
Ras Ħanżir, 177
Re, 144, 145, 161
Red Island of Sardinia, 53
Red overall, 182
Red, 169
Redin, Martin de, 103
Religion, 148, 149, 193
Remarques, 36
Remolaro, 31

INDEX

Ressons, Chev. de, 177
Reuwich, Erhard, 202
Rhodes, 2, 4, 7, 16, 17, 24, 77, 101, 114, 202
Rhodiots, 131
Ricasoli, Francesco, 58, 136
Richard I, 39
Richelieu, 142
Rispolo, Zaccaria, 118
Rochella, 58
Rohan, Emanuel de, 35, 48, 54, 55, 70, 115, 193
Romans, vii, ix, 26, 76
Rome, 2, 3, 8, 64, 91, 92, 114, 123, 124, 131
Romegas, Mathurin de Lescaut, 166
Roosevelt, Franklin D., 5
Rossi, Ettore, 49, 54, 191, 203
Round-shot, 180
Rowers, 130
Royal French Navy, 120
Royal pilot, 118
Ruffo, Fabrizio, Fra, 166
Ruspoli, knight, 70
Russia, 107, 121

S. Elizabetta, 49
S. Zaccaria, 49
Sabotage, 184
Sacre, 167, 173, 166, 174
Sacristy, 149
Saetta, 133
Saica, Muslim, 132
Sailmaking, 199
Sailon, Knight de, 26
Sailor, Maltese, 90, 101, 114, 115, 183, 193
Sails, 2
        Maltese, 198
        weaving of, 198, 199
Saint Rocco church, 152
Sakers, 19
Saladin, 39
Salettina, 133
Saliba, Pietru, 93
Salonica, 21
Salonica, 171, 174, 175, 176
Saluting, 153
Salvago, Girolamo, Fra, 190
Salviati, Admiral, 4
San Antonio, 43, 66, 70, 109
San Carlo, 43
San Claudio, 42, 44
San Filippo, 7, 42
San Francesco di Paola, 70
San Francesco, 41, 43, 168

San Gabriello, 42
San Giacchino, 66, 67
San Giacomo, 21, 42
San Giovanni Battista, 16, 34
San Giovanni, 7, 20, 21, 22, 24, 41, 42, 43, 49, 56, 64, 66, 67, 69, 70, 86, 103, 189, 193
San Giuseppe, 91
San Gregorio, 43
San Luigi, 43, 44, 56
San Michele, 42
San Nicola, 43, 137, 151
San Paolo, 43, 107
San Pietro, 7, 43, 43, 45, 47, 48, 64, 107
San Vincenzo, 53, 70
San Zaccaria, 66, 69
Sanfelice, castle, 56
Sant'Andrea, 45, 48
Sant'Anna, 7, 15, 17-20, 49, 73, 149
Sant'Ursola, 49, 53
Santa Annunciata, 43
Santa Barbara, 50
Santa Caterina, 43, 53, 151, 189, 191
Santa Croce, 6, 7, 42
Santa Elizabetta, 68, 69
Santa Fede, 42
Santa Ferma, 50
Santa Lucia, 50
Santa Maria della Neve, 70
Santa Maria della Vittoria, 7, 190
Santa Maria di Filermo, 53
Santa Maria Madalena, 190
Santa Maria, 7, 15, 16-7, 42, 43, 49, 56, 68, 69, 78, 79, 129
Santa Rosalia, 43
Santa Teresa, 49, 70, 106
Santabarbara, 36, 37
Santissimo Crocifisso, 103
Santo Spirito, 109
Sanz, Emmanuele, 151
Sapienza, 199
Saqqajja, Niche of St Paul at, 177
Saracens, 152
Saragosa, 3
Sardinia, 50, 70
Savoy, 9
Scaloccio, a, 32
Scarabelli, G., 203
Sceih el gebel, 152
Schellinks, W., 190
Schilling, Knight, 23
School of navigation, 120
School, 115
Schwarts, Berthold, 175
Scopoli, 22, 51
Scurvy, 144

Sebille, 40, 41, 138
Second World War, 5
Secret service, Order's, 58
Senglea, 17, 89, 189, 190, 196, 200, 202, 203
Sensile, 32
Sfax, 73
Sheating, 18, 19
Sheer bastion, 196
Ship's arsenal, 189
    biscuit, 37, 144
    clerk, 36
Ship-building, 68
Ship-of-the-line, 14, 53, 65-7, 68, 69, 73, 74, 109, 129, 149
Ships, Muslim, 113, 121, 125
Ships-of-the-line, 189, 191, 193
Shipyard's stores, 200
Shipyards, 189, 190
Shoes, 141
Shore-to-shore sailing, 96
Sicarians, 152
Sicilian squadron, 118
Sicilian, 8, 91
Sicily, 4, 15, 70, 92, 93, 94, 103, 106, 109, 193
Siege of 1565, 202
Signals, 134, 135, 136
Signals, Book of, 129
Sixth rate, 74
Sixtus V, Pope, 149
Skiffs, 19
Slaves, 8, 17, 21, 22, 32, 36, 45, 46, 59, 65, 96, 131, 138, 139, 140, 141, 142, 144, 148, 151, 156, 171, 172, 198, 199, 200, 205
    Christian, 154
    Female, 199
    Muslims, 151
Sleep, 141
Small pistols, 143
Snow, 39
Soldiers, 182, 193
    Maltese, 130, 134, 139
Soleiman Rais, 24
Sonnini, C.S., 35, 54
Sopravesta, 182
Spain, 2, 4, 20, 44, 63, 65, 94, 107, 114
Spalliera, 33, 139, 149
Spaniards, 57, 106
Spanish, 7, 66, 117, 118
Spanish armada, 73
    capitana, 41
    coasts, 94
    fleet, 78
    squadron, 69

Speed, 30
Speronara, 14, 56, 64, 89, 90, 91, 92, 96, 100, 107, 110, 189
Speronare di guardia, 92
Sperone, 100, 103
Spinola, Balì, 130
Spur, 102
Square-rigging, 13, 14, 44, 97, 98, 191
St Angelo, Fort, 17, 19, 24, 134, 175, 202
St Elmo, 190, 191
St Francis of Assisi, 154
St George's day, 23
St James cavalier, 137
St John, 77
St Julians, 17
St Mary's Rock, 58
St Paul, 1
Standia, 77
Stove, 38, 39
Stromboli, 179
Suetonius, 39
Suffren, Admiral de, 121
Suleiman the Magnificent, 2, 5, 24
Sulphur, 175, 176
Sultana, 24
Surgeon, 36
Susa, 24
Swastika, 5
Sweden, 107, 171
Swedish, 10, 101
Swivel gun, Venetian, 173
Swivel guns, 48, 165, 167, 172
Syracuse, 6, 14, 143

Tabernacle, 33
Tagiora, 24
Tambouret, 45
Tar raft, 195
Tartana di Malta, 111
Tartana, viii, 14, 51, 89, 49, 74, 78, 99, 99-101, 103, 104, 106, 149, 189
Tarxien, vii
Taurisano, 81
Tavern, 36, 37, 139
Temericourt, 123
Terminology, 13
Test, 172
Testa di moro, 64
Third rate, 66
Third rate, 66, 118, 153
Tommasi, Bartholomew, Balì, 177
Tools, 169
Touch hole, 171
Toulon, 9, 48, 67
Tourville, admiral, 121
Towers, 145

INDEX

Towers, Coastal, 58
Trattato d'Artiglieria, 184
Trattato della Trigonometria i, 117
Trattato di Navigazione, 117
Tratto Pratico della Manovra de, 117
Treasury, Order's, 17
Trieste, 70
Trinitarians, 154
Tripoli, 20, 23, 93, 101, 121, 199
Tripolitan, 115
Tromboncini, 48
Trumpet, 181
Trumping, 94
Tunis, 96, 101, 106
Tunisian, 26, 53, 94
Turk, 59, 76, 93, 97, 106, 124, 125, 133, 134
Turkey, 10, 39, 126, 129
Turkish, 8, 9, 23, 24, 26, 51, 53, 57
Turkish armada, 4
    assault, 202
    caramousal, 22
    cargo-ships, 21
    fighting ships, 133
    fleet, 133
    forces, 5
    guns, 166
    navy, 136
    royal galley, 181
    ships, 47, 131
    sultan, 126
    vessel, 130
Turks, 2, 4, 5, 8, 9, 10, 21, 22, 24, 26, 152, 154, 156, 166, 171

Ubaldini, M.U., 203
Uniforms, 130
United States of America, 107
Università, 121
University, 115
Upper Barracca, 190
Urban VIII, Pope, 123
Ursoline sisters, 133
Uzzino, Giovanni, 118

Vagabond, 157
Valbelle, Admiral, 120
Valera, Censu, 51
Valette, Jean de, 24, 155, 202

Valletta, 17, 27, 34, 41, 63, 67, 115, 134, 136, 171, 176, 177, 190, 191, 192, 196, 204
Vandal corsairs, 73
Vandal leader, 73
Varie Osservazioni di Porti, 117
Vassallo, G.A., 41, 42, 113, 134
Vaubois, General, x
Vendosme, James d', 123
Venetian fleet, 136
Venetian, 8, 63, 73, 74, 202, 113, 126, 132
Venice, 7, 9, 20, 65, 73, 76, 77, 78, 92, 114, 124, 202
Verdalle, Hugh de, 21, 64, 131, 155
Viaticum, 149
Vilhena Codex, 138, 193, 168
Vilhena's law, 141
Villafranco, 3
Villeneuve, Admiral, 91
Visscher, C.J., 79
Viterbo, 3
Vittoriosa, 24, 35, 64, 115, 138, 171, 189, 190, 192, 197, 198, 200, 202
Vivion, Lieutenant, 49
Voluntary knights, 145

Warships, 130
Water, 38
Western European coastline, 99
Wignacourt Museum, Rabat, 149
Wignacourt, Alof de, 65
Windus, Captain, 18, 19
Wine, 36, 37, 144
Wismayer, J., 203
Wood basin, 193
Wood charcoal, 176
World War I, 90
Worm and hook, 169
Ximenes, admiral, 41
Ximenes, Francisco, Grand Master
Xprunara, Maltese, 90-3
Yugoslavia, 5
Zamora, Emanuel, Fra, 51
Zante, 9, 58
Zoara, 134

Żabbar Sanctuary Museum, 29, 67, 98, 104, 110

239